The collection of essays by prominent historians of the Reformation explores the experience of religious reform in 'national context', discussing similarities and differences between the reform movements in a dozen different countries of sixteenth-century Europe. Each author provides an interpretative essay emphasising local peculiarities and national variants on the broader theme of the Reformation as a European phenomenon. The individual essays thus emphasise the local preconditions and limitations which encountered the Reformation as it spread from Germany into most of the countries of western and central Europe. Together they present a picture of the many-sided nature of the Reformation as it grew up in each 'national context'. The book includes examples of countries where the Reformation was strikingly successful, as well as those where it failed to make an impact. A final comparative essay seeks to understand the different 'Reformations' as variations on an overall theme.

This volume forms part of a sequence of collections of essays which began with *The Enlightenment in national context* (1981) and has continued with *Revolution in history* (1986), *Romanticism in national context* (1988), *Fin de siècle and its legacy* (1990), *The Renaissance in national context* (1991), *The Scientific Revolution in national context* (1992), and *The national question in Europe in historical context* (1993). The purpose of these and other envisaged collections is to bring together comparative, national and interdisciplinary approaches to the history of great movements in the development of human thought and action.

The Reformation in national context

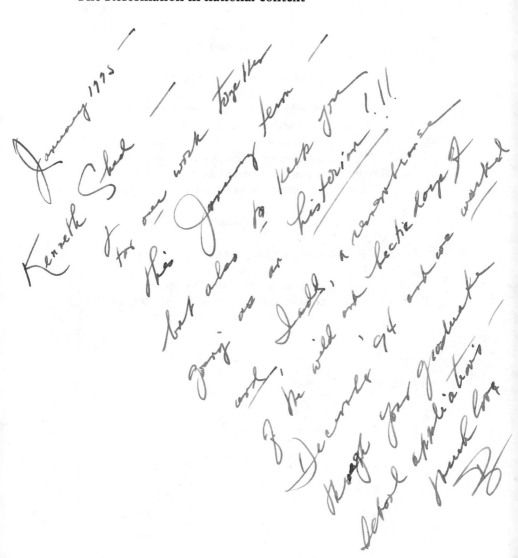

*Volumes edited by Roy Porter and Mikuláš Teich*


*Already published*

The Enlightenment in national context
Revolution in history
Romanticism in national context
*Fin de siècle* and its legacy
The Renaissance in national context
The national question in Europe in historical context
The Reformation in national context (with Bob Scribner)
The Scientific Revolution in national context


Forthcoming

The Industrial Revolution in national context: Europe
and the USA
Drugs and narcotics in history
Sexual knowledge, sexual science: the
history of attitudes to sexuality

# The Reformation in national context

*Edited by*

Bob Scribner
*Clare College, Cambridge*

Roy Porter
*Wellcome Institute for the History of Medicine*

and Mikuláš Teich
*Robinson College, Cambridge*

CAMBRIDGE
UNIVERSITY PRESS

Published by the Press Syndicate of the University of Cambridge
The Pitt Building, Trumpington Street, Cambridge CB2 1RP
40 West 20th Street, New York, NY 10011–4211, USA
10 Stamford Road, Oakleigh, Melbourne 3166, Australia

First published 1994

Printed in Great Britain at the University Press, Cambridge

*A catalogue record for this book is available from the British Library*

*Library of Congress cataloguing in publication data*

The Reformation in national context / edited by Bob Scribner, Roy Porter, and
Mikuláš Teich.
    p.   cm.
Includes index.
ISBN 0–521–40155–0. ISBN 0–521–40960–8 (pbk)
1. Reformation – Europe. 2. Europe – Church history – 16th century. I. Scribner,
Robert W. II. Porter, Roy, 1946–. III. Teich, Mikuláš.
BR307.R4   1994
274′.06 – dc20   93–7922   CIP

ISBN 0 521 40155 0 hardback
ISBN 0 521 40960 8 paperback

CE

# Contents

# Notes on contributors

WIEBE BERGSMA is a research fellow at the Fryske Akademy, Leeuwarden, Netherlands and has published various articles on the Reformation in the Low Countries.

PATRICK COLLINSON is Regius Professor of Modern History at Cambridge University and author of numerous works on English protestantism, including *The Religion of Protestants* (1982) and *The Birthpangs of Protestant England* (1988).

JULIAN GOODARE is a Royal Society of Edinburgh Research Fellow in the University of Edinburgh, working on the finances of the Scottish state 1560–1637 and is currently preparing a book on *The Government of Scotland 1560–1625*. His 1989 Ph.D. thesis on the Scottish parliament won the Hume Brown Senior Prize in Scottish History.

MARK GREENGRASS is Senior Lecturer in Modern History at the University of Sheffield. He has published *France in the Age of Henry IV* (1984) and *The French Reformation* (1987), and has edited *Conquest and Coalescence. The Shaping of the State in Early Modern Europe* (1991).

OLE PETER GRELL is a Carlsberg Fellow at the Wellcome Unit for the History of Medicine, University of Cambridge. He has published articles on the Danish Reformation as well as the monograph *Dutch Calvinists in Early Stuart London* (1989), and has edited, with Andrew Cunningham, *Medicine and the Reformation* (1993).

HENRY KAMEN is Professor of History at the Institut Mila i Fontanalsin Barcelona. He is the author of several books on early modern Spain, the latest of which is *The Phoenix and the Flame. Catalonia and the Counter-Reformation* (1993).

FRANTIŠEK KAVKA has published in both Czech and German numerous works on the Hussite movement, the history of the University of Prague and economic and political problems of the sixteenth century. From 1964 he was Professor of Czech History and head of the Institute of History at

Charles University. In 1970 he was obliged to give up his activities in teaching and scholarship, and returned to them only in 1990.

KATALIN PETER is Scientific Councillor at the Institute of History of the Hungarian Academy of Sciences and has published books and articles on the history of early modern Hungary, especially in recent years on the Reformation.

BOB SCRIBNER is Reader in the Social History of Early Modern Europe at Cambridge University and Fellow of Clare College. His most recent publications include *Popular Culture and Popular Movements in Reformation Germany* (1987); *The German Peasants' War: A History in Documents*, with Tom Scott (1991); *The Reformation in Germany and Switzerland*, with Pamela Johnson (1993).

SILVANA SEIDEL MENCHI is Professor of History at the University of Trent and has worked on various aspects of humanism and the Reformation in Italy. Her numerous publications in Italian, German and English include *Erasmo in Italia 1520–1580* (1987).

JANUSZ TAZBIR, is Professor in the Institute of History, Polish Academy of Sciences, Warsaw, of which he has been a member since 1983. He has numerous publications in several languages on the history of Polish culture and religious movements. He is editor-in-chief of the annual publication *The Renaissance and Reformation in Poland* and his more recent publications include *La Republique nobiliaire et le monde. Etudes sur l'histoire de la culture polonaise a l'époque dau baroque* (1986); 'The popular impact on the discovery of America in East Central Europe', *The Polish Review* 3 (1993); and *The Reformation in Poland* (1993).

KASPAR VON GREYERZ is Professor of History at the University of Zurich, and has published on the Reformation in Germany and Switzerland, the historiography of popular religion, and religious autobiographies of the seventeenth century. His most recent book is *Vorsehungsglaube und Kosmologie. Studien zu englischen Selbstzeugnisse des 17. Jahrhunderts* (1990).

# Introduction

*Bob Scribner*

'The Reformation' is the general label historians use to describe the series of upheavals in the religious life of Europe during the sixteenth and the first half of the seventeenth centuries. Its historical significance is assured because it touched not simply personal belief, but had a profound impact on the social, political and economic spheres. The church was shaken to its foundations, many of its institutionalised expressions were fatally weakened and even abolished in countries where the Reformation was most successful. It laid down patterns of religious allegiance which still persist today, dividing communities and nations, and provoking violent wars, confrontations and even revolutions as men and women of one religious mind set sought to impose their views on those holding another. The intensity and bitterness of conflict in Northern Ireland in our own age is a late echo of the religious confrontations of the Reformation period.

The Reformation began in Germany in the 1520s, with the 'Luther affair', the controversy precipitated by Martin Luther's attack on indulgences and the indulgence trade in October 1517. The subsequent furore spilled over from being a disagreement among theologians and churchmen into the wider public sphere, quickly drawing into its wake questions of politics, social grievance, popular religious discontent, constitutional and legal issues from the level of the Empire down to the smallest communities. It quickly spread beyond the borders of Germany, first into German-speaking territories such as Switzerland and Austria, into lands such as the Low Countries, then across more substantial linguistic borders into England, Scandinavia, France, Italy and into Eastern Europe. Carried by the printed word, but more potently by personal, academic and economic networks, news of the German example quickly encouraged imitation in many other lands. However, local conditions and interests dictated that the Reformation did not develop everywhere in the same way and at the same pace. Although ideas, and especially religious ideas, find ways to penetrate even the most formidable political barriers, the patterns of development in the Reformation inevitably partook of the characteristics of the major states and territories in which it took hold. In Scandinavia, England and Scotland, religious reform was initially hesitant but was helped along the path of Reformation by decisive royal action, imposing change from above. In France and the Netherlands, the movement for reform was initially repressed, only to break out with revolutionary force in a following generation. In Italy and Spain, attempts at religious reform seemed to be sickly growths, easily uprooted by the willing hand of authorities who perceived the dangers of strange plants in their own gardens. In Eastern Europe – Poland, Hungary, Bohemia – the story was different and more complicated because of the more complex nature of the societies and polities in those places.

The Reformation, therefore, is a subject which is pre-eminently suited for viewing 'in national context'. Its many variations have given rise to multiple historiographies, each country in which it took substantial root developing an indigenous tradition of historical explanation, recounting how religious reform came about in that particular land and developing distinctive interpretative emphases. However, in the manner of older theories of the origins of mankind, all variants looked back to a moment of monogenesis in the 'Luther affair' and through the founding fathers of the German Reformation. The history of the Reformation as a European phenomenon has, therefore, oscillated between seeing it as a matter of local variants on a central theme, and emphasising the peculiarities and distinctiveness of local traditions. The difference in conceptualisation is sometimes captured in contrasting titles, for example, between the 'The Reformation in England' and 'The English Reformation'.

The past couple of decades in Reformation historiography have seen substantial changes in interpretation of the phenomenon. There has been a conscious attempt to transcend the rigidities of confessional historiography, in which one's interpretation of the Reformation was closely tied to the self-justification of one's own religious creed. There have been many new impulses to wider understanding of the Reformation as a broader phenomenon by social and political historians, who have argued that it cannot be understood simply in terms of abstract ideas or idealist perceptions of historical change. Emphasis has shifted to exploration of the dissemination and reception of new religious beliefs, to study of implementation and institutionalisation of consequent changes in religious life, and to the limiting conditions imposed on even the most idealist religious reformer by the realities of daily life. Thus, there has been in many countries a resurgence of local studies of the Reformation within its national context, and detailed specialist works have proliferated to the point where any comparative general overview is almost impossible.

Such developments provide the occasion and justification for this collection of essays. On the one hand, it seeks to offer a summary overview of the best recent work in many countries of Europe where the Reformation made a significant impact; on the other hand, it provides an opportunity for comparative reflections on the similarities and differences involved in local experiences of Reformation. It emphasises local context, indigenous pre-conditions and limitations, but still seeks to understand the different 'Reformations' as variations on an overall theme. Each author was asked to provide not a comprehensive factual account, but an interpretative essay emphasising local peculiarities and national variants on the broader theme of religious reform. The subject matter of most of the chapters that follow is self-evident, with the major theatres of reform claiming a chapter each: Germany, Switzerland, Scandinavia, England, Scotland, France and the Low Countries. Developments in Eastern Europe are represented by chapters on Poland, Bohemia and Hungary, while the chapters on Italy and Spain seek to explain why the Reformation never took off in either of these lands, apparently no less ripe for religious reform. Chapters were also planned on two cases of particular interest, Austria and Ireland, and on how the Reformation tradition established itself in the New World, but the intended authors were unable, for various reasons, to supply essays for this volume. Some account has been taken of these and other examples in a final chapter, which attempts a comparative overview. If no comprehensive synthesis seems to emerge, perhaps it is because Chairman Mao's dictum on the consequences of the Russian Revolution is equally applicable to the religious upheavals of the sixteenth century: it is still too early to say.

# 1    Germany

*Bob Scribner*


The German Reformation began in 1520, when the 'Luther affair', the debate among churchmen, scholars and theologians provoked by Luther's 1517 attack on indulgences, became a significant issue in the political agenda of the German-speaking territories of the Holy Roman Empire. The development of 'Luther's cause' from an academic dispute into a major public confrontation was a gradual process, in which many elements were added consecutively to the initial conflict until they produced a chain reaction involving theological ideas, religious conviction, political interests, social grievance, economic repercussions and the tortuous manoeuvring of international diplomacy. From the very beginning, the German Reformation was not, as its propagandists (and subsequent confessional historians) were to claim, a clear, pure, invigorating stream from which one had only to drink to take refreshment, but a heady brew containing many compounds whose effects on those who imbibed it were not always calculable. Thus, the four or five years after 1520 were years of rapid change, confusing upheaval and dizzying leaps into the unknown, often described as the 'wild growth' of the Reformation, in analogy with the exuberance of a garden which has received too much heat and water all at once. It was driven forward not by cool-headed discussion and debate, but by passionate polemic and fevered propaganda, rather like a too enthusiastic application of growth hormones to already overlush vegetation.[1]

In the years 1520–3 the growing demands for religious change developed into forms of direct action, challenging and then dismantling the old apparatus of religious worship and institutionalised forms of church life. This activity took on a new note from 1523, when social grievance came to dominate the public agenda, reaching its peak in the revolutionary upheaval of the German Peasants' War. The defeat of the rebels of 1524–5 brought a calming of the fevered pace of reform, as secular rulers imposed their authority in the name of social order, either repressing reforming impulses or channelling them into more approved patterns of change. From 1526 there emerged the first forms of 'reformation' directed by secular princes, alongside a more wary attitude towards religious change on the part of

4

urban authorities. By 1529–30, these forms of reformation had become sufficiently cohesive for some authorities implementing change to assemble themselves as a political party, the 'Protestants', those asserting their right to take charge of religious reform within their own territories and professing allegiance to a set of theological principles justifying their actions. From this point, the German Reformation was well-established as a divisive and determining factor in the politics of the Holy Roman Empire, a position it was not to yield until the middle of the next century.

The features that stand out in this story are the suddenness of the upheaval, the radical and dramatic nature of the changes it initiated, and its far-reaching effects in every area of life. There are three central questions to be addressed in an essay of this kind, which seeks to determine the 'national' peculiarities of the German Reformation. First, why should the Reformation have broken out in Germany in the first place? Second, what were the characteristics, peculiar to Germany, once it had begun? Third, in what sense did Germany provide a model for the development of reform elsewhere? The third question will be discussed only briefly, since many of the issues involved will be addressed in the final essay in this volume.

## Why Germany?

To seek reasons why a historical event occurs first in one place and not in another could be considered an idle enquiry, rather like asking why lightning should strike one tree in a forest and leave others untouched. We might be tempted to take such a view if we regarded the Reformation as a matter of pure contingency, as merely dependent on the providential whim that produces 'great men' in history. Yet once we begin to regard it as a complex process involving the interaction of many historical agencies – not just religious, but social, economic, political and ideological – we can approach it akin to the ways in which historians have explored phenomena such as revolts, revolutions or social movements. We can then speak of preconditions, of enabling or limiting structures within which events unfold, and of distinctive modes of thought and action which leave their imprint on such a phenomenon even as they are changed by it. Despite the danger of oversimplification, we can validly single out three broad areas of concern – political, cultural and religious – which played preconditioning roles in the development of the Reformation in Germany.

An important precondition is seen in the *political structures* prevailing in 'Germany' during the two or three generations before the Reformation.[2] German territories were characterised by fragmented politics under the limp hand of weak emperors, who had no significant institutions to provide a focus for unified political activity on an imperial level and who did not possess the resources to create such institutions. Thus, German politics were determined by polycentrism and factionalism, as Machiavelli observed shrewdly in 1508, commenting that neither the cities nor the princes wished the emperor to be great or strong because he would dominate and reduce them to an obedience not dissimilar to that exercised by the King of France over his subjects. The comparison is illuminating. Although the role of Holy Roman Emperor was not lacking in charisma of office, it certainly lacked charisma of hereditary royal power comparable to that attached to the rulers of France. The emperors did wield a certain amount of power in Germany and could dispense patronage and status by grants of office or title, but the number of carrots they could offer was limited by their continual impecuniousness, while the stick they could wield to compel obedience was thin and fragile. The Habsburgs may have regarded the office as a family possession, but the mere fact that the Holy Roman Emperor was an elected ruler was a fatal weakness. An imperial election required the investment of a good deal of money, time and political energy to achieve a satisfactory result, and the necessary horse-trading often tied the hands of the successful incumbent. Machiavelli believed in 1508 that the Emperor was better placed than in the past, for there were no longer great princes who dared openly oppose his designs; on the other hand, however, the Emperor could easily be frustrated by the simple non-compliance or non-cooperation of the princes and effectively reduced to impotence.[3]

Although the Emperor's position as a ruling monarch was weak, there was among the German political nation a strong attachment to the idea of the Empire, understood as the 'Holy Roman Empire of the German Nation'. The concept embodied a providential mission assigned to the German nation, and represented an enormous ideological force for unity for any ruler who could mobilise it for his political purposes. Maximilian I came close to doing so, using skilled propaganda to attach the ideals of empire to his own foreign policy, but ultimately he was unable to overcome the conviction of the German princes and cities that he was pursuing purely dynastic policies in the interests not of the 'German nation' but of the house of Habsburg. However, the potential remained, and was perhaps most effectively drawn upon by the nationalist elements of the early Reformation.

The role of *the church as a political entity* was a further distinct feature, most notably in the shape of the great prince-bishops, independent territorial rulers who necessarily involved the church in power politics. The same was true of the next level down the ecclesio-political hierarchy, the rich and powerful abbeys and imperial foundations, ruled by prince-abbots who were also major players in the game of imperial politics. This game was played out not only to preserve and extend their territories – bishoprics and abbatial lands – but in the struggles of various noble houses who sought dynastic advancement by occupying these great offices of the church. Noble families not only provided the incumbents of bishoprics and abbacies, but also the bulk of the canons sitting in the chapters which elected these dignitaries. Throughout its higher offices, the German church was distinctively a nobles' church. It was one of the features that was both to provoke demands for reform and to set limits to the expansion of the Reformation impulse.

Germany was also distinctive for its *developed urban life*, such that even the Florentine Machiavelli marvelled at the riches and power of its cities. Germany was covered by a dense network of almost two thousand towns, constituting an elaborate web of urban interests and influence, spread more or less uniformly across the countryside, but with regions of greater urban density in south-west and in central Germany. The sixty-five 'imperial cities', those subject only to the Emperor, have often been accorded a disproportionate amount of attention in the story of the Reformation, inviting comparison with great urban republics elsewhere. Yet it is somewhat misleading to compare the most powerful imperial cities such as Nuremberg or Augsburg with the urban republics of Italy, since the German imperial cities were certainly not republics and fear of the Emperor's intervention was a continual factor in their political decision-making. However, they did enjoy a high degree of political independence, as did certain other great towns nominally subject to the rule of a territorial prince but which had gained considerable autonomy of political and economic action. It was this which made not just the imperial cities but many territorial towns the seedbeds of the Reformation: independent or semi-independent politics, flourishing communal life and a vibrant civic political culture. German towns of all kinds may have had greater freedom of movement than their Italian counterparts, which were more avowedly republican in their constitutions but were faced increasingly with external limitations on their freedom of political action. We can say, therefore, that constitutional form was less of a deciding factor in the Reformation than political opportunity. Neither in Italy nor in France, where there were strong ties between the Crown and the 'bonnes villes', was there comparable freedom of urban action. The towns of the Low Countries in some respects enjoyed political independence akin to that of their German sisters. However, they too found themselves under increasing pressure from their sovereign lord at the beginning of the sixteenth century, which meant that urban defiance of princely authority was purchased dearly, at great economic, political and social cost.

Just focussing on these three major entities within the Holy Roman Empire, without taking account of minor princes, independent nobles or the peasantry, reveals an important structural feature that allowed movements of religious dissent to grow and flourish. At the end of the fifteenth and beginning of the sixteenth century, the Empire experienced enormous problems of order and public peace, expressed in its inability to deal with a complex range of issues on which firm action across its territories would have benefited all: control over banditry and feud, the lack of a uniform coinage or excise system, the absence of an efficient and effective legal system capable of resolving numerous political, economic and social conflicts. The problem of order was attested by cases of disputed princely succession, by contested elections in ecclesiastical foundations, by instances of princely or noble lawlessness and by internal upheavals in more than three dozen towns in the decade before the Reformation. In all such cases, there was no legal authority strong enough to compel immediate assent to a negotiated settlement, and political disputes often dragged on for many years at great cost to rulers and subjects alike. Thus, maverick princes could only be pulled into line by the investment of a good deal of time and money in forming coercive alliances and raising military force, while towns facing internal disputes fell prey to the predatory instincts of outside powers, whether secular or ecclesiastical princes, who offered to mediate at a price. The Swabian League had been created in 1488 in the south-west as a trouble-shooting alliance to settle disputes among its members and to enforce compliance to the law if necessary, but its workings were slow and cumbersome and its response uncertain, given the strong element of self-interest involved in its operations. Its most notable success, the expulsion of the lawless Duke Ulrich of Württemberg from his territories in 1519, was a unique achievement, and the 1520s were cruelly to expose its inadequacies. The significance for the emergence of the Reformation is self-evident: breaches in legality, as church structures were dismantled, pious foundations ignored, cloisters sequestered and incumbents ejected from clerical benefices, could take place without fear of rapid legal retribution, subject only to the constraints of political expediency.

Such features explain the ease with which religious dissent and heterodoxy spread in the early 1520s, especially given the conviction that there was legitimate disagreement about whether Luther and his supporters should be repressed or supported. Charles V was unable to mobilise the enormous wave of idealistic fervour for the concept of the Empire that arose on his accession, since this was attached more fervently to the idea that Luther's struggle against the papacy was a means of asserting the rights of the German nation. The Emperor remained dependent on cooperation of various subordinate authorities to carry through his condemnation of Luther, but where they chose to sit on their hands and to be uncooperative, the new ideas were allowed free rein to develop. Significantly, it was largely within the boundaries of prince-bishoprics, those powerful territories that so aroused the ire of reforming critics, that the movements were inhibited and checked in the long-term. The Reformation was never able, through massive dissent and disobedience, to capture a major bishopric or, more than temporarily, a major residential episcopal city. It was also effectively checked in principalities whose rulers took a firm repressive line, as in Albertine Saxony up to 1539 or in Bavaria. Low levels of urbanisation may have played a part in the latter territory, but scarcely in the former, where it was decisive action by the ruling prince that denied the Reformation movements any political and legal freedom to unfold.

These broadly structural features were complemented by *the nature of German politics*, by which we understand the goals, tactics and strategies pursued by the main independent actors in German public life, whose relatively broad-meshed and informal nature allowed scope for a wide range of political activity. This encompassed, for example, the petty, creeping expansionism by lords such as successive Abbots of Kempten, who sought to enlarge their territorial control by exchange of serfs and by imposing servile status on their peasant tenants; and the calculating policy of princes such as Magnus I of Saxony-Lauenburg (1507–43) who ruthlessly pursued his goal of mediatising the bishopric of Ratzeburg, first by rigging an episcopal election and then by imprisoning and coercing his uncooperative nominee. It included the machiavellian politics pursued by the city fathers of Erfurt, who sought to play the town's overlord, the Archbishop of Mainz, off against its contractual protectors, the Dukes of Saxony, or the ambitious plans of some towns for territorial expansion which led them to acquire serfs and act as feudal landlords.[4] All the acquired skills of political chicanery, duplicity, manoeuvring, opportunism, calculation and risk-taking played their part in the ability of towns and princes successfully to introduce and maintain religious heterodoxy and innovation.

A major goal of German politics at all levels well before the Reformation was to submit the church and its agencies to secular control. This ranged from the attempts of princes such as the Dukes of Saxony to gain rights of presentation to bishoprics and important canonries and to place their offspring in the highest church offices, over the nakedly coercive policies of Magnus of Saxony-Lauenburg, to the desire of towns to take charge of ecclesiastical institutions such as hospitals or to control the appointment of their parish clergy. The great point of dispute in this regard was the struggle over legal jurisdiction, secular authorities seeking to submit the clergy to secular courts and denying the rights of church courts to cite lay people before them in non-spiritual matters. We must note the relative backwardness of Germany in this regard. There was no uniform privilege *de non evocando*, of not being cited before foreign courts, gained in England since the fourteenth century as a means of preventing legal disputes being referred outside the country to papal jurisdiction; there was no mortmain legislation comparable to that in England and France, which restricted the alienation of secular property into clerical hands; and there were no consistent agreements limiting to German patrons the rights of presentation to importance benefices.

In the wake of the fifteenth-century conciliar movement, many lands established national churches, either through exploiting papal weakness in the wake of the Great Schism, as did England and France, or by rebellion and assertion of the rights of an independent national church, as occurred in Bohemia. But Germany had nothing similar to the Concordat of Bologna of 1516, which formally conceded to the King of France the right to nominate to nearly all the bishoprics, abbacies and major benefices in the kingdom. Instead, German lands were a rich picking ground for foreigners seeking ecclesiastical benefices, especially Italian favourites at the papal court or those able to tap into the network of patronage whose centre was Rome and the Curia. Everyone in German public life was aware of what was involved in securing a national church: this much had been learned from the Hussite upheavals in Bohemia. Concerted national action based on ethnic allegiance could assert local control against foreign rights and privileges, even achieve the virtually autonomous status of the Bohemian church. However, many Germans were also aware of the negative aspects of the process: protracted internal upheaval, invasions by maurauding Hussite armies and the fanaticism of religious militants, reviving memories of the bloody campaigns required to uproot heresy in earlier centuries.

No one who played any part in public life was unaware of the potential dangers of religious schism, yet the gains of ecclesiastical independence were seen to outweigh the losses, and numerous voices were raised throughout the latter part of the fifteenth century demanding the bridling of Rome and the creation of a truly national German church. What was lacking was opportunity and a leader, and in the search for the latter many chose to fix their hopes on a mythical figure, the prophetic emperor, the 'Third Frederick', who would revive religion and chastise Rome and the Roman clergy. Desire for reform was thus powerfully bound up with desire for a national church. It is singularly ironic, therefore, that it was the very lack of a national church and the very weakness of central authority that allowed the development of the polycentric Reformation movements which became the bearers of reform, rather than the more centralised reforms instituted elsewhere, in England or Scandinavia. At the same time the German reform movements inherited the anti-Roman and anti-papal religious and cultural nationalism of the fifteenth century – a historic combination of two different kind of centrifugal force, which so easily tore the thin fabric of the 'imperial church' (*Reichskirche*), that pale shadow of the national churches elsewhere.

Let us now consider some of the equally distinctive *cultural presuppositions* for Germany's reforming path. There is no doubt about the vitality of German cultural life during the century prior to the Reformation. To take one important indicator, the number of German universities increased continually throughout the fifteenth century, growing from the three young foundations (Heidelberg, Cologne, Erfurt) in existence in 1400 to a total of fourteen by 1506.[5] The German student population expanded disproportionately to the German population as a whole, which suffered decline of that period. There was thus an absolute and a relative increase in the numbers of those with university education – by 1500 there were five times as many students enrolling at university as a century earlier. Founding a university could be a matter of civic pride, as in the case of Cologne, Erfurt or Basel, but the pattern of steady expansion was primarily caused by the desire of sovereign princes to have the prestige of a university offering higher education to their subjects and training potential civil servants. There is a strong possibility that Germany was by 1520 over-supplied with men of higher education, the numbers of graduates far outstripping available demand in princely or civic chanceries, and many found lesser employment as teachers and in the church, perhaps in poorly beneficed positions. If so, one of the important preconditions for the German Reformation was a large pool of intellectual talent, discontented with the opportunities available, and especially with a system riddled with pluralism, favouritism, simony and foreign (Roman) control. The robustness of German intellectual life in the fifteenth century, therefore, was matched by an equally high degree of discontent, even alienation, among its intelligentsia.

Many *German humanists* certainly bore all the blemishes of alienated intellectuals. Historians of the Reformation have perhaps focussed too much on humanism and too little on the wider intellectual and cultural activity outside that movement. This is largely a result of swallowing too readily the propaganda of the sixteenth-century humanists, who presented themselves as voices crying in the wilderness, struggling against the envy of obscurantist hordes. We now know that German intellectual life on the eve of the Reformation was more vital and more variegated than the humanists claimed and that the basic principles of humanism, especially interest in the literature and values of classical antiquity, had penetrated far deeper than was once commonly assumed. It is useful to distinguish between broadly humanist principles and attitudes and the self-conscious movement promoting those values in education, society and religion that we know as German humanism. The widespread diffusion of the former actually enabled the rise of the latter.

German humanism was a peculiarly local variant, however, growing out of the wider interest in humanist studies. The early humanist movement in

Germany had distinctive but limited enthusiasms – initially it focussed strongly on the liberal arts and on poetry and was strongly anti-institutional, setting up a polarity between humanist approaches to letters and scholasticism, the reigning intellectual orthodoxy at all German universities. It began only late in the day to concern itself with the formalities of higher education and with curriculum reform. Where it was based in the universities, it neglected the higher faculties of law, medicine and theology, so that its proponents were accorded junior status and rarely gained positions from which they could decisively change the curriculum. It did influence basic programmes in many schools and transmit its more general principles into civic and princely politics, but German humanists up to the second decade of the sixteenth century still displayed the stridency of outsiders demanding to be taken more seriously.

Many humanists worked themselves up into a reforming zeal just at the moment when their cause began to make more progress in German institutions. This was the zeal both of the ambitious and the discontented, and it was seasoned with a large dash of cultural assertiveness, born of a desire to show that German letters were not backward by contrast with those elsewhere, especially in Italy. Thus, the surge of German cultural nationalism on the eve of the Reformation, largely advanced by self-conscious humanists such as Ulrich von Hutten, was a complex affair, socially, culturally and psychologically. Its combination of intellectual vitality and immaturity in some ways matched the vitality and immaturity of German political development, of which its advocates were only too aware. The yearning to assert German and humanist cultural values easily became mixed up with the desire for more vibrant political development; whether this was to be via the Empire or via powerful local princes was the ongoing ambiguity of German political life. Here perhaps the general rule applied, that national feeling is always more strident when the 'nation', however that term is constructed, is weakest as a real entity.

Alongside humanism, perhaps the most well-known cultural precondition of the Reformation is *the development of printing*, usually mentioned as the indispensable tool for the dissemination of evangelical ideas in the 1520s. Printing was neither a mere technological advance, nor a tool laying idle until the Reformation took it up and put it to effective use; it was rather part of wider social and cultural processes that pre-dated the Reformation. It is important to call attention to certain aspects of these processes in order to understand how far the early culture of print prepared the ground for the Reformation movements. Germans of the later fifteenth century were proudly conscious of that fact that printing was an indigenous invention, regarding it as a special sign of divine blessing. This was no mere metaphor, for early printing had a potently religious dimension, reflected in the overwhelmingly religious nature of the output of the printing press to 1500. The printing press was also born and nurtured in the context of urban culture, especially in great urban centres such as Cologne, Nuremberg or Augsburg – there were a few monastic presses, but these tended not to stay the distance. Yet the most striking feature of the early centres of printing is that they were either university towns or episcopal residences, and bishops and other clergymen played a major role as instigators, authors and readers of printed works. Indeed, many reform-minded clerics seized upon the new invention as a providential means of furthering the cause of religious revival – and for many that meant improving the religious life of the laity. This in turn meant translating religious books into the vernacular, ranging from lives of the saints, works of popular mysticism and prophecy, prayerbooks, penitential handbooks and works of popular devotion at one end of the market, through to weightier and more expensive academic books, including vernacular editions of the Bible, at the other. There was general agreement that vernacular works of piety would strengthen lay religion and promote the cause of religious reform, although learned clerical opinion was more divided on the issue of how far the Bible should be put in the hands of lay people, who might follow the path of earlier heretics and derive from it propositions contrary to the authority and teaching of the church. Some feared that once the laity had access to the vernacular Bible, they would say: 'We now have in our hands the holy Scripture, and can know and expound for ourselves what is necessary for salvation, and need neither the church nor the pope.' This was certainly the fear of such an effective populariser as Geiler von Keysersberg, who held that it was no good thing to print the Bible in German, just as it was dangerous to give a child a knife with which it might cut itself.[6] The more conservative-minded went even further, and in 1485 the Archbishop of Mainz issued a mandate prohibiting the translation into German of any kind of theological work on the ground that this would falsify sacred truth. The advocates of the vernacular upheld the contrary view, expressed by the author of one Cologne chronicle, who in 1499 praised printing as a special gift of God which enabled every person to read, or have read out to him or her, the way to salvation.[7] Printing thus contributed to a campaign to improve the religious education of the laity, a campaign that pre-dated the invention of the printing press, but which was given a new immediacy by it.

It is a matter of dispute how far printing widened literacy – it could be said that the latter was more a pragmatic need occasioned by commercial and craft activity or that it arose from a desire for social mobility, in its turn dependent on higher levels of education. We know that commentators around 1500 were aware of a widespread desire to read, a desire that printing may have met but did not necessarily create. We can plausibly postulate a widening readership, although its social profile is hazy. It may have been more heavily urban than rural, more clerical than lay, more male than female. However, we can point to one significant feature – that many of those most active in vernacular religious publishing encouraged active lay reading and emphasised the importance of lay participation in the work of religious reform virtually to the point of idealising the 'unlearned laity', that is, those literate in German but not in Latin. When early Reformation propaganda presented the lay person as the appropriate bearer of God's reforming Word, as more learned in the truths of religion than the highly trained scholar, it was drawing on this tradition; and when it presented the ideal evangelical Christian as the bible-reading layman, it had merely brought it to fulfilment.

Finally, we must mention religious life in Germany, a complex subject of which I wish to highlight only two points, the desire for religious reform and the incredibly wide range of matters encompassed by the phenomenon of 'religion', which made the task of thoroughgoing reform almost insurmountable. For people of the fifteenth and sixteenth centuries, 'religion' involved not merely questions about salvation and piety (the conduct of a consistently godly life). It also included pastoral aspects (the offering of consolation) and fulfilled a functional purpose (a means of coping with the material problems of daily life, often through recourse to 'magical' means and remedies). All these features flowed from the recognition that spiritual, personal and material dimensions of the human condition were dependent on the sustaining power of the divine. However, religion also had its complicated social, economic and political aspects, and any attempts at reform invariably became entangled in the web of such interests. The Reformation offered a new approach to the question of salvation, but also found itself constrained by these other aspects of religious life, for example, falling prey to political or social interests, or finding that popular attachment to magical remedies persisted despite Protestant attempts to condemn them as 'superstitious'.[8]

The recognition of the need for reform was widespread throughout fifteenth-century Germany. Indeed, the idea of 'reform' had a long tradition there and at certain levels had progressed far and wide, possibly further than elsewhere. The absence of a national church meant that reforming attempts were piecemeal and could appear inadequate, certainly to those who yearned for reform through some single agency such as the pope, the emperor or a general council of the church. Yet in many towns, villages and dioceses steps were undertaken that provided a foundation for the reforms of the sixteenth century. Civic authorities sought to take control of many aspects of religious life, including control of morals, appointment of pastors and the disposition of religious services. They sought to influence provision for pastoral needs, and to direct collective religious life. In many villages, parishioners sought to exercise control over the appointment of their parish clergy so that the religious services they provided could be more effectively integrated into daily communal life. Many bishops sought to train a more professional clergy, both through raising standards of clerical education, and by providing the parish clergy with more precise instructions on how to carry out their job. Here the printing press met the needs of episcopal reform, supplying uniform liturgical books, prayerbooks, handbooks for confessors, manuals for parish priests, and collections of biblical readings (postillen) for each Sunday and feastday of the year from which sermons might be constructed. The large-scale investigation of the state of the parish clergy involved in the episcopal visitation was undertaken, while church authorities began to clamp down on the more over-enthusiastic and theologically dubious manifestations of popular religion. There was the active campaign to encourage lay religious reading, mentioned above. There was a revival of preaching in the vernacular, especially through the creation of funded preacherships on lay initiative, while reforms were undertaken of many monastic houses, often at the initiative of, and aided by, secular authorities. Historians have yet consistently to assemble and evaluate all the various aspects of effective reforms before the Reformation, but we know enough to say that the reforming process was well under way before 1517, and that the Reformation benefited immensely from the entire process. Summing up what has been said in this section, we could say that all these features created a bundle of enabling preconditions within which an essentially German response to a new impulse for religious reform emerged. All the political, cultural and religious features mentioned here contributed to the peculiarity of the German Reformation.

## The peculiarities of the Germans

Religious reform erupted in Germany in the 1520s and was consolidated in the 1530s, following a decade of religious and social ferment. New forms of ecclesiastical organisation began to appear from 1526, the lead being given by Ernestine Saxony, the Landgraviate of Hesse, the duchy of Württemberg and certain imperial cities. Once these new churches had presented the forces of Catholic orthodoxy with a *fait accompli*, there was no chance of reversing the process of reform and schism. What were the salient features of this process that we now know as the Reformation? We could list as many as a dozen aspects that characterise the process, even if they do not describe it exhaustively. The distinctive theologies of the Reformation are not a major focus of attention here and will be left out of the discussion, although they are presupposed in examining the nature and conditions of their reception.

First, the movement of reform originated in the *intelligentsia*, who quickly responded to the 'Luther affair' as it reverberated in university circles, along humanist networks and among senior churchmen and politicians, before breaking surface as a matter of massive public interest. The leading advocates of the new ideas were men of high learning, part of an educated elite, who might have been expected to take a leading role in public, intellectual and religious affairs. They helped to develop the emerging Reformation as a matter of high theological debate alongside the more instinctive religious emotions aroused by Luther, whose early popularity among a wider public rested more on his devotional works than on his theological treatises. Thus, 'Luther's cause' had a double aspect from the beginning: it was a dispute among churchmen and theologians, but also a matter of wider popular concern with piety, salvation and the state of religion. Part of the skill of the leading supporters of the new cause was to project it as essentially a concern of ordinary lay people, while developing complex theologies justifying deviation from previous orthodoxy.

Second, reform originated in an *urban context*, partly because it grew out of debate among the intellectual elites located in the towns, but also because cities were the natural cultural and political centres in which the debate could attract a wider audience and a mass following. This does not mean that there were not those in the courts of princes or even bishops who found themselves attracted by the new ideas – for example, such leading reformers as Wolfgang Capito and Ulrich von Hutten were part of the retinue around the Archbishop of Mainz, Albert of Brandenburg. Nor was interest lacking in noble castles and on noble estates, or in great monastic or religious foundations such as the Premonstratensian Abbey of Belbruck in Pomerania, whose members provided almost all the key figures for the Reformation in Pomerania, as well as the leading reformer of North Germany, Johannes Bugenhagen. More lowly rural dwellers could also hardly have been ignorant of the 'Luther affair' within a year or so of its emergence as a matter of public debate – if nothing else, they visited urban markets and heard the local gossip about such matters. However, the scene of the reforming action tended to be in urban centres such as Wittenberg, Erfurt, Strassburg, Nuremberg, Zwickau, and in many other smaller towns throughout the southwest and central Germany. The towns served as pace-setters and innovators, forcing territorial rulers to take notice of the speed and extent of change, or at least of the intensity with which change was demanded. Dealing with religious upheaval from the outset meant encountering and coming to terms with it in an urban setting.

Third, there was the *conjuncture of religious and social dissent* that turned the demand for reform into a wider movement for change. In the towns it was clear from the earliest days, for example in Wittenberg, that demands for religious change could be linked to social and political grievances and have far-reaching consequences. This made the initial movements a form of social dynamite, requiring only the right kind of detonator to set off a larger explosion of discontent. The detonator was sometimes supplied by anticlericalism, sometimes by inept attempts of secular or ecclesiastical authorities to repress the new ideas, sometimes by impatience for reform. By 1523 it was clear throughout Germany that the ferment of religious dissent had become a broad-meshed demand for 'reformation', a radical alteration in the religious, social and sometimes political features of contemporary life. By late 1524 this spilled over into the upheaval that became known as the 'German Peasants' War', a religiously legitimated revolution, albeit one that failed in most of its primary objectives.[9]

The *linguistic unity* of religious revolt is a fourth distinctive feature. Not only were most of the really significant debates conducted in German, but the German language was continually invoked as the divinely chosen bearer of the new ideas, a means of making evangelical truth clear and accessible to all. The Swabian pamphleteer, popular preacher and former Franciscan, Eberlin von Günzburg, saw it as a sign of the truth and reliability of the new teachings that they were expressed in German, so that every one could encounter and reflect on them. We cannot speak of any uniform German language in this period, for dialects were predominant and there was a vast difference between, for example, Low German and the German spoken in Switzerland. However, the degree of similarity in the written language overcame the differences in dialect and the different variants were sufficiently cognate to minimise problems of translation. That many parts of north Germany used Low German dialect was no significant barrier to the spread of new religious ideas, although it sometimes complicated appointment of preachers and contributed to regionalised development in patterns of reform. Luther's works were quickly translated into Low German, helped by the fact that Wittenberg lay close to the linguistic boundary between Low German and East Middle German, and there were enough students from the north who were fluent in both tongues. They provided the preachers able to cross this minimal divide to enable ideas to spread widely across the Germanophone territories.[10] This clearly influenced the emergence of a 'reformation public opinion', constructed on the basis of pre-existing communication and opinion networks in the vernacular, and using the powerful interface of oral, written and printed communication.[11]

Fifth, *anticlericalism* played an undoubted part as a spur to reform and as a vehicle for popular religious dissent. It might be overstating the case to claim it as a prime mover or as the fuel of the Reformation movements, but its contribution is undeniable.[12] The phenomenon of anticlericalism predated the Reformation, indeed, it existed virtually as an ideological resource in the political armoury of the day, predicated upon the presence of the clergy as a privileged social group within most polities. It could always be invoked by shrewd politicians to divert popular passions from other more embarrassing political, social and economic issues. It also had complex psychological dimensions, based on hatred, envy and fears for salvation – hatred of the arrogant behaviour of some clerics, envy of their privileged life-style and fear that the salvation of all was at risk because of their failures. In the early Reformation it was used in all these ways to inspire negative feelings about the old religious regime and, more importantly, to move people to take positive action. It often stirred up baser emotional instincts while invoking a morally elevated cause, creating fear and loathing of the 'papists', arousing anxieties and playing on popular emotion. Many riots and violent disturbances were provoked by whipping up anticlerical feelings, so providing the occasion for suspending the old forms of worship, expelling priests, monks and nuns and 'cleansing' churches of the alleged impurities of the 'priests of Baal', the idolatrous worshippers of false gods. Especially in the towns, civic leaders used it opportunistically or manipulatively to get their own way in the matter of reform, while militant reformers used it to put pressure on the reluctant and to create solidarity among their committed followers. Although it was not a constant or indispensable feature of the Reformation, the entire character of that process would have been different without it.

We should highlight, sixth, the importance of *propaganda* for the rapid and polemically effective spread of dissident ideas. Indeed, it can be said that the Reformation was a massive exercise in propaganda in all its complex forms and manifestations. Propaganda was both negative and positive: it both criticised and exposed the shortcomings of the established religious regime, as well as advocating alternatives. We would misunderstand its nature if we saw it merely a means of inducing intellectual conviction, for propaganda contained many emotional elements. It dealt in revelations with the power of prophetic utterances, not only calling attention to known abuses, but showing their inner religious connections and drawing out their complex cosmic significance. Thus, many religious grievances were shown to be part of an elaborate structure of systematic exploitation and deception on the part of the papal church, in effect part of a diabolical conspiracy designed to frustrate God's plan for human salvation and to condemn as many as possible to the torments of hell. It thus relied on a shock-effect, by unmasking the hitherto revered (the papacy, the clergy, sacred events such as the Eucharist) and showing them as works of the Devil, masks behind which the Antichrist went about his terrible work. We should not underestimate the impact of such revelations on the religious psyche of the time. The success of the Reformation relied on the willingness of many people suddenly to abandon a system revered by their ancestors over many generations. This was only possible by arousing such deep anxiety about their chances of salvation within that system that they were willing to reject it totally and immediately. It was an essential role of propaganda to arouse this anxiety and to maintain solidarity among those thus converted to evangelical views. Without it, the Reformation movements would have been signally ineffective.[13]

We should next mention, seventh, the unique *freedom of movement* which allowed dissent to unfold unhindered by political repression or ecclesiastical discipline. All movements require both social and political space to emerge and develop; political space in the sense that political authorities permit the free dissemination of their ideas and ideals; social space in the sense that particular social groups are receptive to these ideas and see them as relevant to their own spiritual and material needs. Political space was assured by the reluctance of secular authorities in many towns, lordships or principalities to enforce papal and imperial condemnations, to censor printing and preaching, and to hinder the free dissemination of ideas. Especially important, however, was securing a favourable response from those in key positions of authority. Leading politicians such as the city mayors Bernhard Besserer in Ulm or Adolarius Huttener in Erfurt, city secretaries or legal advisers such as Lazarus Spengler and Christoph Scheurl in Nuremberg could smooth the path of reform. Scheurl played the key role of mediator, since he actually introduced Luther's ideas into Nuremberg as early as 1517 and ensured that they found a favourable hearing among the ruling elite. It was often a decisive feature of the successful progress of reform in so many towns that it could rely on a group of supporters in the ruling town council. Their political influence or decisions facilitated the development of dissident ideas and occasionally fostered them directly. If they took no positive action in support of 'the Gospel', it was almost as important that they either neutralised resistance or provided protection for the advocates of the new beliefs. The primary demand of any local reform movement was for someone to preach the 'pure word of God'. Once this demand was achieved and preaching was permitted to proceed relatively unhindered, the way was open for more radical chances in the liturgy and in the structure of the church. Thus, the 'preaching mandates' issued by so many town councils have rightly been seen as the foundation charters of the Reformation – they gave the green light for the work of reform to proceed apace. But they depended on the available political space which allowed them to work.

Social space was ensured both by political permissiveness and by the very broad-meshed nature of the early evangelical message, which did not exclude any social group from its implications. Even the clergy, the major target of negative polemic, could win approval and acceptance by internalising and acting upon evangelical ideas, turning to preaching or fulfilling a genuinely pastoral role. Monasticism was perhaps most marginalised, but even here evangelical monasteries and foundations came to be accepted as long as they conformed to the new principles. Thus, it was possible for the evangelical movement to take root in almost every group in society. Although the new ideas may have made their greatest impact on the clergy, the urban classes seemed to be the preferred target audience closely followed by the peasantry. The idealisation of the 'common man' as the bearer of the work of the Gospel contributed much to the ready reception among both these social classes. The term was wonderfully ambiguous, sending signals both to the formal citizen of urban communes, who thought of himself as 'the common man' *par excellence*, but also to the rural classes, where it had some of the connotations attached to the modern notion of 'the common people'. It is true, however, that the gender specification of the term rather hindered its appeal to women, and we must look to other kinds of resonances in the early evangelical message to understand female responses.

This calls attention, eighth, to the importance of *gender differences*, an issue that presents the Reformation historian with considerable problems. Most evangelical propaganda was gender specific, aimed at the 'common *man*', while the idealised lay Christian in the person of the 'evangelical peasant' or the 'evangelical burgher' was usually a male figure. There were very few female pamphleteers or evangelical activists to serve as role models attracting women to the new movements. On the other hand, women had a particularly strong attachment to female saints, who were seen as powerful intercessors in childbirth and for the alleviation of female ailments. How, then, did evangelical ideas appeal specifically to women? There are two possibilities to consider. First, the long medieval tradition of female piety focussing on the person of Christ and with its own complex gender-specific dimensions, found a focus in the evangelical message of Christ as sole saviour. Second, the emphasis on the all-importance of the Word of God as a means to salvation presented a gender-neutral religious message. Taken with the idea that lay people could themselves take up and read the Scripture, this may have encouraged women to take charge of their own spiritual lives, especially when linked to the anti-sacerdotal aspects of much of evangelical thought. Just as with medieval mystical thought, which had a powerful appeal to women, the evangelical message offered an unmediated access to piety and salvation, and one with which women could identify within their own gender-specific religious circumstances.

However, it is difficult to know how far such considerations may have moved women to participate in the more active aspects of the evangelical movements. We know that women were present in many demonstrations and disturbances, sometimes they took more prominent roles, deriding priests, attacking monks and nuns, mocking the newly discredited expressions of orthodox religious practice. However, the evidence is sparse by comparison with that of male activity, even allowing for the gender bias in official accounts. In a world which reserved active political roles, including those of dissent and rebellion, almost exclusively to men, it required a greater leap for women to feature prominently as individuals, rather than a part of wider collectivities. In one major area of female life, nunneries, the evidence for female response is not without its problems. There was certainly a mass exodus from convents as a result of the Reformation, but the reasons are complicated. In many cases, fathers or brothers of evangelical conviction simply fetched their daughters or sisters home without consulting their preferences. Some women undoubtedly welcomed release from a cloister to which they had been consigned more for secular than for religious reasons. Yet the emptying of the nunneries often occurred more through external political action, as a result of riot or disturbance, because of the Peasants' War, or in consequence of secularisation of monastic houses by ruling authorities. We can point to many women who remained attached to their collective religious life and resisted evangelical reform, others may have continued it informally after their expulsion, living in private houses in the manner of beguines. We can rarely trace former members of female religious orders; often they are most visible as the wives of the new preachers, and this status may have appealed to such women as a way of continuing a religious vocation outside the cloister. The role of ordinary wives and daughters, however, remains completely in the dark for lack of wider research. Evidence about the activities of women attracted to radical religion shows that they took on active roles as disseminators of their new found belief, in some cases putting away unbelieving spouses and entering new spiritual unions with fellow believers. Much more research is required in this field, but in general we can say that the overall effect of the Reformation was not the freeing of women to take more active religious roles, but their subjection to a strengthened form of moralising patriarchy.[14]

Ninth, there is the importance of *communalism*, roughly speaking, the manner in which ideas of reform grew out of a desire for wider communal control of religion, religious life and the institutionalised church, and the way in which this communal impulse shaped the type of reform envisaged by some Reformers. The desire of small communities to take charge of their own affairs was undoubtedly a major feature of both urban and rural politics in the late middle ages, based on an idealised understanding of the commune as a form of collective life enabling maximum participation and control of local government. This communal impulse extended to religious life, especially in the demand for parish communities to take charge of parish finances and to appoint and dismiss their own pastors, who were expected to provide the religious services essential both for salvation and for this-worldly consolation. The Reformation clearly benefited from the communal impulse, since many early Reformation principles echoed those of communalist ideals. Traces of communalism can be found in all parts of Germany, but communal movements were stronger and more developed in south Germany and Switzerland, where they undoubtedly coloured the kind of religious demands and organisation that emerged out of religious reform. However, the communal impulse was no uncomplicated matter, since it was easily undermined by the inherent tendency in most sixteenth-century communities towards oligarchy, or at least towards the privileging of elite groups who were able to assert their own self-interest in the name of an idealised commune. Thus, the notion of the commune was more an ideal-type, a set of aspirations which each interest group sought to fill out according to its own understanding. Yet there was an important moment in which the secular aspirations of local communities coincided with the ideals of the early Reformation, with the notion that each community should take charge of its own religious affairs. This 'communalist conjuncture' helped give the Reformation movements a powerful political and social momentum to turn what might have been isolated collective strivings into a more universal cause.[15]

The tenth characteristic is the *centrifugal tendency of reform*, away from a national church and a diocesan model towards a more localised church, understood in terms of smaller social and ecclesiastical units. One of the most striking features of the first places to be reformed was the manner in which they spoke of themselves as separate churches, undoubtedly in conscious imitation of New Testament models, speaking of the 'church of Wittenberg', the 'church of Erfurt', the 'church of Strassburg', almost in the same tones as the church at Corinth, the church at Ephesus, the church of Jerusalem. As the new churches began to organise themselves, they were set up on this model, as almost independent local congregations, their status ensured by the right to elect their own pastor. The Reformations carried through by the princes in their own territories mirrored this localising tendency, rejecting the older episcopal structure which organised the church into large (sometimes impossibly large) dioceses, which were then sub-divided into deaneries. Instead, the structure of the church was grafted onto the secular administrative structure. Administrative districts varied in size in sixteenth-century Germany and could encompass a few villages or take in a couple of market towns and a hundred villages. However, they were usually focussed on a district seat, either a market town, a castle-town or some other urban central place. This gave the structure of the new churches a distinctively local character, and provided a more manageable focus for pastoral and religious life than the older dioceses. Religious grievances which could not be settled with the pastor could now be referred to a Superintendent and/or a district official, both located in a nearby town at most a few miles distant. Only in very rare circumstances were villagers forced to take the matter further, to the territorial ruler at his court or capital. It is true that a centralised ecclesiastical bureaucracy did grow up eventually, detracting from some of the localised character of religious life. Moreover, the right of each community to elect its own pastors was often attenuated into a more passive right merely to accept an outside nominee, but even here a local community could occasionally assert its local independence in the name of evangelical tradition.[16]

The importance of *sovereign authority* (*Obrigkeit*) for ensuring a successful institutionalisation of reform is the eleventh feature to discuss. Religious reform in any community involved considerable upheaval: alteration to religious ceremonies, the restructuring of ecclesiastical benefices, the abolition of monastic foundations and other religious institutions, the cessation of pious foundations and endowments, often the reordering of parish structures and finances, and infringement of episcopal rights. These were steps fraught with innumerable social, political and legal dangers and therefore not matters to be undertaken lightly. The legal problems were multiple and complex: sequestration of church property was a breach of property law, intervention in appointments to benefices infringed the secular legal rights of patrons, while the cessation of religious endowments and foundations was a breach of private contract. If undertaken by an inferior authority, i.e. someone holding authority devolved from above such as a landlord or a territorial town, there was the danger that the superior authority would intervene to oppose the changes or take action against the offenders. At best, it could involve protracted and costly lawsuits, or it could provoke a feud or other form of coercive action.

In this situation considerable advantages were enjoyed by sovereign authorities as holders of magisterial office equipped with prerogative powers and the coercive forms of lordship and domination, responsible to no lord other than God and the Emperor.[17] It was for this reason that some imperial cities were able to innovate quickly and efficiently – legally they had only the Emperor to fear, although there was still the danger of citation before the Imperial Chamber (*Reichskammergericht*) by those whose privileges or rights they had infringed. However, there was a view on the part of princes and independent nobles that corporative entities such as cities were not bearers of sovereignty, since they were dependent on the consent of their citizens, whereas the notion of sovereign authority was personal and hierarchical, flowing downwards from above, with responsibility only to those in the superior ranks of hierarchy. In this view, only princes of the empire were the real bearers of sovereignty. In practice, what counted was the coercive force attached to the status of a superior authority, and smaller polities such as imperial cities found that even possessing the status of an *Obrigkeit* was of little practical use when it came to negotiating with other powers. An imperial city such as Schwäbisch Hall found, for this reason, that reform was only possible in piecemeal and hesitant fashion in its eighteen rural parishes, where the patronage rights were in the hands of eight different patrons, including three religious foundations, one count of the empire and members of the local nobility. Although it possessed in theory the same sovereign authority as other immediate members of the Empire, it was bound by pragmatic limitations. Its sovereignty did not extend beyond imposing reform within its own area of undisputed competence within the city. However, had it possessed a complete control over its villages, it would have been able to innovate there thoroughly and at will, as the city of Strassburg was able to do.[18]

Finally, we should not overlook the considerable influence exercised by *ecclesiastical institutions* on the possibilities of reform. In the first instance, we should mention the German bishoprics, most of which were powerful territorial states in their own right and which in general proved immune to the forces of evangelical reform within their borders. The Reformation movements were unable to convert any major bishopric to evangelical ideas by pressure from below, although it sometimes looked during the Peasants' War as though this was a likelihood, not least when Würzburg was occupied by a peasant army and the Archbishopric of Mainz capitulated to the rebels in the first week of May 1525. These successes proved to be as short-lived as the evangelical movements in a large number of episcopal residential towns – Würzburg, Bamberg, Trier, Mainz, Passau, Freising, Eichstätt and Salzburg. Even evangelically minded bishops were rarely able to carry their bishopric with them, as two bishops of Cologne discovered in the 1540s and 1580s. The nub of the problem was often found in the episcopal chapter, responsible for electing the bishop and which often retained a strong degree of influence over the affairs of the bishopric. Many chapters may have contained individual members inclined to the new ideas, but self-interest persuaded the majority of the canons to remain with the old church. Thus, the cathedral chapter of Magdeburg held back the Reformation in that diocese for almost a generation, until resistance was finally broken by a combination of expulsion from the city and the appointment of an evangelical archbishop as an expression of the dynastic politics of the rulers of Brandenburg. It was only late in the second half of the sixteenth century that the gradual election of Protestant canons enabled the election of Protestant bishops and opened the possibility of a reformation of the bishoprics, only to find this path blocked by imperial action.[19]

Some bishoprics in central and north Germany did turn Lutheran, but largely as a result of outside interference, under the impact of the dynastic policies of local princes, as occurred in the Saxon bishoprics of Merseburg, Meissen, Naumburg-Zeitz and Wurzen in the 1540s, or in Hildesheim under the influence of the duke of Braunschweig. In other bishoprics the gradual permeation of Protestantism lamed the territory, rather than being able to convert it completely, as occurred in the bishoprics of Speyer and Worms, where the pockets of orthodoxy existed like islands in a Protestant sea. In the many bishoprics that survived the Protestant onslaught, the possibility remained for active Counter-Reformation policies which preserved large chunks of German territory in both north and south as areas of continuing Catholic allegiance. The same was true of other powerful institutions such as abbeys or urban foundations. The vitality or resilience of these institutions kept reform at bay. Many were indeed sapped by the depredations of the Peasants' War, yet many such as Kempten or Weingarten recovered from this setback and remained bastions of Catholicism.

## Model Germany?

I have tried to single out some distinguishing aspects of the German Reformation, both in its preconditions and in the way in which it developed as an ongoing and many-sided process. It cannot be claimed that many of the features described here were unique to Germany, although a more careful comparison with other forms of Reformation will be attempted in a later essay. However, in the light of the preconditions and structural features highlighted in the first part of this essay, the course of the Reformation in Germany was hardly surprising. The concatenation of preconditions and characteristics do add up to create something that was unrepeatable in exactly the same form. In one banal sense the German Reformation was only truly unique in having been first in time, although this involved rather more than the biological accident of Luther being born and working in Thuringia-Saxony. Like the first in any series of revolutions, it could serve as a model to imitate in similar or even dissimilar circumstances, but under three conditions, summed up in the terms 'the leap in the dark', the 'pacemaker function' and the 'awful warning'.

Much of the distinctiveness of what unfolded in Germany arose from the first of these, the fact that what emerged as 'the Reformation' truly involved a leap into the unknown. Once the conviction had set in that the old form of religion was no longer acceptable and the old shape of the church untenable, the advocates of reform faced a confusing dilemma, for they had no models on which to build a new kind of church. Despite claims to be returning to the 'primitive church', the reformers were forced by the logic of their own position to strike out in a new direction. Much of the first generation of reforming activity was, of necessity, a matter of trial and error. The first years of the Reformation were marked by an enormous wave of creative religious fervour, presenting a very wide range of possibilities for change with a freshness that was never to be repeated in subsequent waves of reform. Some alternatives were rejected on theological or ecclesiological grounds, others for social or political reasons. Others were simply the result of pragmatic decisions that later came to have the force of custom. Indeed, the normative Lutheran model was one which opted, as far as possible, for gradual change rather than sudden and dramatic change. However, once a range of alternatives had been identified, it tended to set out an agenda of possibilities for imitation or avoidance and so provided a limiting framework.

It was its role in setting the agenda that gave the German Reformation a pacemaker function that no other variant of reform was ever quite able to emulate. The kinds of solutions to the problem of reform worked out there provided a benchmark against which all other variations on the theme of religious reform were to be judged, whether from the side of heterodoxy or orthodoxy. Thus, attempts to carry out reform within the broad structure of existing belief, such as the Erasmian reform undertaken by princely authority in Jülich-Cleves, or the caesaro-papalist reform initiated in England by Henry VIII ('Catholicism without the pope'), were forced into the mould established by and for the German Reformation. Even the distinctive approach initiated in Switzerland by Zwingli was seen primarily in relationship to the evangelical pattern to the north, helped by the early political checks to Zwinglianism within the Swiss confederation.

At least part of the mould bore the label 'an awful warning', referring to the danger of revolutionary social and political upheaval linked to dissent in religion. The 'awful warning' was associated most specifically with the danger of widespread peasant upheaval, so that most authorities both inside and outside Germany kept a wary eye out for warning signs of like occurrences. This did not prevent peasant insurrection linked to a religious cause, as both France and Austria were to learn, but in some sense being forewarned was to be forearmed, and no subsequent chain of events came as close to creating a comparable revolutionary upheaval originating in the peasantry. It would attribute too much to the ability of people of the sixteenth century to master the tidal wave of events often associated with movements on the scale of the Reformation to argue that they could learn wholly effective lessons from what happened in Germany in the 1520s. But orthodox opponents of reform clearly benefited from the German experience to know rather more effectively how to nip dissent in the bud or to inhibit its progress. On the other hand, supporters of reform had precedents to imitate and mistakes to avoid, but above all traditions to follow and heroes and martyrs to emulate.

NOTES

1 The term *Wildwuchs* to describe the period 1520–5 was not coined by Franz Lau, as claimed in Andrew Pettegree, ed., *The Early Reformation in Europe* (Cambridge, 1992), p. 16, but dates from the early part of this century, although I have been unable to trace its first usage precisely.

2 There was, of course, no sixteenth-century entity corresponding to the word 'Germany'. Here I use it to designate the German-speaking territories of the Holy Roman Empire, but excluding other germanophone parts of Eastern Europe and the Habsburg lands in Austria and the Tyrol. This highly artificial division is simply a convenient means of establishing boundaries with several other contributions in this volume.

3 Machiavelli's account of German affairs is in his *Opere*, vol. II, *Arte della guerra e scritti politici minori*, ed. Sergio Bertelli (Milan, 1961), pp. 195–215, the passages referred to on pp. 210–12; an extract translated in David Webster and Louis Green, eds., *Documents in Renaissance and Reformation History* (London, 1969), pp. 59–61.

4 For examples of such serf-owning towns (Basel, Solothurn, Freiburg im Breisgau), see Claudia Ulbrich, *Leibherrschaft am Oberrhein im Spätmittelalter* (Göttingen, 1979), pp. 136–215.

5 I have excluded two earlier imperial foundations, Prague (1348) and Vienna (1365). The German universities were Heidelberg (1385), Cologne (1388), Erfurt (1392), Leipzig (1409), Rostock (1419), Greifswald (1456), Freiburg im Breisgau (1460), Basel (1460), Ingolstadt (1472), Trier (1473), Mainz (1477), Tübingen (1477), Wittenberg (1502), Frankfurt/Oder (1506).

6 The quotation is from the anonymous author of a manuscript sermon of 1515, put in the mouth of a lay Christian taking advantage of the vernacular Bible, cited in Johannes Janssen, *Geschichte des deutschen Volkes* (7th edn, Freiburg im Breisgau, 1881), vol. I, p. 607.

7 The debate about making restricted knowledge available to ordinary people was not just confined to religious matters, but affected other areas of professional competence such as law and medicine. Vernacular editions of medical manuals or handbooks would enable the unskilled to treat themselves at little expense or, in the case of the law, expose the limitations of the professionals who charged so highly for their services. It was a debate that continued well into the seventeenth century; see Bob Scribner, 'Heterodoxy, Literacy and Print in the Early German Reformation', in *Heresy and Literacy c. 1100–c. 1530*, ed. Ann Hudson and Peter Biller (Cambridge, 1994), pp. 255–78; Klaus Schreiner, 'Laienbildung als Herausforderung für Kirche und Gesellschaft', *Zeitschrift für historische Forschung*, 11 (1984), pp. 257–324, especially pp. 279–87.

8 These aspects of religious life discussed in more detail in Bob Scribner, 'The Reformation and the Religion of the Common People', in *The Reformation in Germany and Europe. Interpretations and Issues, Archiv für Reformationsgeschichte, Sonderband* (Gütersloh, 1993), pp. 204–24; the problem of popular magic in Robert W. Scribner, 'The Reformation, Popular Magic and the

*Entzauberung der Welt'*, *Journal of Interdisciplinary History*, 23 (1993), pp. 475–94.

9 For these aspects see Peter Blickle, *The Revolution of 1525* (Baltimore, 1981); Peter Blickle, *Communal Reformation. The Quest for Salvation in Sixteenth-Century Germany* (Atlantic Highlands, N. J., 1992); and with a somewhat different interpretation, Tom Scott and Bob Scribner, eds., *The German Peasants' War. A History in Documents* (Atlantic Highlands, N. J., 1991).

10 There is no comparable study of the diffusion from Wittenberg into North Germany to that by Manfred Hannemann, *The Diffusion of the Reformation in Southwestern Germany 1518–1534* (Chicago, 1975).

11 For the points in this paragraph see C. J. Wells, *German. A Linguistic History to 1945* (Oxford, 1985), pp. 179–216. A slightly more qualified view, especially stressing the divergence between South Germany/Switzerland and central Germany, is found in Erwin Arndt and Gisela Brandt, *Luther und die deutsche Sprache* (Leipzig, 1987), pp. 32–69.

12 The role of anticlericalism is overemphasised in Hans-Jürgen Goertz, *Pfaffenhass und Grossgeschrey. Die reformatorischen Bewegungen in Deutschland 1517–1529* (Munich, 1987), while describing with great insight many of its central features; it is underestimated by Goertz's critics and by Euan Cameron, *The European Reformation* (Oxford, 1991), pp. 297–9. The comments here are based on my article 'Anticlericalism and the Cities' in Peter Dykema and Heiko A. Oberman, eds., *Anticlericalism in Late Medieval and Early Modern Europe* (Leiden, 1993), pp. 147–66; this volume represents the most extensive discussion of the phenomenon to date. For an earlier view of the theme, see my article 'Anticlericalism and the German Reformation', in *Popular Culture and Popular Movements in Reformation Germany* (London, 1987), pp. 243–56.

13 I have discussed propaganda in more detail in the second edition of *For the Sake of Simple Folk. Popular Propaganda for the German Reformation* (Oxford, 1994).

14 On the subject, see Lyndal Roper, *The Holy Household. Women and Morals in Reformation Augsburg* (Oxford, 1989); Merry E. Wiesner, 'Nuns, Wives and Mothers. Women and the Reformation in Germany', in Sherrin Marshall, ed., *Women in Reformation and Counter-Reformation Europe. Public and Private Worlds* (Bloomington, 1989), pp. 8–28.

15 For 'communalism', see Blickle, *Communal Reformation* and R. W. Scribner, 'Communities and the Nature of Power', in *Germany. A Social and Economic History*, ed. Bob Scribner and Sheilagh Ogilvie (London, forthcoming), vol. I, for criticism of Blickle's 'communalism' thesis, Heinz Schilling, *Religion, Political Culture and the Emergence of Early Modern German Society* (Leiden, 1992), pp. 189–201; and R. W. Scribner, 'Paradigms of Urban Reform; Gemeindereformation or Erastian Reformation?' in *Die dänische Reformation vor ihrem internationalem Hintergrund*, ed. Leif Grane and Kai Hørby (Göttingen, 1990), pp. 111–28.

16 These matters discussed in Scribner, 'Paradigms of Urban Reform', and in 'Pastoral Care and the Reformation in Germany', in *Humanism and Reform. The Church in Europe, England and Scotland 1400–1643. Essays in Honour of James K. Cameron*, ed. James Kirk (Oxford, 1991), pp. 77–97.

17 One should note here that the notion of *Obrigkeit* is different from the concept of sovereignty enunciated and popularised by Bodin, who saw it as unitary and

indivisible power. It certainly involved a hierarchical concept, in which authority could be devolved from higher authorities such as a prince or (ultimately) the Emperor; but it was also linked to the idea of authority of office and plurality of authorities under the overarching notion that all secular authority was divinely ordained. Thus, it excluded any implication that authority derived from the direct consent of the governed, but could include the notion that the governed had to give assent and could withhold it for legitimate reason. The period of the early German Reformation stood at the crossroads of a development from one path (a consensual and contractual view of authority) along another (towards Bodin's notion of sovereignty). The German concept and its development is scarcely alluded to in J. H. Burns, ed., *The Cambridge History of Political Thought 1450–1700* (Cambridge, 1991), chapters 6 and 10.

18  On Schwäbisch Hall, J. Gmelin, *Geschichte der Reichstadt Hall und ihres Gebiets* (Schwäbisch Hall, 1986), pp. 743–5; on Strassburg, James M. Kittelson, 'Successes and Failures in the German Reformation. The Report from Strasbourg', *Archiv für Reformationsgeschichte*, 73 (1982); James M. Kittelson, 'Visitations and Popular Religious Culture. Further Reports from Strasbourg', in *Pietas and Societas. New Trends in Reformation Social History*, ed. Kyle C. Sessions and Phillip N. Bebb (Kirksville, Missouri, 1985), pp. 89–101.

19  Examples in this section are drawn from information in *Territorien Ploetz. Geschichte der deutschen Lände*, vol. I, ed. G. W. Sante and A. G. Ploetz Verlag (Würzburg, 1963).


FURTHER READING

Most of the major items have been mentioned in the notes above, especially in notes 8–9, 12, 15. Euan Cameron, *The European Reformation* (Oxford, 1991) is the best recent introduction, while a useful synthesis of intellectual antecedents is Alister McGrath, *The Intellectual Origins of the European Reformation* (Oxford, 1987). Andrew Pettegree, ed., *The Early Reformation in Europe* (Cambridge, 1992) usefully complements the articles here. There are also many valuable essays in the second edition of *The New Cambridge Modern History*, vol. II, *The Reformation 1520–1559*, ed. G. R. Elton (Cambridge, 1990). A collection of documents that takes account of more recent research is Pamela Johnson and Bob Scribner, *The Reformation in Germany and Switzerland* (Cambridge, 1993).

# 2 Switzerland

*Kaspar von Greyerz*

The first impulse for the spread of the Reformation in the Swiss confederation originated in the cities. Zurich took the lead, followed by Berne and, later, by Basel and Schaffhausen. The role of these towns as territorial lords facilitated its propagation in the countryside, as well as, chiefly due to Berne's Western designs, its spilling over into the French-speaking part of Switzerland. In all three cities a coalition movement of artisans, evangelically minded priests and individual councillors ensured its ultimate success, even against the will of the acting urban regime, as was the case in Berne and Basel.[1] However, the Reformation message did not prove contagious in all cities of the confederation. It ultimately failed in Lucerne, Fribourg and Solothurn.

It has been estimated that in 1500 the population of Switzerland (in its modern boundaries) amounted to slightly less than 800,000 and to above one million inhabitants in 1600. Although the significance of urbanisation for early modern Switzerland should by no means be underestimated, it must be clear that we are looking at cities of a comparatively small size. The most sizeable among them in the sixteenth century were Basel (9,000 – 10,000 inhabitants) and Geneva (approximately 10,000), which in the heyday of Huguenot immigration around 1560 even reached a figure as high as 17,000. Berne had about 5,000 inhabitants, St Gallen 4,500 to 5,500, and Zurich's population ranged between 5,000 and 8,000 persons. The population estimates for sixteenth-century Solothurn, Fribourg and Lucerne range between 2,000 and 4,500 inhabitants.

Zurich took the lead in the Swiss Reformation and its role of pacemaker indirectly rallied the forces of resistance at a relatively early date. This was particularly the case in Central Switzerland, where by 1524 the cantons of Lucerne, Uri, Schwyz, Unterwalden and Zug, in opposition to Zurich's ecclesiastical policy, began to form the nucleus of the Catholic party of the confederation. Within a few years only, this group was joined by Fribourg and Solothurn. In 1528 Zurich and the evangelical party within the confederation gained the support of Berne. This was crucial for the further spread of the movement in Switzerland. In 1529 and especially in 1531, the confrontation between the two parties led to agreements, which created a stalemate stifling the further advance of the Reformation and cementing the confessional factions and fronts for generations to come. The most important underlying principle of these agreements was the principle of confessional parity.

This meant that major confessional conflict was in effect averted in the interest of the political survival of the confederation, a basic consensus that was to govern the policy of the members for generations to come. It was re-confirmed in the Villmergen treaties of 1656 and 1712, which ended renewed outbreaks of open confessional strife, and was maintained down to the creation of the modern Swiss federal state in 1848.

The turmoil of the Reformation reached Switzerland just when the late medieval process of territorial consolidation finally came to a halt by about 1520. The last full members to join the complicated network of treaties, which formed the backbone of the late medieval and early modern confederation, were Basel and Schaffhausen in 1501, and Appenzell in 1513. From then onwards there were thirteen full members: Uri, Schwyz, Unterwalden, Lucerne, Zurich, Berne, Fribourg, Solothurn, Basel, Schaffhausen and Appenzell – in the chronological order of their accession. The city cantons fully matched the rural members in terms of territorial expansion.

A second layer of the network of treaties in question comprised the so-called Associated Members (*Zugewandte Orte*). Among them were St Gallen, Mülhausen in the Upper Alsace, Biel and Rottweil in the Black Forest, as well as the County of Neuchâtel and the Benedictine Abbey of St Gallen. In the course of the sixteenth century, Geneva and the Bishop of Basel also joined their ranks, although, for largely confessional reasons, they were associated only with individual members of the confederation. The Valais and the Grisons formed states of their own, which were, however, closely interconnected with the confederation.

Associate members did not enjoy the same rights as the thirteen full members of the confederation. Generally, they took no part in the government and administration of the Mandated Territories (*Gemeine Herrschaften*), which were subject to the control of some or several of the full members. The area of Baden and its hinterland (the *Freie Ämter*), the Thurgau, the Rhine valley bordering on Appenzell and the Toggenburg region, as well as the areas of Sargans were Mandated Territories, and so were the several bailiwicks, which made up the Ticino in the South. An additional cluster of such territories was administered jointly by Berne and Fribourg in the West. The collectively governed Mandated Territories were to become the particular 'zones of confessional irritation'.[2]

The agreements made by the two confessional parties in 1529 and 1531 and their underlying principle of parity not only put a stop to the further spread of the Reformation, they also inhibited a possible further growth of the confederation by way of additional association as this would have upset the prevailing confessional balance. It was only at the periphery of the confederation that the advance of the Reformation did not come to a halt in 1531. This applies, of course, to French-speaking Switzerland, where the major successes of the Reformation were linked to Berne's occupation of the Pays de Vaud in 1536. In the remote alpine world of the Valais, as well as in the bishopric of Basel, notably at Porrentruy, it made inroads into the educated section of the population, notably during the 1550s and 60s, but failed to generate a broader movement. The ensuing decades witnessed the increasing hold of the Counter Reformation on the hitherto Catholic regions of Switzerland, made evident by the establishment of Jesuit schools in Lucerne, Fribourg and Porrentruy between 1574 and 1591. At the same time, the Capuchins founded monasteries at Altdorf, Stans and Lucerne (1581–9). Although Catholic reform was noticeably slow in gaining a hold on the Valais, the Indian summer of the Protestant Reformation nonetheless remained a short-lived episode.

The following will be in four parts. First we shall look briefly at the course of the Reformation in Switzerland from Zurich in the 1520s to Geneva in the 1540s and 50s. Secondly, I will focus on the impact of the Swiss Reformation on social and ecclesiastical discipline. In part three, we will examine the appeal of the Reformation to the common people. The fourth and final section of this essay will consist of a short conclusion.

## I

In the cities, the century preceding the Reformation was marked by the city council's increasing invasion of monastic and ecclesiastical privilege. The aim of this policy was the gradual integration of the church within the civic community. Similarly, the Swiss cantons managed to expand their control over the church in rural areas 'to a considerable and probably even exceptionable extent'.[3] This was an important precondition of the Reformation.

The Swiss Reformation began in Zurich. Its chief representative during the 1520s was Huldrych Zwingli, common priest at the city's Grossmünster church from December 1518. The simultaneous discovery of St Augustine's theology, knowledge about Martin Luther's quest for reform, and experience of the plague of 1519, turned him into a reformer eager to combine ecclesiastical with social reform, as became apparent, for example, in his fierce opposition to the mercenary system, so dear to many Swiss contemporaries for whom it was a source of income and even of wealth.

Zwingli differed from Luther from the outset in the way he linked inner and outer reform. It is not surprising that they should also differ in their theology of the eucharist, a difference which was to become the symbol for all the points of doctrinal contention separating Protestants of the Reformed (Zwinglian and, later, Calvinist) persuasion from those of a Lutheran faith. While Luther insisted on Christ's physical presence in the eucharist, Zwingli, in the wake not just of Cornelis Hoen but also of Erasmus, interpreted the Lord's Supper as a communal remembrance of Christ's suffering.[4]

Zwingli's marked advocacy of ecclesiastical and social reform soon not only won him a following in Zurich but also a number of influential opponents. In order to overcome the latter he appealed to the city council and was granted a disputation, which took place on 29 January 1523 under the auspices of the city's authorities. It brought Zwingli a decisive victory over his opponents and ensured the continuation of reform which, on Easter 1525, ended with the official introduction of the Reformation symbolised by the abolition of the mass and the official removal of images. Additional reforms of those years encompassed, *inter alia*, the abolition of pilgrimages and of saints' days, the reform of communal poor relief, as well as the city's refusal to renew a treaty with the King of France covering mercenary service. The first Zurich disputation of 29 January 1523 has rightly been claimed to have been a decisive event in the Protestant Reformation in that it laid the ground for the further creation of Reformed communal churches in Switzerland as well as abroad.

From 1523 the Reformation in Zurich was accompanied by considerable socio-religious turmoil in and outside the city, which erupted in acts of popular iconoclasm and which, in 1524, merged with the beginnings of the Peasants' War. Together with a series of disputations held between September 1523 and June 1524 it led the city authorities to order the removal of all images from the churches under their control. In accordance with Zwingli's stern opposition against all forms of what he considered idolatry this ultimately even led to the destruction of all organs in 1527.

However, these measures did not suffice to temper the impatience of some of the more zealous sections of the rural population, who expected a combination of a thorough reform of the church with social reforms, such as the abolition of the tithe.[5] The most radical among them joined the Anabaptists.

The polarisation between the confessional parties dividing the confederation increased considerably after the powerful city of Berne adhered to the Reformation in the spring of 1528, especially since Berne, Biel, Zurich, Constance and Strassburg concluded the *Christliches Burgrecht*, a mutual defence treaty. By 1529, a confessional war between the evangelical party, especially Zurich and Berne, and the Catholic cantons of central Switzerland became inevitable, not least in view of the increasing confessional conflict in the government of Mandated Territories, such as the Zurich hinterland (*Freie Ämter*) and the Thurgau, which were ruled jointly by Reformed and Catholic members of the confederation. The first confrontation ended peacefully, however, as bloodshed was avoided at the last minute. The First Peace of Kappel of 1529, as we have seen, made the principle of confessional parity a basis for future reconciliation. So too, did, the second treaty of Kappel of 1531. This second treaty was not beneficial to the further growth of Protestantism. In fact, it was to stifle its further advance. It sealed the defeat of Swiss Protestantism at the hands of its Catholic opponents in two battles of October 1531, in the first of which Huldrych Zwingli and a considerable number of Zurich's political leaders perished.

The treaty of 1531 was to govern confessional matters within the confederation up to the mid-seventeenth century. It led to the dissolution of the *Christliches Burgrecht* and to the reinstatement of the Abbot of St. Gallen, whom the Reformation movement had deprived of most of his possessions. It had a particularly pernicious effect on the hold of Protestantism in the Mandated Territories. It entailed a return to Catholicism in the *Freie Ämter*, in Gaster and Uznach, and notably in the towns of Rapperswil, Bremgarten and Mellingen, as well as a partial reversion to the old faith in the Rheintal, and it curtailed any further progress of the Reformation in these jointly governed regions. The outcome of the battles of 1531 for a while led to a serious crisis of Zurich's rule, especially in the territories subject to the city's control.

In Berne, the autonomy of the city authorities in ecclesiastical matters was very highly developed on the eve of the Reformation. It is not surprising, therefore, that, when a small but influential Reformation movement began to take shape in 1522, which occasioned the first open conflicts regarding the interpretation of the church's tradition, the city-councillors evaded the bishop's jurisdiction and took matters into their own hands. They held a disputation between the reforming priest Georg Brunner and his adversaries and decided that Brunner was to continue to preach since he did so according to the scriptures. Ernst Walder has pointed out that this argument was completely in line with the council's late medieval ecclesiastical policy, that the council used the appeal to the authority of the bible above all as a political justification for not involving the bishop. Did considerations of a religious nature only play a secondary role? It is difficult to gauge Walder's thesis on the basis of the available evidence. But it should be added that it is useful in pointing to important aspects of continuity in line with other recent research on the political, cultural and social aspects of the Reformation.[6] It is true, however, that the Bernese authorities stuck to their temporising insistence on scriptural preaching throughout the next five years despite the growth of the Reformation movement in the town led by the painter, writer and politician Nikolaus Manuel (1484–1530) and by the reformer Berchtold Haller (1492–1536).

Ultimately, in the spring of 1527, it was pressure from the city's artisans, which overcame the opposition of some influential councillors and brought about a decision in favour of holding a disputation. This took place in January 1528 and led to the official introduction of the Reformation both within the city and its extended territory. A consultation of the rural population (*Ämterbefragung*) was held on 23 February 1528 in the Bernese countryside, which yielded a handsome majority in favour of the Reformation. In spite of this, the abolition of the old order for a while met with some fierce peasant resistance in the Bernese Oberland.

Next to the Reformation in Zurich, the movement's success in the powerful republic of Berne had the most decisive effect on the history of the Reformation in Switzerland. The case of Schaffhausen, where a Reformation movement formed around figures such as the physician Johannes Adelphi and the reformer Sebastian Hofmeister (1476–1533), provides a good illustration for this. After the Peasants' Revolt of 1524–5, which caused considerable unrest in this city, Schaffhausen did not follow Zurich's example. Instead, the council banned Sebastian Hofmeister, and there was a kind of stalemate until the orderly Reformation in Berne cleansed religious reform from the opprobrium of causing social unrest. On 29 September 1529 the Great and Small Council together finally opted in favour of abolishing Catholic worship in the presence of a delegation composed of emissaries from Zurich, Berne, Basel, St. Gallen and Mülhausen. A week later, it joined the *Christliches Burgrecht*.

In St. Gallen, where the new order was introduced in the spring of 1527, the progress of the Reformation movement, headed by the learned Joachim Vadianus (1484–1551) and by Johannes Kessler (1502/3–1574), was accompanied by uncontrolled acts of iconoclasm, much as in contemporaneous Basel, following the council's decision on 23 February 1529 to secularise the church of the Abbey. The council soon came to regret this rash decision taken against the recommendations received from Zurich. In 1532, in the wake of the Protestants' defeat at Kappel, the city authorities had to restore the abbot's secularised possessions at great cost, and the uniformly Protestant community henceforth had to tolerate the continued presence of the ancient Benedictine monastery in town.

The residence of the prince-bishop in former times, Basel managed in 1521 to cut the last constitutional ties linking its council elections to the participation of the bishop. In the same year, unlike Zurich, it acceded to the alliance with France along with other members of the confederation. After a group of priests began to adhere to the Reformation, the council interfered for the first time in 1523 by silencing a vociferous group of conservatives at the university and by appointing the reformers Conrad Pellicanus (1478–1556) and Johannes Oecolampadius (1482–1531) as professors of theology. While the former soon moved on to Zurich, the latter was to become Basel's main reformer.

Following the example of Zurich, the council issued a mandate enjoining scriptural preaching, soon to be imitated in Berne and Strassburg. However, this marked a half-way position, and the Basel authorities were in fact reluctant to take any more decisive steps in favour of reform after that.

In 1525 an open socio-religious revolt in town by the unruly vintners, gardeners and weavers could be averted. After the turmoil subsided, even a temporary backlash occurred in that influential councillors encouraged clerical defenders of Catholicism in their endeavours. But there was a clear change of heart in 1526, when the Catholic cantons of central Switzerland failed to participate in Basel's renewal of its treaty with the confederation. This experience decisively strengthened the friends of reform. However, the final breakthrough of the Reformation, more and more impatiently awaited by the city's artisans, was still slow in coming. It took increasing open unrest within the community, acts of spontaneous iconoclasm, and, finally, an open revolt against the oligarchical role of the council on 8 and 9 February 1529, which forced the latter to exclude twelve conservative members, before the Reformation could triumph.

In the rural cantons of Appenzell and Glarus and in the Grisons of Eastern Switzerland, the principle of *communal* decision played an important role. In Glarus matters remained in a delicate balance down to the spring of 1528, when individual cases of iconoclasm led to the convocation of a series of *Landsgemeinden* (regional meetings of all full citizens), in which a solution to the confessional problem was sought. It became clear that the evangelical party constituted a majority, but, at the same time, the deep divisions within the community on account of the Reformation became apparent. At the *Landsgemeinde* of 2 May 1529 a guarantee for domestic peace in confessional matters was ultimately found in the principle that each individual community should have the right to decide for or against the Reformation. Implicitly, this amounted to an official recognition of the Reformation, which survived the difficult years after 1531, even though it had not managed entirely to replace Catholicism. A similar decision was taken by the *Landsgemeinde* of Appenzell as early as April 1525. Here, too, the effect of the Second Peace of Kappel of 1531 was to halt the further advance of Protestantism.

In the Grisons a great many communities followed the example of the town of Chur, where the Reformation managed to establish itself in 1527. Chur was also the seat of a bishop who was the major feudal lord of the surrounding valleys. The spread of the Reformation combined in a major part of the Grisons with opposition against the secular power of the bishop and peasant resistance against the latter's feudal privileges, as is demonstrated by the Ilanz Articles of 1524 and 1526. These document not only the secularisation but also the communalisation of episcopal rights, such as those of territorial rule, of hunting and fishing, as well as of appointing pastors, which the combined peasants' and Reformation movement successfully put into effect.[7]

Let us now turn to French-speaking Switzerland, which, short of the lower Valais and some smaller Mandated Territories, embraced the Reformation almost in its entirety from the 1530s onwards. In the country of Neuchâtel and the adjoining domaine of Valangin (which together form the modern canton of Neuchâtel) the indefatigable preaching of Guillaume Farel (1489–1565) helped prepare the ground, so that a meeting of Neuchâtel's burghers on 4 November 1530 officially voted for the abolition of Catholic worship, albeit by a fairly narrow margin. This decisive step was preceded by widespread acts of iconoclasm. In neighbouring Valangin, the territorial lords saw themselves forced to introduce the Reformation when Berne conquered the Pays de Vaud from the hands of the Duke of Savoy in 1536. In Lausanne and the Vaud, *Messieurs de Berne*, as their new subjects called them, lost no time in decreeing the abolition of Catholicism by mandates issued in October and December 1536, and in establishing an initially small group of Reformed preachers. Likewise they soon began to reform the schools, founded the Academy of Lausanne and reorganised poor relief.

An important precondition of the Reformation in Geneva was the rallying of the forces favouring a close alliance with the Swiss confederation, which, in 1526, resulted in the first treaty of *Combourgeoisie* being signed between Geneva, Fribourg and Berne. This alliance was, at the same time, an expression of the will of an influential group of Genevans to free this episcopal city from the rights of the bishop and the Savoyard embrace, which threatened the independence of the city. It was under Berne's protection that the religious renewal got going with Guillaume Farel beginning to preach there from 1532.

The abolition of the old order, and, thus, the establishment of Geneva's complete independence, came after an unsuccessful attempt to lay siege to the city on the part of the Duke of Savoy and Berne's reaction in the form of the invasion of the Savoyard country surrounding the Lake of Geneva in 1536. The new order suffered its first serious crisis, when Farel and John Calvin (1509–64), whom Farel had recruited as a fellow reformer, were banned by the Genevan councillors for having dared to criticise the latters' life-style. This banishment was reversed when Ami Perrin, subsequently one of the reformers' chief opponents, acting on behalf of the city government, brought Calvin back from Strassburg in 1540.

During the next two decades this remarkable man was to make this city, to which he returned only reluctantly, into a Protestant Rome. He achieved this against formidable opposition raised against him by the clans of the Favre and Perrin families, who resisted his attempt to impose a strict moral conduct on all Genevans regardless of their social rank. Calvin ultimately won this confrontation, lasting from 1546 onwards, after a political landslide in 1554 brought several of his supporters into the Small Council. In 1555 Ami Perrin and his closer friends were banished from Geneva while some of his associates were executed. This marked the ultimate victory of Calvin's reform. The city government was henceforth headed by the representatives of a new generation of politicians who believed in the image of 'a republic prostrated before God'.[8]

## II

The Upper-German Reformation (and that includes the Reformation in German-speaking Switzerland) differed from the Lutheran Reformation elsewhere in the Holy Roman Empire in the greater importance it attributed to the 'sanctification' of the individual member of a church and of the parish community as a whole.[9] The particular emphasis on church discipline (*Kirchenzucht*) and moral control (*Sittenzucht*), which characterised the Swiss Reformation from the outset, was adopted by the Reformation in French-speaking Switzerland and especially by that of Geneva. It was an area in which the interest of church and secular authorities coincided. In this respect, the Swiss ministers everywhere became the mouthpiece of the secular government's drive for the reform of manners; countless were the mandates in question which the pastors regularly had to read from their pulpits. Although many men of the church would have liked to act independently in these matters, nowhere in Switzerland, not even in Geneva, did they manage to wrest the control and initiative over this reform of manners from the secular government. Zwingli firmly believed in the role of the Christian magistrate in this respect, whereas other reformers, such as Oecolampadius, who wished to establish the right of ministers to excommunicate unruly members of the church, failed to get what they were striving for.[10]

There are three areas in which the new emphasis on communal discipline was particularly visible: poor relief, schooling and the institutionalised control of public morality.

The reform of public welfare policy brought about the organisation of the communal support of the well-deserving, indigenous poor, who, following the drying up of traditional Catholic almsgiving on account of the Reformation, could no more rely on spontaneous individual donations. Unlike traditional almsgiving the new system categorically excluded the vagrant, and especially the able-bodied, beggar. In Zurich, from January 1525, it rested on the *Mushafen* providing daily food for the poor, as well as on the common chest.

As far as education is concerned, the Reformation in the cities gave a new impetus to the reform of schooling. On occasion this brought about changes even before the final act of introducing the Reformation. In Schaffhausen, for example, the Latin school was reorganised two years before the introduction of the Reformation in 1527. In 1532, the city council also created a new German school for primary education. This was even more than was done by the government of Zurich, where reforms were restricted to a reorganisation and strict supervision of the two Latin schools and the creation of a theological *Hochschule*. Zurich's German schools of that period, however, were privately run institutions.[11] Due to the limitation of space, the fact that from the 1530s onwards the catechism played a crucial role in primary education can be mentioned only in passing.

The most singular creation of the Swiss Reformation was the particular form of matrimonial court it engendered. This first materialised at Zurich in May 1525, and was subsequently imitated by all major Swiss cities, including Geneva. It was this institution in particular that allowed the Reformed alliance of church and state to establish a control of people's moral conduct, which on occasion did not stop short of invading domestic privacy. It also encouraged the spying out of less devout members of the community, as becomes apparent in the matrimonial court ordinance of Basel from 1533, which promised half of the five pound fine for a conviction for adultery to the city guard, who, through his spying, had brought the suspect person to court.[12]

In Berne, the matrimonial court called the *Chorgericht* was established in May 1528. It was constituted of six members, two representatives each of the Small and Great Council, and two preachers. The composition was different in other towns, but nowhere was this institution of moral surveillance manned by the clergy alone. From 1530 a *Chorgericht* was established in every parish of the Bernese countryside, and, only a few years later, this system was introduced into the Pays de Vaud as well. In Geneva, the *consistoire*, which became one of the most important means of Calvin's reform, was founded upon the reformer's return to this city in 1540.

In Geneva, Berne and Basel, the Reformation's quest for enhanced social discipline led to the prohibition of public prostitution. Where the prostitutes were not banished, as in Zurich, close control was institutional-ised. At the same time, the ecclesiastical and secular authorities jointly intensified the battle against excessive drinking in inns and alehouses and at fairs. However, the drive for discipline went way beyond this. The Refor-mation in Switzerland led to attempts at suppressing traditional expressions of popular culture, for example, in the clerical opposition against carnival, where people become, 'inebriated day and night, eat like gluttons, shout like wild beasts and sing inexpressibly base songs' as a contemporary critic exclaimed in disgust.[13] In Geneva and Lausanne, similar criticism led to the suppression of the abbeys of youth in 1538 and 1544, respectively. Church ales also became an object of increasingly stringent moral control.

This attack on specific manifestations of popular culture would, later in the sixteenth century, lead in its most extreme form to the persecution as witches of wise women and sorcerers whose popularity is attested by numerous contemporary sources. However, it must be added that such campaigns did not differ substantially from those simultaneously going on in Catholic areas, and that there were other forms of witch-hunting, too, as in Geneva, where from 1545 onwards alleged witches were repeatedly accused of having helped the spread of the plague.

These are only a few examples taken from the vast field in which the Reformed secular and ecclesiastical authorities jointly developed their efforts at disciplinary reform. The reduction of the number of saints' days, more radical than in Lutheran Germany, and the introduction of marriage and baptismal registers almost immediately after the final abolition of Catholic worship are additional cases-in-point. What was the reaction to all these measures? Were they wholeheartedly accepted?

## III

The Reformation message was conceived by a relatively small number of reformers, disseminated in town and countryside by a more numerous group of evangelically minded preachers, and, finally, received by the mass of common people. This complicated process could involve alterations and shifts in emphasis due, above all, to differences in the nature of the concerns of daily life, which strongly influenced the reception of sermons, pamphlets and catechism. The initial confrontation between adherents and adversaries of the Reformation among the common people in and around Geneva typically did not concern central theological issues but concentrated on such problems as fasting, the veneration of saints and images, priestly marriage, and the like. Confusion and insecurity on this level of society must have been very widespread.[14]

Although Peter Blickle's thesis of the central role of the communal corporation in bringing about the Reformation locally requires some modification in this respect, he is almost certainly correct (at least as far as German-speaking Switzerland is concerned) in suggesting that the Reformation became much more authoritarian and lost a good deal of its communal support after 1525. After the suppression of the Peasants' Revolt, there was a clear loss of interest in the Reformation on the part of those common people, who had linked social with religious reform, such as the Basel weavers and the peasants of the Zurich countryside, because the reformers, jointly with the secular authorities, had disavowed such a conception of reform. This disavowal resulted in a 'divorce between doctrine and life'.[15]

In German-speaking Switzerland this divorce was intensified on the political level by the fact that the Reformation so strengthened the power of the urban authorities, that the traditional *Ämteranfragen* (the consultation of the common people district by district on important issues), repeatedly used by the authorities of Berne and Zurich during the crisis of the early Reformation period, fell into disuse after 1531. This development gave expression to the increasingly authoritarian hold of the cities on the countryside.[16]

The year 1525 also marks the point at which the movement of Anabaptism definitively veered from the course of the official or magisterial Reformation. One of the several birthplaces of sixteenth-century believers' baptism was Zurich, where on 21 January 1525, Conrad Grebel baptised the former priest Georg Blaurock in the house of Felix Manz. At the same time, Anabaptism found many adherents in the villages surrounding Zurich. Many of these Brethren were involved in the Peasants' Revolt, which spread across northern and eastern Switzerland at the same time.[17] Disillusionment with Zwingli's reform combined with deep disappointment about the increasingly authoritarian nature of the Reformation. The result was the growing seclusion and isolation of the Swiss Brethren, who separated from the established church and, with their strict rejection of oath-taking and warfare, initiated a decisive departure from their initial radicalism. Soon after 1525, the surprisingly widespread appeal of their movement led to its harsh and cruel suppression, especially by the city councils of Zurich and Berne. As a movement, Swiss Anabaptism was contained to German-speaking Switzerland and largely failed to take root in the French-speaking part of the country.

Given the almost total lack of specific modern research, the longer term impact of the Reformation in Switzerland is as yet very difficult to measure. It is certain, however, that it was more significant in the urban setting than in the countryside, where the spread of the Reformation was not only slowed down by the fact that many evangelical preachers were former priests, whose resonance was limited as far as bringing about the new order was concerned, but also by the strong attachment of the rural population to forms of traditional Catholic culture. Thus, to cite only one of several possible examples, the Bernese rulers of the Pays de Vaud complained in an ordinance of 1548 that reform had so far made only little progress, that Catholic and magical belief and practice were still widespread, that torches continued to be lit on the first Sunday of Lent, that the water of certain public fountains was still considered by many people to contain miraculous powers of healing, that wise women and sorcerers could still count on a considerable clientele, and that officially abolished Catholic feasts were still being celebrated.[18]

For Geneva, however, research on baptismal names has suggested that the impact of Calvin's reform from 1550 onwards was considerable. For Zurich during the early modern period, Markus Schär has drawn similar conclusions, although it must be added that his findings have by no means remained undisputed.[19] We should nonetheless not overlook the fact that these observations concern only the urban environment.

To date we also lack a detailed study of the common people's Protestant culture. In trying to outline its contours, Richard Weiss has pointed to the fact that the Swiss Reformation strongly relativised the traditional role of 'community and tradition' and that this involved a basic rejection of most traditional popular culture by the Swiss reformers. A result of this was the significant reduction in the number of annual feasts and the general asceticism which accompanied feasting as well as worship, to the extent, for example, that playing the organ was reintroduced in Zurich's churches only in the course of the nineteenth century. The religion of Swiss Protestants was above all, as Weiss has emphasised, a religion of the book, a fact epitomised by the claim of a Zurich schoolmaster in 1653 that all those who could not read and write would in time go to hell.[20]

How successful was the Protestant reform of schooling? A Zurich dissertation published a decade ago suggests that it was unusually successful in the Zurich countryside, where between 30 and 40 per cent of the adult population in the years 1650 to 1700 were able to read.[21] These are surprising figures, for we know that in the mid-sixteenth century catechetical instruction in the same region suffered from the negligence of individual ministers and from the resistance it encountered among the rural population. Unfortunately, we lack supplementary studies enabling us to verify these findings for other areas of Switzerland.

What was the impact of other Reformed disciplinary measures? It is almost certain that the attempt to reform church ales seems to have yielded very limited results. I have already pointed to the difficulties the Genevan consistory ran up against during the first decade of its existence. In the neighbouring Pays de Vaud, the effect of the work of these matrimonial courts showed itself only very gradually. In Basel, local youth in 1609 barricaded the door to the meeting place of the matrimonial court because it had suppressed the traditional nightly tricks of youth during the weeks preceding Christmas. However, we lack information as to whether this was an isolated act of resistance or rather part of a general reluctance of youth to conform to the standards which these institutions sought to enforce. The reform of welfare inspired by the Reformation everywhere ran up against the great difficulties presented to the authorities by the dramatic increase in the number of the poor from the mid-sixteenth century onwards, – a result of the contemporary demographic growth.

Despite the provisional nature of the foregoing paragraphs, it is probably safe to claim that the appeal of the Reformation met its limits where it collided with alternative belief systems, such as the widespread attention paid to judicial astrology or the equally prominent resort to traditional, Catholic expressions of popular culture. The latter manifested itself in the resort to exorcisms performed by Catholic priests, the use of sacramentals for magical purposes, and the participation in pilgrimages, to mention only a few examples. However, the range and actual significance of all this needs to be determined by further research.

## IV

If we disregard the rather special case of the Reformation in Geneva, it is safe to say that the Swiss Reformation in its early stages had much in common with the Reformation in Upper Germany. However, there were some important differences, too, especially in respect of the control of Swiss cities over unusually large territories, which facilitated the spread of the Reformation, as well as regarding the central role of mercenary service.

The mercenary question was a central issue of the Swiss Reformation in the years prior to 1531. For Huldrych Zwingli and his close supporters rejection of mercenary service was, like other social problems, inextricably linked to ecclesiastical reform. This linkage also helps to explain the serious obstacles the Reformation encountered in parts of the country. For the regions of Central Switzerland mercenary service was indispensable from an economic point of view. Next to the widespread fear that the Reformation would contribute to the destruction of all traditional authority, the mercenary issue was at the heart of the rejection of the Reformation by the political leadership of Central Switzerland, as well as of Fribourg and Solothurn.

For a moment, the disruptions and tensions created by the Reformation threatened the very survival of the Swiss confederation as a political entity. The danger was averted by subordinating, in the major part of Switzerland, the confessional question to the imperative of political unity at a comparatively very early stage.

## NOTES

1 Leonhard von Muralt, 'Stadtgemeinde und Reformation in der Schweiz', *Zeitschrift für Schweizergeschichte*, 10 (1930), pp. 349–84, here p. 377.

2 Peter Stadler, 'Eidgenossenschaft und Reformation', in *Säkulare Aspekte der Reformationszeit*, ed. Heinz Angermeier, Schriften des Historischen Kollegs, Kolloquien, vol. 5 (Munich and Vienna, 1983), pp. 91–9, here p. 91.

3 Hans Conrad Peyer, *Verfassungsgeschichte der alten Schweiz* (Zurich, 1978), p. 64.

4 See George Huntston Williams, *The Radical Reformation* (Philadelphia, 1962), pp. 34–5.

5 Kurt Maeder, 'Die Bedeutung der Landschaft für den Verlauf des reformatorischen Prozesses in Zürich (1522–1532)', in *Stadt und Kirche im 16. Jahrhundert*, ed. Bernd Moeller, Schriften des Vereins für Reformationsgeschichte, vol. 190 (Gütersloh, 1978), pp. 91–8.

6 See Ernst Walder, 'Reformation und moderner Staat', in *450 Jahre Berner Reformation*, Archiv des Historischen Vereins des Kantons Bern, 64/65 (Berne, 1980), pp. 441–583, here p. 502.

7 See Friedrich Pieth, *Bündnergeschichte* (2nd edn, Chur, 1982), pp. 119–38; Peter Blickle, *Gemeindereformation. Die Menschen des 16. Jahrhunderts auf dem Weg zum Heil* (Munich, 1985), pp. 51–9, and Stadler, 'Eidgenossenschaft und Reformation', pp. 97–8.

8 William Monter, 'De l'evêché à la Rome Protestant', in *Histoire de Genève*, ed. Paul Guichonnet (Toulouse and Lausanne, 1974), pp. 129–83, here p. 143.

9 Bernd Moeller, 'Die Kirche in den evangelischen freien Städten Oberdeutschlands im Zeitalter der Reformation', *Zeitschrift für Geschichte des Oberrheins*, 112 (1964), pp. 147–62.

10 Walther Köhler, *Zürcher Ehegericht und Genfer Konsistorium*, vol. I, Quellen und Abhandlungen zur Schweizer Reformationsgeschichte, vol. VII (Leipzig, 1932), pp. 285–92.

11 Hans Ulrich Bächtold, *Heinrich Bullinger vor dem Rat. Zur Gestaltung und Verwaltung des Zürcher Staatswesens in den Jahren 1531 bis 1575*, Zürcher Beiträge zur Reformationsgeschichte, vol. 12 (Berne and Frankfurt/Main, 1982), pp. 211–14.

12 *Das Tagebuch des Johannes Gast*, ed. Paul Burckhardt, Basler Chroniken, vol. VIII (Basel, 1945), p. 298, note 70.

13 Johannes Stumpf, *Gemeiner loblicher Eydgnoschaft ... Chronik ...* (Zurich, 1548), vol. II, p. 351, cited in Leo Zehnder, *Volkskundliches in der älteren schweizerischen Chronistik*, Schriften der Schweizerischen Gesellschaft für Volkskunde, vol. 60 (Basel, 1976), p. 300.

14 Kurt Maeder, 'Glaubensdiskussion und Meinungsbildung in der Frühzeit der Zürcher Reformation', *Zürcher Taschenbuch* (1973), pp. 12–29, especially pp. 16–17.

15 Heiko A. Oberman, 'The Impact of the Reformation. Problems and Perspectives', in *Politics and Society in Reformation Europe. Essays for Sir Geoffrey Elton*

*on his sixty-fifth birthday*, ed. E. I. Kouri and Tom Scott (London, 1987), pp. 3–31, here p. 7.

16  See Peyer, *Verfassungsgeschichte*, pp. 68–70; Walder, 'Reformation und moderner Staat', pp. 475–6 und 530, and especially Peter Bierbrauer, *Freiheit und Gemeinde im Berner Oberland, 1300–1700*, Archiv des Historischen Vereins des Kantons Bern, vol. 74 (Berne, 1991), pp. 230–88.

17  Hans-Jürgen Goertz, 'Aufständische Bauern und Täufer in der Schweiz', *Mennonitische Geschichtsblätter*, 46 (1989), pp. 90–112.

18  Henri Vuilleumier, *Histoire de l'eglise réformée du Pays de Vaud sous le régime bernois* (Lausanne, 1927), vol. I, pp. 368–9.

19  Markus Schär, *Seelennöte der Untertanen. Selbstmord, Melancholie und Religion im Alten Zürich, 1500–1800* (Zurich, 1985).

20  Richard Weiss, 'Grunzüge einer protestantischen Volkskultur', *Schweizerisches Archiv für Volkskunde*, 61 (1965), pp. 75–91, especially pp. 76–87.

21  Marie-Luise von Wartburg-Ambühl, *Alphabetisierung und Lektüre. Untersuchung am Beispiel einer ländlichen Region im 17. und 18. Jahrhundert*, Europäische Hochschulschriften, Reihe 1, vol. 459 (Berne and Frankfurt/Main, 1981), pp. 27ff and 247ff.


FURTHER READING

A useful general introduction is provided by Rudolf Pfister, *Kirchengeschichte der Schweiz*, vol. II: *Von der Reformation bis zum Villmerger Krieg* (Zurich, 1974), and by Gottfried W. Locher's broadly conceived *Die Zwinglische Reformation im Rahmen der europäischen Kirchengeschichte* (Göttingen and Zurich, 1979). Peter Blickle, *Gemeindereformation* (see notes above) highlights the role of communalism in the Swiss and South German Reformation. To date there is no comprehensive social history of the Swiss Reformation. The *Geschichte der Schweiz und der Schweizer* (Basel and Frankfurt/Main, 1991), especially Martin Körner's contribution offers some useful background information. Hans Conrad Peyer, *Verfassungsgeschichte der alten Schweiz* (Zurich, 1978), is indispensable in respect of the constitutional aspects. For Zurich, besides G. W. Locher's work, George Potter's *Zwingli* (Cambridge, 1976), offers a valid treatment in English. The most authoritative work on Zwingli in taking account of modern research is Ulrich Gäbler, *Huldrych Zwingli. Eine Einführung in sein Leben und sein Werk* (Munich, 1983).

The most recent biography of the reformer of Geneva is William J. Bouwsma, *John Calvin. A Sixteenth-century Portrait* (Oxford, 1987). A comprehensive look at the Genevan Reformation is offered by E. William Monter, *Calvin's Geneva* (New York, 1967); see also Monter's article cited above. For Berne, an introduction is provided by Kurt Guggisberg, *Bernische Kirchengeschichte* (Berne, 1958). On Anabaptism, Claus-Peter Clasen, *Anabaptism – a Social History, 1525–1618* (Ithaca, N.Y. and London, 1972), still offers a good overview, although this should now be read in conjunction with more recent contributions, such as that by H.-J. Goertz cited above. For other important aspects of the Swiss Reformation see the works cited in the notes above, as well as Hans R. Guggisberg, 'The Problem of "Failure" in the Swiss Reformation. Some preliminary reflections', in *Politics and Society in Reformation Europe. Essays for Sir Geoffrey Elton on his Sixty-Fifth Birthday*, ed. E. I. Kouri and Tom Scott (London, 1987), pp. 188–209, who analyses the 'failed' urban reforms; Kurt Maeder, *Die Via Media in der Schweizerischen Reformation. Studien zum Problem der Kontinuität im Zeitalter der Glaubenskämpfe* (Zurich, 1970), who investigates the links between humanism and the Reformation, and A. Zimmerli-Witschi, *Frauen in der Reformationszeit* (Zurich, 1981), who looks at the role of women. A good introduction to the social function of the Reformed ecclesiastical court in the wake of the Swiss Reformation is provided by a case study by Heinrich Richard Schmidt, 'Die Christianisierung des Sozialverhaltens als permamente Reformation. Aus der Praxis reformierter Sittengerichte der Schweiz während der frühen Neuzeit', in *Kommunalisierung und Christianisierung. Voraussetzungen und Folgen der Reformation, 1400–1600*, ed. J. Kunisch and P. Blickle, *Zeitschrift für historische Forschung* Beiheft 9 (Berlin, 1991), pp. 113–63.

# 3    France

*Mark Greengrass*

The central drama, and fallacy, of the French Reformation lay in the attempt to win over the support of the monarchy.[1]

On 23rd August 1535, John Calvin completed the famous preface to his first major religious treatise which he had decided to christen the *Institution of the Christian Religion*.[2] Barely twenty-six years old, he was in a 'quiet hiding place' in exile at Basel. Not able to speak the language of the inhabitants, his friends were mainly among those who had taken flight from religious repression in France. Some, like Calvin himself, had been forced to retire hastily during the storm which had broken out in the wake of the 'Day of Placards' in Paris and other provincial cities during October 1534. Fearful of greater persecution to come and aware that his friends in France were already dead or imperilled, Calvin wrote in a tone of cold anger. The 'fury of certain wicked persons' was at large; through fraud, villainy and treason, they sought to exterminate the true religion from France by 'prison, exile, proscription and fire' on both land and sea.

It would be readily understandable if Calvin had dedicated the preface to a member of his family, to his humanist mentors, or even the memory of his close friends who had stayed and paid the price. Calvin directed it instead to the French king Francis I, whom he had never met (and would have disliked if he had), and who would have been unlikely to read it. The preface tells us why. Calvin wanted those in authority in France to know that Protestants were not antisocial revolutionaries, and that they had nothing in common with the Anabaptists at Münster. Protestants believed in the institution of the Christian religion, the foundation of society. They were there to defend it from those who sought, through injustice, 'to wrest the scepters from the hands of kings, to cast down all courts and judgments, to subvert all orders and civil governments, to disrupt the peace and quiet of the people, to abolish all laws, to scatter all lordships and possessions – in short to turn everything upside down'.[3] The king should know that the persecution of Protestants, undertaken in his name, was, therefore, unjust and unnecessary. Calvin hoped, so the preface implied, that Francis I would one day become the patron of Protestantism in France.

Was this such a foolish thought? Around him, Calvin saw German princes, Scandinavian monarchies and the English king breaking away from Rome. For much of that decade, Francis I had sought closer diplomatic relations with them. In addition, France had vigorous native printing presses, some of which had already been producing discreet translations of Luther and crypto-Protestant literature, and this was reinforced by works in French published in the Rhineland.[4] There had been a transformation in educational provision through the establishment of municipal colleges, later viewed by Catholics as the harbingers of heresy.[5] Calvin had personal experience of various Protestant-tending groups, '*cénacles*', congregating in French towns and cities.[6] He had been involved in organising house-groups (*manducations*) at Tours in 1534 which were probably still flourishing a decade later.[7] Perhaps he was told of the penetration of evangelical ideas in the parishes of the cathedral town of Meaux or amongst the outworking cloth-villages of Normandy and elsewhere.[8] French humanism had a profound influence upon him, as upon others, and his intellectual development was testimony to the way in which it had been, at least for some, a conduit for reformed ideas.[9] One of the places where Calvin had first sought refuge after the Day of Placards was at the little court of the king's sister, Marguerite de Navarre. She made no secret of her sympathy for religious dissent although her spiritual pilgrimage would never be confined within a narrow confessional path. It would not have been surprising if Calvin had reckoned that, if only the French king were persuaded of the justice of the case, a reformation would swiftly follow.

In retrospect, Calvin's dream of a French monarchy sympathetic to Protestantism withered in his own lifetime. Why was this so? Why, to be precise, did the French monarchy never become Protestant, or even tolerant of Protestant opinions in France save under the pressure of abject necessity? Historians have traditionally approached this question in several distinctive, but complementary, ways, influenced (at least until comparatively recently) by enduring differences of approach along confessional lines. Some would argue – by concentrating on an analysis of the institutions of the French monarchy and their operation – that there was something 'structural' in the French polity which made it particularly difficult for its rulers to abandon the traditional religion. Others, secondly, have tended to suggest that it was because of the particular kind of Reformation which France engendered – the kind shaped by Calvin. A further approach, recalling the strength of the narrative history of the French Reformation as it was written in the previous century, suggests that the failure of the French monarchy to patron Protestantism was because the right political circumstances never occurred to make it possible. Finally, it is possible to argue that the 'failure' and 'success' implied in the preceeding sets of propositions is too stark and naive a way of approaching the history of the French Reformation.

## The 'Great Monarchy of France'

The French monarchy was perceived and projected in the sixteenth century as a sacral institution. Its kings were charismatic leaders, both literally (by virtue of the chrism or holy unction with which they were anointed during their coronation) and in a Weberian sense.[10] The rituals of the monarchy (royal baptisms, coronations, funerals) presented France's 'Most Christian king' as 'God's elect', his theocratic powers (such as the power to heal scrofula) mystically devolved to him.[11] It was not difficult to imagine the French king as a prophetic figure, his victories inspired by God.[12] At the same time, French kings were reminded of how they were sustained and embraced in a mystical communion by the loving obedience of their people so long as they maintained the faith.[13] During the coronation service, French kings, their hands on the Gospels, took the 'oath of the kingdom'.[14] From 1215, its last clause solemnly included the promise to be diligent in expelling all heretics (as defined by the Church) from the realm. It was a promise which Catholic propagandists would regularly return to during the religious troubles.[15] It would have required a stubborn, not to say rash, monarch openly to challenge these assumptions, deeply rooted in the fundamental traditions of the French monarchy, proudly evoked by its kings.

Close to the king at the ceremonial events of the monarchy, were the great officers of the crown, the Chancellor, the Constable, the *Grand Maître de l'Hôtel*. Drawn from the most conservative families of the French aristocracy, these individuals represented the continuity of monarchical tradition and symbolised its governing cadres.[16] Only two of the holders of these three great offices were either Protestant or sympathetic to Protestantism during the sixteenth century; their fates are indicative of the degree to which the traditional religion and institutions of France were integrally related. The Chancellor Michel de l'Hôpital was not a Protestant but, upon the encouragement of the queen mother, Catherine de Médicis, he became the architect of the first edict of toleration in 1561. He was eventually hounded out of his post in 1568, unworthy (so his critics claimed) of the office, and he died in disgrace.[17] From early on, Admiral Gaspard de Coligny had made no secret of his reformed faith. He found himself fighting a blood feud with the Guise family which culminated in his assassination ten years later in 1572, the prelude to the Massacre of St Bartholomew.[18]

The great officers of state had automatic rights of entry to the king's council. So, too, did the French cardinals who also had rights of precedence over other councillors in its deliberations. It is difficult to imagine French politics in the sixteenth century without a cardinal close to the epicentre of power, playing a leading role. These advisers were regular reminders to the French king, should he need it, of the dangers of novelty and change. Although the king's closest councillors were by no means always chosen from amongst their number, any monarch would have found it extremely difficult to counter the combined weight of opinion, unanimously expressed, of the great crown officials. We know very little of the deliberations of royal councils. The religion of the monarch, a private *arcana arcanorum* (mystery of mysteries), was, in any case, none of their concern. But monarchical traditions and territorial integrity were. They knew that the monarchy, though very old as to its origins, was recently established in many of its spheres of influence. Brittany, Picardy, Burgundy, Provence and much of the Gascony had only been acquired during the previous century. France was a huge country, its monarchy still aggressive and acquisitive. It had no unity of language, national identity, legal customs or history. Only religion and the monarchy held it all together. Change the one and, or so it would have seemed, you threaten the other – not least because many of these newly acquired regions were, and would remain, bastions of orthodoxy, scarcely touched by the Reformation. Lorraine (France's Catholic frontier), Picardy (birthplace of the noble Catholic League), Brittany (where Catholics and local traditions were almost synonymous) would all look potentially vulnerable in a period dominated by France's wars with its neighbours.[19] How could the French monarchy be sympathetic to change without threatening its fragile, territorial unity?

Beneath the officers of the crown and the council lay the intricate institutions of the French monarchy, particularly its law courts, the *Parlements* of Paris, the provincial *Parlements* and the subordinate courts. Officers of these courts swore to uphold the Catholic faith when they took up their posts.[20] Increasingly during the first half of the sixteenth century, they purchased their offices from the crown and were, therefore, virtually irremovable by the king. Some senior office-holders had an exalted and austere view of their own status and responsibilities, assuming that justice and the maintenance of the right religion in the realm were almost synonymous.[21] Although some of the lesser courts, particularly those in the Protestant strongholds of the civil wars – Nîmes, Montauban and La Rochelle, for example – eventually contained mostly Protestant judges, and although office-holders in general played a disproportionately large role in the Huguenot cause, especially in the French Midi, only a small minority of senior magistrates declared their Protestantism openly.[22]

## The prosecution of heresy

Judges were at the apex of what one historian of the central Middle Ages has called a 'persecuting society' – that is to say, a set of institutions and attitudes which were manipulated by governing groups to promote the need for a consensus in society through the preservation of the purity of the majority and the persecution of minorities.[23] Since the thirteenth century, the ecclesiastical Inquisition had combined with royal justice in France to secure and sustain orthodoxy. But the ecclesiastical Inquisition had become rusty by 1500, and it had difficulty in actively and effectively persecuting the Waldenses of the Alps, the last of the medieval heresies in France. Persecution is always a demonstration of social power and in this instance – as again in the 1530s in Provence – there was the active collaboration of a group of local judges and *clerici*, using persecution as a weapon of intrigue.[24] The sovereign courts generally reacted with suspicion towards clerical power and local intrigue but even greater hostility towards anything which smacked of a loss of social discipline. The first 'massacre' of the French religious troubles was ordered from above when the *Parlement* of Provence authorised the destruction of the Waldensian community of Cabrières in 1543.

When the Reformation first appeared in France it is significant that it was factional interests, court intrigue and some of the senior magistrates who instituted repression, not the king. It was to Francis I that some members of his court and family looked to protect their friends and clients from investigation for heresy by royal and ecclesiastical courts, just as others looked to him to prosecute heresy. The first wave of repression began, in fact, during the king's captivity in Spain. In the course of the Day of Placards, as R. J. Knecht had demonstrated, it was the *Parlement* of Paris which began rounding up suspects in the city, closing the bookshops, instituting processions of penitence, even before the king had arrived back in the city from his chateau on the Loire.[25] But the pressures on the French king to promote the prosecution of heretics were, in fact, considerable. Not to have stood by the judiciary in the prosecution of Protestantism would have been tantamount to the French king rejecting the kind of consensus with his people which was the bedrock of the monarchy. It would take a political crisis of considerable magnitude within the monarchy itself to release it from the pressures of the 'persecuting society'.

The trouble was that France was no longer the traditional society it had been in the Middle Ages. Social change created more powerful mechanisms for dissent so that the prosecution of heresy created frustration, failure and anxiety amongst its promoters. How many Protestants were judicially investigated, let alone how many were eventually put to death from 1523 (the date of the first Protestant 'martyr') and the death of Henry II in 1559 is a matter of speculation. The French legal system was decentralised and the records are far from complete. The number of cases brought before the courts up to 1559 was probably in excess of 5,000 and may have been as high as 8,000.[26] At all events, it was certainly the highest number of 'victimless crimes' prosecuted by the French state, during a period when justice was generally perceived as the compensation of particular injuries to particular individuals. There was a gathering pace of prosecution, reflecting as much the changes in statute (broadly speaking, an increasingly precise codification of the public manifestations of heresy so that they could be judged as *cas privilégiés* by the royal courts) and methods of prosecution (an increasing use of state organisms for coercion) as the growth of heresy itself.

With the growth of prosecutions, however, came a nagging sense of frustration. Nearly all heresy cases began with a denunciation until the 1550s when, with the growing activity of Protestant congregations, groups of suspects could be caught in the act. Some denunciations were made to further personal ambition as much as religious purity and, in the ensuing judicial investigations, the testimonies were often inconclusive or difficult to assess. Magistrates were by no means always sure of the crime they were looking for. When summoned to appear before the royal courts, many suspects chose flight, not surprisingly since the judicial process gave them few opportunities for defence. The courts were understandably reluctant to confer a martyr's crown and had to try to match the punishment to the popular perception of the crime. Punishments tended to go in waves, broadly related to the prevailing perceptions of threat to the common weal at large, with punishment by burning reserved for those cases where an exemplary sentence was required to purify a community and broadly to advertise the dangers of heresy. But each wave of persecution inevitably fed the worst fears of its advocates; the more suspects were investigated, the more heresy appeared to be on the increase. The legal system became the target for these frustrations. Francis I and Henry II's chancellors invoked a variety of devices to try and make the system work better. *Parlements* were suspended and replaced by Parisian judges on commission. Judges on assize (*grands jours*) were despatched to regions which were remote from the immediate influence of the sovereign law courts. Particular attention was paid to the possibility of heresy among the judges themselves. There was a proposal for a French version of the Spanish Inquisition from the cardinal de Lorraine in 1555 although it was resisted by the Paris *Parlement*.[27] The cardinal, in turn, accused the magistrates of encouraging heresy through their exaggerated respect for legal niceties and their own prerogatives.[28] These anxieties culminated in the remarkable *lit de justice* (a royal visitation to the Parlement in Paris), held in June 1559. It took place following the peace of Câteau-Cambrésis and was overshadowed by the forthcoming wedding of the king's daughter to the Spanish king Philip II. Henry II heard a sequence of judges cast doubt upon the procedure, legitimacy and effectiveness of the persecution of heresy. The king demonstrated his anger immediately. Two judges were arrested forthwith, followed by several more shortly afterwards. One, Anne du Bourg, who refused to retract what he said, was tried and executed in a notorious and highly publicised trial. The whole affair only served to demonstrate how deeply rooted the new religion had become in France and reinforced the growing, paralysing sense of failure.[29]

The failure to halt the spread of the Reformation in France was hard to disguise, especially by the 1550s. Although there was some success in the control of the French printing press, the importation and distribution of heretical books had proved impossible to curb. Royal decrees were only enforced with difficulty in the more distant parts of legal jurisdictions. Pockets of immunity continued to exist for Protestantism almost every-where within France, but particularly in the big cities and on the domains of the powerful nobility. These are the environments in which the Calvinist churches of France tended to congregate. Their First National Synod, held in the summer of 1559, was in humiliating defiance of royal will. Historians have no way of knowing precisely how many Protestant congregations there were in France by this date but contemporaries had no doubts as to their number and support; 'Heresy has penetrated so deeply that it has corrupted almost all the nobility and a portion of the French people' said the Venetian ambassador Barbaro whilst the traditional-minded curé of Provins, Claude Haton, reckoned that 'a quarter' of the nation was infected.[30]

The sense of anxiety spread to orthodox France as well. This is of importance, if only because historians have tended to neglect the complex reactions to the Reformation from 'traditional France' in favour of examin-ing it through Protestant eyes and witnesses. Claude Haton is a good indicator of this anxiety. For him, the appearance and spread of heresy in France induced in him a measure of panic, a sense that the world which he understood and in which he felt secure, was completely threatened. Comets, prodigious happenings, unnatural births, became signs of God's wrath and the imminent destruction of Christendom. Like many others, he read the almanacs of Nostradamus 'which predicted so many things to come in Christendom, especially its desolation, and particularly in France and Germany ...'.[31] His sense of disjuncture extended towards a fear of all change: 'With the opulence of wealth and the peace which was enjoyed in France, social ambitions increased throughout the orders in society. The attire of men and women was disturbed by new fashions, something which was greatly displeasing to some of the older folk of both town and country-side who predicted a terrible future for France, and in the near future'.[32] Only more rigorous executions, more public burnings, would succeed in restoring the wholesomeness of communities which felt polluted, defiled and fundamentally challenged. The writer and poet Artus Désiré, author of over seventy works (mainly published in the 1550s) expressed the collective psychosis of traditional France in violent and eschatalogical language.[33] Heresy was a hydra-headed dragon, polluting the streams and rivers of the kingdom. It would bring God's judgement in its wake. Calvin was the messenger of Antichrist. The king and the nation must rise up as one to protect the French Jerusalem.

There were undoubtedly places in France where the popular sense of anxiety about heresy had become so manifest that it resulted in action on the streets. There is evidence to suggest that, in some localities, crowds were beginning to take matters into their own hands in the later 1550s, wanting to organise their own bloody and ritualistic punishments of suspected Protestants.[34] The prosecution of heresy had fundamentally divided France by 1559. On the one hand there were Protestant congregations growing in confidence and numbers by the day and, on the other, Catholic communities fundamentally threatened by them. The French monarchy was committed by everything in its traditions to the maintenance of the traditional religion but, despite the increased sense of power in the French state, the prosecution of heresy, undertaken in its name, had lost it the underlying consensus in the nation upon which its authority ultimately relied.

### A Calvinist Reformation

France was the largest kingdom to face a Calvinist Reformation. Up to 1559, the Reformation of large principalities had been largely (although not exclusively) Lutheran. This had conserved many of the established practices and rituals of the Catholic church and it had suited the traditional societies that governed. The Lutheran princely Reformations succeeded in providing a secure and enduring basis for the confessional arrangements of Germany, Scandinavia and England. What made the Calvinist Reformation more threatening to a monarchy like the French?

It was, firstly, a 'refugee reformation', its forms dictated from outside the kingdom rather than within. Religious refugees from the French kingdom followed Calvin to the cities of the Rhineland and Switzerland. About seventeen 'stranger churches' were established in Strassburg, Geneva and elsewhere at various stages during this period.[35] These 'little flocks of Jesus Christ' (Calvin's term for them) struggled against their own fractiousness and the hostilities of their host communities to establish (*dresser*) their churches. These cities had mostly already witnessed the impact of the 'civic' Reformation, a Reformation whose confessional basis had been very broad (stretching through civic Lutheranism to Zwinglianism and Anabaptism). There had been much experimentation with new forms of lay piety and ecclesiastical structures. This 'civic' Reformation had been generally corrosive of established rituals, images and ecclesiastical practices and its social appeal had been broad. Sometimes it had appeared revolutionary. For a variety of reasons, however, the 'civic' Reformation tended to run out of steam around 1550 and there were few places where they survived that decade with its innovations intact. Calvinism, the religion of the refugees, shaped the diverse experimentation of the 'civic' Reformation into a theology and an ecclesiology which would endure and survive, albeit mostly as a minority religion.

The experience of exile had an enormous effect upon Calvin. In our pluralist world we are in danger of underestimating the degree to which being separated from family, milieu, established sociabilities and loyalties mattered in the sixteenth century. Calvin knew all about losing one's sense of belonging and described it graphically. He repeatedly referred to it in his Biblical Commentaries and his sermons, reinterpreting for his own age the exile of the Hebrews in the Old Testament or the sense of alienation in the psalms.[36] Exile both heightened his own sense of anxiety at the loss of a former world and also, more importantly, strengthened his resolve to create a new one. He learnt a great deal in Martin Bucer's Strassburg, where he spent three important years helping to minister to the French stranger community from 1538 to 1541. When he returned to Geneva for a second time in 1541, it was to shape a new order, one in which the 'abyss' of the old, which God would surely punish for its fearful confusion and shameful wickedness, would be replaced by a thorough and total Reformation, not just of the church but of all society as well.

Historians have often overestimated the influence of Geneva upon the French Reformation but, during the last decade of Calvin's life, from 1554 to 1564, it gave it its enduring shape.[37] New congregations looked to Geneva, their 'new Jerusalem', to appoint their ministers, to settle their disputes, and to provide them with a sense of moral and intellectual ascendancy.[38] Refugees came from France in increasing numbers in the late 1550s threatening to swamp the city's native population.[39] They had a permanent effect upon the success of Calvin's Reformation there, as well as upon the city's economy.[40] They provide historians with a crude 'litmus test' of the social and geographical appeal of Protestantism within France during these years.[41] Although Geneva's company of pastors could not satisfy more than a fraction of the requests for ministers, the publications of the Genevan presses, Calvin's foremost amongst them, enjoyed an extraordinary appeal in France during the years from 1557 to 1562. Gathering numbers, a sense of imminent victory, coupled with the organising power of the Calvinist nobility put together the national French church which, in its first synod of 1559, agreed the French 'Confession' and 'Discipline' which broadly mirrored the new world order as preached from Geneva. The 'Confession' outlined in unambiguous terms the stark faith of Calvinism, shorn of ritual, imagery and traditional symbols. The 'Discipline' was enforced through consistory courts which enjoined upon the faithful a sobriety and decorum which challenged in many respects the ways of life of traditional – particularly rural – France.[42] If Genevan Protestantism only managed to enjoy the active adherence of a small minority of the population of the more urbanised northern Netherlands in the early seventeenth century, where the political and social conditions lay much more in its favour, it is hardly surprising that its French counterpart was destined to remain a religion of a minority of its population, probably never more than 10 per cent.

Looked at in the narrowest perspective, there was little in what Calvin said, or what emerged from Geneva, which directly undermined the authority of the French monarchy. Calvin was, as we now know, more cautious than contemporary Lutherans in expressing anything other than the doctrine of passive obedience.[43] Rulers were to be obeyed because they were instituted by God's ordinance. Biblical injunctions told us we should regard them as Gods. If a magistrate were a tyrant, that did not undermine his legitimacy to rule. Against tyranny there was little to be done beyond suffering, praying to God for deliverance, or taking up voluntary exile. There were, however, ambiguities – the result of tensions within his own thought as well as resulting from the pressures of events (and particularly those in France) upon him. From the 1541 edition of the *Institution* onwards he began cautiously to accept the case for a 'constitutional' opposition to a tyrant based on the legitimate authority of the 'lesser magistrate'. But at no stage could Calvin's – or Genevan – thought be categorised as a 'creed for rebels' during Calvin's lifetime and it was not because Calvinism directly challenged the authority of the French monarchy that it appeared so dangerous.

In the broader perspective, however, Calvinism did challenge the traditional, almost mystical, public perceptions of the French monarchy and its destiny. The Calvinist Reformation was desacralising, deritualising, and demythologising. By refusing to accept transubstantiation and the fundamental assumptions about the manifestation of holy power which lay behind that doctrine, Calvinists were 'sacramentarian'. Iconoclasm was also a fundamental feature of the French Calvinist Reformation. Going far beyond the traditional, often anonymous and generally limited, gestures, of defiance of the holy power of images, Calvinist iconoclasm was far more aggressively desacralising.[44] Crucifixes were daubed with excrement and shrines desecrated. In northern France, iconoclasm remained at the stage of elementary gestures but in the Midi it became more systematic, paralysing the organisms of authority which might seek to control it. This accompanied an iconoclasm towards other aspects of holy power too. Preachers were interrupted during their sermons, clergy mocked in the streets and catholic processions held up to ridicule. Dislike and fear of priestly power was demonstrated in the satirical anonymous broadsheet literature of the early 1560s.[45] The Roman church had often been referred to by Calvin as the old world gone mad, a world of fools, 'dogs', 'beasts', 'ravening wolves' and these were the images commonly employed to mock the clerical order in the streets of French cities. This was just the prelude to physical attacks by Calvinist crowds on the priesthood, often of revolting brutality. Claude Haton provides a (literally) stomach-turning account of the treatment meted out to one obstinate priest in Provins.[46] The context of this iconoclasm was, especially from 1561 until the coming of civil war in April 1562, the Protestant sense of 'triumphalism'.[47] Huguenots crowds often accompanied iconoclasm with the singing of Psalms (in the French metrical version, one of the most enduring contributions of the Reformation to French culture). Breaking up the old order became a demonstration of God's Providence, acting in accordance with his Word. The triumph of the new order over the old was surely close at hand. 'Tue les Papistes! Monde nouveau!' cried the Protestant crowd in the massacre at Nîmes in 1567.[48]

For the French monarchy, this was anathema. A different perception of holy power inevitably meant a changed perception of secular power too. If images were not holy, what were the consequences for the sacral monarchy? If the only chrism there was lay in the conscience of individuals, did that not imply that obedience to the French monarchy was no longer to be embedded in its populace as a mystic union between prince and people? Did not the popular Reformation, which the iconoclastic forces in the French Reformation foreshadowed, presage dreadful revolt? Already in August 1558 there had been an attempted assassination of King Henry II by a Protestant student named Cobache, who cried out as he lunged forward with his knife: 'Dieu m'a commandé que je tue!' (God has commanded me to kill you!) or, in another account: 'Ha! Ha! Polletion il fault que je te tue!' (Ha!, Ha! Pollution, I shall have to kill you!).[49] The following year the king was killed in a jousting accident by a nobleman, Gabriel de Montgomery. Montgomery subsequently led Protestant forces in 1562 and, passing through Le Mans, the local royal bailiff is said to have remarked: 'Adieu la Messe: voicy celluy qui a tué un Roy. Il en tuera ung aultre' (Farewell to the Mass: there's one who had killed one King. He will kill another).[50] The Catholics of Gaillac were told by one of the (Protestant) royal officials of the town:[51]

Allez, idolâtres, caphards ... on ne fait que commencer le jeu, le temps vient et est bien près que l'ancienne Babel sera destruicte, s'il n'y a rois, princes, evesques, ny prestres qui la puisse defendre ou garder. Nos esglizes sont déjà assez fortes pour la ruyner.
(Go, idolaters, hypocrites ... the game has barely begun, the time has come when the ancient Babel will be destroyed, there are no kings, princes, bishops or priests who can defend or guard it. Our churches are already too strong to ruin.)

## The politics of 'Non-Reformation'

If Genevan-style Protestantism was to succeed in France, it would have to be enforced by public authority, by royal fiat. Were there any periods when political events seemed conceivably to force the French monarchy to turn Protestant or, of its own volition, to become the promoter of Protestantism in France? Three periods are worth closer attention: 1551–2, 1561–2 and 1589–93.

If there was ever a moment when there was a possibility that a French king would break with Rome and perhaps, in time, accept a moderate Lutheran or Anglican-style Reformation, it occurred in 1551. In dispute with the Papacy over a number of issues, but particularly over French influence in central Italy and the proposed recall to its second session of the Council of Trent, which the French king regarded as an Imperialist event,[52] Henry II responded by strengthening his alliances with the German Protestant princes. He recalled his cardinals from Rome and issued letters to French bishops to undertake visitations of their dioceses in order to attend a National Council of the Church which would (or so it was implied) reform the ills of the Church. It is just conceivable that this assembly, had it met, might have found itself the mouthpiece for a groundswell of Gallican opinion in the Church which might have persuaded the king, sufficiently aroused by Papal intransigence, to break with Rome. Pope Julius III certainly regarded the Council as the beginnings of schism and reminded Henry II of the enormous powers the French monarchy exercised in the Church as well as the respect in which it was regarded in Rome. In any case, the French cardinals were astute in preventing any rupture, emphasising the imminent dangers of sacramentarian heresy in the kingdom. Their insistence had its effect and, in the midst of the crisis, Henry II published the repressive edict of Châteaubriant. Within the year, his differences with the papacy were a thing of the past and he was alarming German Protestant princes and Strassburg with his occupation of the Lorraine bishoprics of Metz, Toul and Verdun. This was the period when Calvin finally gave up hope for any support for the Reformation from the French monarchy. The nearest it ever came to a National Council for the Church was a decade later at the colloquy summoned to Poissy in 1561 by Catherine de Médicis. There, in the midst of a political crisis, the cardinal of Lorraine proposed a Lutheran-style resolution for Protestant grievances.[53] But times had moved on and the Calvinists rejected the offer, fearing that the cardinal was merely trying to split the ranks of the Reformed and that, if he was sincere in his offer (they entertained many doubts), he would never carry the rest of the French episcopacy, let alone the monarchy, with him. The cardinal of Lorraine's next port of call was the last session of the Council of Trent, the conclusion of whose deliberations marked an end to any possibility of resolving France's growing divisions by means of a council.

In retrospect, the years 1561–2 marked the climax of the French Reformation.[54] The remarkable political conjuncture of a royal minority, bankruptcy and an upsurge of factionalism in the French aristocracy ensured the collapse of the machinery for the prosecution of heresy and a sudden weakening of the monarchy itself. Protestantism appeared, albeit briefly, not as the religion of a prosecuted minority but the possible religion of a majority of France. People from all walks of life went along to Protestant sermons, confessed the faith, or at least were prepared to give it a hearing. These were the 'wonderyears' of the French Reformation, surprising everyone, including Calvin in Geneva. He was overwhelmed with requests for pastors. Copies of the Psalms sold by the thousand and the printing presses of Geneva kept people awake at nights as they coped with demand.

For a brief period following the death of the young king Francis II and the accession of his boy brother Charles IX in December 1560, French Protestants also thought that political events were moving their way. French constitutional law was quite explicit that kings who were not of age (i.e. not fourteen years old or in their fourteenth year) had to be tutored by a regent or a regency council. Many precedents pointed in favour of his oldest relative, Antoine de Bourbon, King of Navarre, becoming regent. In contrast to the great officers of state, the *seigneurs du sang* had a reputation for political dissent and would provide the political leadership for the Huguenot cause.[55] When the news of Francis II's death reached him, Calvin immediately despatched a letter to Antoine, not at that moment in the Midi, advising him to assert his rights.[56] But Antoine de Bourbon was vacillation itself and, by the time he reached the French court, the king's mother Catherine de Médicis had arbitrarily declared herself regent. If the rivalry between the great officers of the crown, especially the Constable Anne de Montmorency and the *Grand Maître* François de Guise, had not been so intense, she would have been stopped. As it was, a critical moment for the

French Protestants to influence the direction of the French monarchy passed by and it never recurred.

One of Catherine's earliest political decisions (the *lettres de cachet* of January 1561) was to begin to dismantle the machinery for prosecuting heresy. Yet, although this was readily announced, the anxieties which had reinforced and sustained Protestant persecution still remained. As the year 1561 wore on, so more alarming and savage Catholic popular violence broke out on the streets of France's cities, attempting to eliminate the pollution of heresy in their midst, often by means of physical attacks upon suspected Protestants.[57] At the massacre of Vassy, the duke of Guise stormed a Protestant congregation in Champagne and killed about fifty worshippers in cold blood. Sectarian violence combined with aristocratic factionalism in a lethal cocktail which was to reappear more than once in the tragic sequence of civil wars which dominated France's history from 1562 until 1598.

There were moments during the years 1561–2 when it looked as though the French Reformation might have been a truly 'popular Reformation', converting sufficient of the populace of France to its ranks by its own peculiar force of rhetoric and persuasion in order to convince the regent queen to change her religious allegiance. That this did not happen was, at least in part, because the leadership of France's Protestants was not at all convinced that it wanted a Reformation to occur 'from below'. Calvin, Beza, the pastors at the early National Synods and the emerging Protestant consistorial elites were almost as obsessed at the dangers of disorder ('libertinism', 'atheism', 'epicureanism' – the language of panic adopted by the Calvinist magistrates and consistories) posed by iconoclasm and desacralisation as the French monarchy itself. Patience, modesty, sobriety, obedience, acceptance to what Providence decreed, became a neo-stoic credo preached to, and eventually believed by the majority of, French Protestants. God sent trials and tribulations in order to test the faithful; the faithful should expect to suffer for the greater glory of God. So, although there were towns (especially the urban 'republics' of the Midi) where consistorial discipline did not go unchallenged, and attempts were made to modify the Calvinist Discipline to reflect a more 'popular' Reformation in the 1560s, these were in the end defeated.[58] The socially disruptive features of the Reformation were occluded. At the same time, the aristocratic leadership of the Huguenot cause was at pains, at least until the death of the prince of Condé in 1569, to stress that it was fighting in *defence* of the monarchy against the evil (Guisard) forces which surrounded it.[59] That the Huguenot cause was led by princes of the blood was a guarantee of its fundamental loyalism; for who else had a more legitimate interest in the defence of the monarchy? In this fashion, the monarchomach forces in the French Reformation were deflected and defused. It was one of the paradoxes of the

French Reformation that, just as the 'popular' elements of the French Reformation were finally put to rest in French Protestantism, so Huguenot monarchical loyalism, the counterpart, faced its greatest challenge in the Massacre of St Bartholomew in 1572.

The Massacre of St Bartholomew, or rather the sequence of massacres in Paris and the provinces which took place in the autumn of 1572, was the culmination of the sectarian tensions and monarchical crisis of the French religious troubles. It is an event which still provokes historical controversy.[60] Contemporaries encased the Massacre in a 'metahistory' which eventually transmuted St Bartholomew into a Catholic/royalist and Protestant set of mythologies.[61] As a sequence of events it is only explicable in terms of the previous decade. Significantly, contemporaries sought to explain it in terms of the recent past. To Catholic commentators like Guy du Faur de Pibrac and Pierre Charpentier, the assassination of Coligny and the subsequent massacres had been monarchical self-defence. The Calvinists had intended to kill the king and overturn the social order. It was a Catelline conspiracy and 'monarchomach' Protestant political writings after the massacre were but demonstrations *post facto* of covert Huguenot intentions throughout the 1560s. The people of Paris had rallied to the endangered monarchy, doing what came naturally to them. There was 'no other nation which so reverently, so religiously and piously honoured the estate of royalty, nor was there one which demonstrated a more vehement loving affection and greater fidelity towards its sovereign prince'. Charles IX had been projected before the public as the innocent boy-king who would, one day, come into his own and avenge the enemies of the crown and true religion. Far from trying to excuse or minimalise the royal involvement in the massacre, they sought to emphasise it.

For Protestant commentators, however, St Bartholomew was a betrayal of the recent past. The Huguenots had been fundamentally loyal to the monarchy, despite provocation, and their reward was treachery. They had warned of the malevolence of royal councillors, especially Catherine de Médicis, and they had been proved tragically correct. The massacre had been premeditated and planned from on high. The monarchy had become a tyranny and was no longer worthy of their loyalty. They had always suspected that Catholics had wanted to eliminate the new religion by force and this had been the intention of St Bartholomew. Whatever the distortion introduced on either side, the fact remains that, after the events of 1572 it was difficult for either the French Protestants or the French monarchy fully to trust one another again.

France did, of course, have a Protestant monarch for four years, from 1589 to 1593. He was king of less than half the kingdom and the ineluctable process which led to his abjuration acts as a summary of the political forces which kept the French monarchy, despite all the pressures placed upon it during the civil wars, Catholic. A few days after his accession in August 1589, Henry IV called the great officers of the kingdom before him to ask for their loyalties. He knew that he would not get them as a Protestant – indeed over half his predecessor's army had already melted away, refusing to serve a heretic king.[62] So, by the famous Declaration of St Cloud, Henry IV agreed that he would undertake to be instructed in the Catholic faith within six months if they would give him contingent, provisional oaths of loyalty. This they did, although he did not keep his promise, at least not to the timetable of it. Over the next four years he attempted to win France over by military force. Even with the support of Elizabeth I, the Swiss and the German Protestant princes, he failed. Most of the major provincial strongholds held out against him, despite his sieges at Paris and Rouen. Of the cities with *Parlements* residing in them, only Bordeaux, close to his ancestral lands, declared for him. And, if urban France would not support its Protestant king, there was little likelihood that rural France would provide either the means or the morale to sustain his campaign for the kingship.

Prominent Protestants like Sully were realistic enough to see that the king had no choice. So it was that, at the abbey of St Denis (symbolically, for it was the mausoleum of the kings of France), just outside Paris, that Henry IV made his act of abjuration in July 1593. It was not just Paris, but the whole of France, which was worth a Mass.

The monarchy provides a key answer to the question why there was a 'Time of Troubles' but no 'Reformation' in France. Yet the Reformation had an enormous impact. The Protestant minority maintained its national unity and coherence, despite the inherent regionalism of France and the punishing effects of the civil wars. Its churches retained the loyalties of their congregations, even though consistorial discipline was sometimes uninviting. It eventually achieved a measure of public recognition from the monarchy in the pacification at Nantes (1598), privileges and protection which were enforced in the localities by a revived royal authority, capable of mastering the forces for sectarian disorder which had dominated the country for a generation. But the sacral basis of the French monarchy remained, and was strengthened by monarchical absolutism; the seeds of revocation were being sown at the same time as the edict of Nantes was being enforced.

NOTES

1 Georges Livet in Pierre Chaunu, ed., *The Reformation* (Gloucester, 1989), p. 168.
2 Text, with discussion of date, translated into English in J. T. McNeill and F. L.

Battles, eds. and trans., *Institution of the Christian Religion*, Library of Christian Classics vol. XX (London, 1961), pp. 9–31.

3 *Ibid.* p. 10.

4 J.-F. Gilmont, ed., *Le Réforme et le livre. L'Europe de l'imprimé* (Paris, 1990). Cf. W. G. Moore, *La Réforme allemande et la littérature française* (Strassburg 1930); F. M. Higman, 'Les traductions françaises de Luther, 1524–1550' in J.-F Gilmont, ed., *Palaestra Typographica* (Brussels, 1984), pp. 11–56.

5 G. Huppert, *Public Schools in Renaissance France* (Urbana, Ill., 1984), with the well-documented example of the college in Agen further explored in H. Heller, *The Conquest of Poverty* (Leiden, 1986), chapter 3.

6 Alexandre Ganoczy, *Le Jeune Calvin* (Wiesbaden, 1966), pp. 23–83 for a summary of the evidence of Calvin's contacts with evangelical groups in France in Paris, Noyon and the university towns along the Loire.

7 Emile Doumergue, *Jean Calvin, les hommes et les choses de son temps*, 7 vols. (Lausanne, 1899), vol. I, pp. 59–60. Cf. Heller, *The Conquest of Poverty*, pp. 116–20.

8 Doumergue, *Jean Calvin*, pp. 60–9.

9 On humanism and French reform, nothing replaces the works of M. Mann, *Erasme et les débuts de la réforme française (1517–36)* (Paris, 1934); P. Imbart de la Tour, *Les origines de la réforme*, 4 vols. (2nd edn Paris, 1946), vol. III; A. Renaudet, *Préréforme et humanisme à Paris pendant les premières guerres d'italie (1494–1517)* (2nd edn Paris, 1953). However, J.-C. Margolin, *L'humanisme en Europe au temps de la Renaissance* (Paris, 1981), chapter 3 stresses that humanists responded in different and contradictory ways to religious change, being more coherent in their attitudes towards intellectual, educational and moral reforms, broadly conceived. A good example of his point is provided by the French episcopacy where, according to the most recent survey, the humanist bishops were not predominantly those who eventually embraced protestantism – see F. J. Baumgartner, *Change and Continuity in the French Episcopate. The Bishops and the Wars of Religion* (Durham, N.C., 1986), pp. 123–32.

10 R. Doucet, *Les institutions de la France au XVIe siècle*, 2 vols. (Paris, 1948) vol. I, pp. 72–81.

11 Richard A. Jackson, *Vive le Roi! A History of the French Coronation from Charles V to Charles X* (Chapel Hill, 1984); Ralph E. Giesey, *The Royal Funeral Ceremony in Renaissance France* (Geneva, 1960).

12 Anne-Marie Lecoq, *François Ier imaginaire. Symbolique et politique à l'aube de la Renaissance française* (Paris, 1987), chapter 5.

13 E.g. Claude Seyssel, *The Monarchy of France* (New Haven, 1981), p. 52:

'It is essential that whoever is king here make known to the people by example and by present and overt demonstration that he is a zealous observant of the Christian faith and wishes to maintain and augment it to the best of his ability. If the people had another opinion of him, they would hate him and perhaps obey him but ill. Moreover, this people would impute all the troubles that came to the realm to the erroneous creed and imperfect religion of the king.'

14 Jackson, *Vive le Roi!*, pp. 57–8.

15 E.g. amongst others, Jean Talpin, *Institution d'un Prince Chrestien* (Paris, 1567), which reminded the young king Charles IX that he must follow his sacral destiny and resist heresy, assisted by the united prayer and mystical adoration of his people.

16 Doucet, *Les institutions de la France*, chapter 3.
17 J. Héretier, *Michel de l'Hôpital* (Paris, 1943).
18 J. Shimizu, *Conflict of Loyalties. Politics and Religion in the Career of Gaspard de Coligny* (Geneva, 1970); R. J. Knecht, *The French Wars of Religion* (London, 1989), pp. 106–7 for the promises undertaken by Guisard clients to avenge Francis, duke of Guise's death. N. M. Sutherland, *The Massacre of St Bartholomew and the European Conflict* (London, 1973).
19 E.g. A. Croix, *La Bretagne aux 16e et 17e siècles. La vie, la mort, la foi* (Paris, 1981).
20 R. Mousnier, *La Vénalité des Offices* (Rouen, n.d.), chapters 2–3.
21 J. Dewald, *The Formation of a Provincial Nobility* (Princeton, 1980); J. K. Powis, 'Order, Religion and the Magistrates of a Provincial Parlement in Sixteenth-Century France', *Archiv für Reformationsgeschichte*, 72 (1980), pp. 180–97 (concerned with the magistrates of the *Parlement* of Bourdeaux). Cf. R. A. Mentzer, 'Calvinist Propaganda and the Parlement of Toulouse', *Archiv für Reformationsgeschichte*, 67 (1976), pp. 284–300.
22 J. Garrisson-Estèbe, *Protestants du Midi (1559–98)* (Toulouse, 1980), p. 28.
23 R. I. Moore, *The Formation of a Persecuting Society* (Oxford, 1987).
24 E. Cameron, *The Reformation of the Heretics* (Oxford, 1984), especially chapter 2. Cf. G. Audisio, *Les Vaudois du Lubéron. Une minorité en provence (1460–1560)* (Mérindol, 1984).
25 R. J. Knecht, *Francis I* (Cambridge, 1982), pp. 248–52.
26 M. Greengrass, *The French Reformation* (Oxford, 1987), pp. 32–8. The best detailed studies of the legal prosecution of heresy are N. Weiss, *La Chambre Ardente* (Paris, 1889); R. Mentzer, 'Heresy proceedings in Languedoc, 1500–1560', *Transactions of the American Philosophical Society* (Philadelphia, 1984); N. M. Sutherland, *The Huguenot Struggle for Recognition* (New Haven, 1980), chapters 2–3; D. Kelley, *The Beginning of Ideology* (Cambridge, 1981), especially chapter 6.
27 J. A. de Thou. *Historiarum sui temporis*, 7 vols. (London, 1733), vol. I, p. 559.
28 See A. Franklin, 'La Mercuriale du 10 juin 1559', *Bulletin de la Societe d'Histoire de Protestantisme Français*, 30 (1881), pp. 49–56, especially p. 52.
29 *Ibid*. D. Kelley, *The Beginning of Ideology*, chapter 4.
30 M. N. Tommaseo, ed., *Relations des Ambassadeurs Venitiens sur les affaires de France au XVIe siècle* (Paris, 1838), vol. II, p. 55; Claude Haton, *Mémoires contenant le récit des événements accomplis de 1553 à 1587 . . .* , ed. F. Bourquelot, 2 vols. (Paris, 1857), vol. I, p. 163.
31 Haton, *Mémoires*, pp. 25–6.
32 *Ibid*. p. 112.
33 D. Crouzet, *Les Guerriers de Dieu*, 2 vols. (Paris, 1990), vol. I, pp. 191–201 ('Un personnage essentiel. Artus Désiré'). This fundamental work has radically reshaped our perception of the French Reformation and its perspectives have shaped various sections of this chapter.
34 *Ibid*. chapter 6.
35 Philippe Denis, *Les églises d'étrangers en pays rhénans (1534–1564)* (Paris, 1984).
36 See W. Bouwsma, *John Calvin* (Oxford, 1988), chapter 1, especially pp. 16–17.
37 See the classic work of R. Kingdon, *Geneva and the Coming of the Wars of Religion in France* (Geneva, 1956).

38 Janine Garrisson, *Les Protestants au XVIe siècle* (Paris, 1988), chapter 6, especially pp. 172–9.
39 E. W. Monter, 'Historical Demography and Religious History in Sixteenth-Century Geneva', *Journal of Interdisciplinary History*, 9 (1979) pp. 399–427.
40 Liliane Mottu-Weber, *Genève au siècle de la Réforme. Économie et Refuge* (Geneva, 1987) provides the most complete investigation of the effects of refugees upon the Genevan economy in the sixteenth century.
41 P. Geisendorf, 'Métiers et conditions sociales du premier refuge à Genève, Mélanges Antony Babel' (Geneva, 1963), pp. 239–49. This was the first of a number of attempts to analyse the social appeal of French Protestantism which has led to a number of detailed local studies. Altogether they have produced a number of (often mutual contradictory) hypotheses, sometimes resting on rather simplistic social analysis and reductionist logic. Rather than providing a convincing explanation of the impact of the Reformation in France on their own, they are a complement to such an explanation. See Greengrass, *The French Reformation*, chapter 3 and D. Crouzet, *Les Guerriers de Dieu*, vol. I, chapter 1.
42 Garrisson, *Les Protestants au XVIe siècle*, chapter 7; cf. part one.
43 Q. Skinner, *The Foundations of Modern Political Thought*, 2 vols. (Cambridge, 1978), vol. II, part three.
44 C. M. N. Eire, *War against the Idols* (Cambridge, 1986), chapter 8; D. Crouzet, *Les Guerriers de Dieu*, chapter 7.
45 E.g. 'The Great *Marmite* Overturned', reproduced in P. Benedict, *Rouen during the Wars of Religion* (Cambridge, 1981), p. 55.
46 C. Haton, *Mémoires*, vol. I, pp. 256–60; The Protestant agressors

'luy fendirent le ventre par le nombril qu'on appelle le bouteril, et par là tirèrent environ demy aulne et plus de ses boyaux, qu'ilz lièrent et attachèrent à un petit arbre, et l'ayant mis tout à nud, en le foytant avec des verges, le contraignirent de tourner à l'entour dudit arbre, jusques à ce que tous les boyaux furent demellez et envellopez à l'entour dudit argre'.

(. . . split his belly at the navel which one calls the belly-button and out of it they took around half a yard or more of his guts, which they tied to a small tree, and having stripped him naked so that his penis hung out, they forced him to turn himself around the tree until all his guts were unravelled and wrapped around it . . .)

47 D. Richet, 'Aspects socio-culturelles des conflits religieuz à Paris dans la seconde moitié du XVIe sièclé, *Annales ESC*, 32 (1977), pp. 764–89; explored further in D. Crouzet, *Les Guerriers de Dieu*, vol. I, chapter 9.
48 L. Ménard, *Histoire civile . . . de Nismes . . .*, 5 vols. (Paris, 1644–58), vol. V, p. 11.
49 *Ibid.* p. 750.
50 D. Crouzet, *Les Guerriers de Dieu*, vol. II, p. 36.
51 'Mémoires de Mathieu Blouyn', *Chroniques du Languedoc*, vol. II (1876), p. 10.
52 M. Venard, 'Une réforme gallicane? Le projet de concile national de 1551', *Revue d'histoire de l'église de France*, 67 (1981), pp. 201–25.
53 D. Nugent, *Ecumenism in the Age of the Reformation. The Colloquy of Poissy* (Harvard, 1972); N. M. Sutherland, *Princes, Politics and Religion, 1547–1589* (London, 1984), chapter 7.
54 These climactic years still await their modern historian. There remains L. Romier, *Le Royaume de Catherine de Médicis. La France à la veille des guerres de religion*, 2 vols. (Paris, 1925).

55  A. Jouanna, *Le devoir de révolte* (Paris, 1989).
56  Memorandum partially translated in G. R. Potter and M. Greengrass, *John Calvin* (London, 1983), p. 167.
57  N. Z. Davis, 'Rites of Violence', in *Society and Culture in Early Modern France* (London, 1975); D. Crouzet, *Les Guerriers de Dieu*, chapters 4–5.
58  R. Kingdon, *Geneva and the Consolidation of the French Protestant Movement, 1564–72* (Geneva, 1967).
50  D. Kelley, *The Beginning of Ideology*, chapter 7.
60  J-L. Bourgeon, 'Les légendes ont la vie dure. À propos de la Saint-Barthélemy et de quelques livres récents', *Revue d'histoire moderne et contemporaine*, 34 (1987) pp. 102–116.
61  R. M. Kingdon, *Myths about the St Bartholomew's Day Massacres, 1572–6* (Harvard, 1988) provides the most recent account of protestant mythologies. D. Crouzet, *Les Guerriers de Dieu*, vol. II, chapters 11–12 provide the most sophisticated analysis upon which I have drawn for these remarks.
62  See M. Greengrass 'The public context of the Abjuration of Henry IV', in K. Cameron, ed., *From Valois to Bourbon. Dynasty, State and Society in Early Modern France* (Exeter, 1989), pp. 107–26.

# 4    The Low Countries

*Wiebe Bergsma*

## Introduction

During an enforced exile at Emden in East Friesland, a Calvinist from the present province of Groningen wrote a chronicle in the 1590s. The anonymous author had been forced to leave his home as a Calvinist and an opponent of the Spanish king Philip II. In his exile, he came to reflect on the history of his times. The anonymous author was clearly a Protestant. Even the flourishing of agriculture, he believed, was due to the influence of Luther and the Reformation in general, for new methods of farming were a gift from God. He suspected Catholic priests of illicit affairs with nuns, greed for money and hypocrisy. He describes the Spanish soldiery as cruel; his father had seen for himself how a Spaniard hanged a soldier. Our Calvinist also finds much to astonish him: the many exiles from England and France in Emden, the great deal of chaff among the wheat, the many Anabaptists in the Netherlands, the turbulent baptists of Munster, the followers of Franck, the divisions in Lutheranism, but above all he is amazed at the great following of the spiritualist David Joris of Delft. According to our spokesman, there was no greater tempter than this David Joris, with his many followers particularly among prominent people. Mohammed had led a wild, murderous, thieving, untaught people in the stony wastes of Arabia. David Joris, on the other hand, had not misled poor and simple people, but rich, prosperous and educated citizens of a shrewd and clever population. With amazement, the chronicler summarises the variety of heretics and sects that were to be found in the Netherlands in the sixteenth century: turbulent baptists, followers of the former Frisian pastor Menno Simons, all kinds of spiritualists and all manner of other sectarians.[1]

This chronicler illustrates in his own way the more important developments in the sixteenth-century Netherlands in the political and ecclesiastical fields, but he also shows how relative the national context is. The Reformation in the Netherlands was an 'international' event *par excellence*. Local circumstances determined the concrete form taken by the Reformation. Great reformers such as Luther, Zwingli and Calvin did not appear in the Netherlands. Desiderius Erasmus had much influence in many fields, but he did not found a church of his own.

Around 1500 the seventeen provinces of the Low Countries formed a motley patchwork, which was gradually incorporated into the Burgundian-Habsburg Empire. A hundred years later seven provinces had joined together in the period of the Eighty Years' War or Dutch Revolt, in which the Calvinists with their theories of resistance played a leading role, to form the Republic of the Seven United Netherlands, a unique political system in the *ancien régime*.

The Reformation in the Netherlands was not guided from above, as was the case in a number of countries and cities of Europe. The heretical tendencies in the Netherlands could not count on the sympathy of Charles V and later of Philip II. The churches which came into being in the Netherlands did not resemble the Anglican or Lutheran state churches, the Genevan theocracy of Jean Calvin or the Swiss civic reformations. In the Netherlands, as elsewhere, we can listen to a cacophony of heretical voices, humanists and Erasmians, sacramentarians and Anabaptists, Lutherans and Calvinists, Jorists and Franckists, Schwenckfeldians, Loists and Familists, to name only a few. In 1585 a Spanish soldier wrote that there were seventeen different religions and ninety-four different sects in Antwerp, a remark which illustrates religious pluriformity but also the relativity of figures and numbers when dealing with religion.[2] Powerful impulses for reform came above all from the south and the commercial metropolis, Antwerp. Here too, the first executions of heretics took place. Decades later, it was from here that the iconoclastic fury was to spread across the whole of the Netherlands. But because of the course taken by the Dutch Revolt, ultimately the South remained Catholic, and the North became a Republic which was at least nominally Protestant.

The inhabitants of the Low Countries were thus able to choose from many, sometimes bizarre, variants of Christianity in the sixteenth century. An encyclopaedic description of this great religious pluriformity and religious anarchy is not appropriate in the context of this volume. In this contribution I wish to pay special attention to the Anabaptists and the Calvinists, who were both of great importance in the history of the sixteenth-century Netherlands and who both offered a permanent alternative to the old *Ecclesia romana*. In both North and South the new religious movements grew up in spite of persecution, both laid great stress on the forming of communities, and both emphasised ecclesiastical discipline within those communities. During the sixteenth century, both lost ground in the South, but succeeded in winning the support of many in the North. The differences in social position between Anabaptists and Calvinists were however very obvious: the Calvinists were the privileged, they evolved from the victims of persecution to the persecutors in the sense that their preachers did everything they could to oppose the Anabaptists. The baptists rejected every link with the state, while the Calvinists supported a tie between the church and the state – or vice versa.

I shall merely sketch the main outlines, as I see them.[3] It is unavoidable that the familiar story of Munster must be retold. I shall not go into the questions of *outillage mental*, popular belief, the problems of christianisation and dechristianisation, the gulf between the proscribed norms and the way they were experienced in practice, and the problems of popular culture and popular belief.

### Religious pluriformity

Around 1500 there was a unitary Catholic Church in the Netherlands as elsewhere. In villages and towns, there were numerous churches, chapels and monastic houses. Masses were read, regular and secular clergy performed their duties, indulgences were sold, saints invoked, fasts held and last wills and testaments often referred to the salvation of the soul. Much has been published about the involvement of the ordinary laity, and the last word on this subject has certainly not been said, but one fact is clear: as is evident from the criticism increasingly heard in the fifteenth and sixteenth centuries, for many people the Catholic Church had lost some of its meaning, in a religious sense, in the years 1520–30. A hundred years later many church buildings were still intact, but they had been put to another use. The preacher took the place of the priests, celibacy was no longer expected of the clergy, the hierarchical organisation of the church had been replaced by a presbyterian system, saints' days had disappeared, images had often been removed, as had altars and other visual elements, masses had been replaced by the communion service, memorial masses had been abolished, the number of services had been reduced, most monasteries had been closed and the Catholics formed a tolerated minority in a society which allowed the Reformed Church a privileged position.

As early as the later middle ages, there were all kinds of movements which criticised the Catholic Church and wished to purge it of all manner of abuses, for example the Modern Devotion of Geert Grote. Nonetheless, attempts to reform the church and the monastic orders in the fifteenth and sixteenth centuries ended in complete failure. Criticism from within became sharper and sharper. Vitriolic criticism also came from many humanists, Desiderius Erasmus the first among them. Erasmus' *Praise of Folly* was much read in the sixteenth century. In spite of their criticism of the Catholic Church, the humanists often remained loyal to it. In the 1520's much criticism was levelled at the mass, with doubt being cast on transubstantiation in particular. Wendelmoet Claesdochter, executed at The Hague in 1527, said of the mass during her trial: 'I think your sacrament is bread and flour, and what you think is God, I say that it is a devil.' To the question, what she thought of the sacrament for the dying ('What do you think of the Holy Oil'), she replied 'Oil is good for a salad or to rub your shoes with.' From the twenties one can speak of an undifferentiated movement for renewal with a multiplicity of heretical voices.[4] Important points in dispute were confession, indulgences, purgatory, the intercession of Mary and the saints, monks, images and fasting, but above all the mass and the real presence of Christ in the bread and wine during the mass. Thanks to the art of printing, many could become acquainted with all these heretical opinions through the works of popular dramatists or 'rhetoricians', pamphlets, tracts and other prose works. But most dissidents did not go so far as to break with the Catholic Church.

The first to separate themselves from the Catholic Church and form their own communities, were the Anabaptists. 'Fleeing from Babel, we entered Jerusalem'; thus the Anabaptists experienced their exodus from accursed popery.

### Menno's people

Historians have been quarrelling about the origin of the baptist movement for centuries and the Anabaptists of the sixteenth century themselves engaged in violent debate about their origins. Nowadays, it is at least agreed that their origin is not to be sought among the Waldensians. In recent times the emphasis has been placed on various points of origin, or to put it in more impressive terms, there has been a shift from a monogenetic to a polygenetic explanation of Anabaptism. Here I shall retell the classical tale.[5]

The reformation begun by Zwingli led, among other things, to the removal with the support of the civic authorities, of images from churches in 1523 and the abolition of the mass in 1525. That reformation was welcomed by Conrad Grebel and Felix Mantz, but they criticised the way in which it had been achieved, namely the active involvement of the civic magistracy in ecclesiastical life. They wanted a church community without spot or stain, with preachers who were paid by the members of the community themselves, and they also propagated a strict church discipline. They felt that the sacrament of baptism was only intended for true believers. A new-born child cannot have any faith, they reasoned, and so they rejected infant baptism and practised the baptism of adults. In January 1525 the first baptism took place. Thus the Donatists of the age of Augustine found 'followers' in the sixteenth century.

The Anabaptists may have rejected the involvement of the authorities in the Church, but the authorities involved themselves with the Anabaptists, in the form of repression. In 1527 Mantz became the first Anabaptist to be sentenced to death by drowning. This was the start of a rigorous persecution in Europe. The gallows and the stake were unable to contain the movement, and it spread like an oil slick across the German Empire, the Tyrol and Moravia.

An important role in Anabaptism was played by the Swabian furrier and Lutheran lay preacher, Melchior Hoffman (c. 1495–1543). Hoffman was a strongly eschatological thinker. He proclaimed the coming of a new heaven and a new earth. Strassburg was to be the new Jerusalem. From that city, the new Elijah prophesied, the 144,000 of the Book of Revelation would go throughout the world to spread the new faith. Hoffman was thrown into prison in Strassburg and died in total solitude in his cell.

Hoffman converted many to Anabaptism. In the years 1530 to 1532 he preached in the Netherlands and at Emden. In Emden he baptised around 300 persons at Whitsun 1530, townsfolk and peasants, or peasants and servants according to an eyewitness. There were also a great many refugees from the Netherlands in Emden, among them Jan Volkertsz Trypmaker and the Frisian, Sicke Freersz. Both were rebaptised in 1530 and sent to the Netherlands to proclaim the faith. In Amsterdam and Friesland they proceeded to found their own congregations. The Melchiorites soon spread throughout the Netherlands, and many took over the eschatological legacy of Hoffman. The Anabaptists soon formed a numerous flock, with their own congregations in spite of severe persecutions. One of their martyrs' songs claims that there were a hundred converts for every one put to death, and though this is of course a metaphor, it had some historical basis.

Since Hoffman lay in prison and Strassburg remained a mere city in South Germany, a new leader of the Melchiorites came forward in the person of the Haarlem baker Jan Matthijszoon. He sent out twelve apostles to resume the rebaptisms. Two of these apostles arrived on 5 January 1534 in the city of Munster which has ever since been so traumatic for Anabaptists. At least 1,400 people spontaneously had themselves rebaptised. It was not Strassburg but the Westphalian episcopal city which was to be the new Jerusalem. Those who thought differently were driven out of the city, if they had not already taken flight. In February Jan Matthijszoon and his apostles arrived. The churches were destroyed, images removed and books burned. Later, community of property and polygamy were introduced, all as part of the kingdom of God on earth. The city acted as a magnet to the Anabaptists. From North Holland alone, about 3,000 people left for Munster.

The city was at once besieged by the bishop's troops. Jan Matthijszoon led a sally against them in April but was killed. He was followed by Jan van

Leiden, who had himself crowned king of God's kingdom before the cathedral of Munster. The King of Sion led a princely life and even managed to defend the besieged city until 25 June 1535, when he fell into the hands of the bishop. The leaders were cruelly tortured. Their bodies were exposed in cages on the tower of the church of St Lambert; these cages still hang there today.

In Amsterdam, Bolsward, in the Groningen countryside and in Leiden, there were riots which resembled the kingdom of God in Munster. All these events made a great impression on contemporaries. 'Munster' also meant a turning point in Anabaptism. It had dealt itself a heavy blow. From 1535 the baptists were stigmatised. From that time an Anabaptist was not only heterodox, he was also a seditious rebel, a danger to the state and a threat to the commonweal. Persecutions broke out in the Netherlands, although they varied from province to province. Alastair Duke has calculated that in the period 1523 to 1566 about 1,300 people were executed for their beliefs: in Brabant 228, Flanders 265, Friesland 102, Utrecht 31. The majority of them were Anabaptists.[6]

In spite of the persecutions, Anabaptism continued to exert a great attraction. In many places, especially in Holland and Friesland, baptist congregations arose, which were intended to be without spot or stain. Exclusions and discipline were important in these baptist congregations, hence the great internal divisions and the countless splinter groups in the history of the Anabaptists. Of course, the baptists distanced themselves from the events in Munster, but their reformed and Catholic contemporaries thought otherwise and were eager to remind them of the past events at Munster. The great leader of the baptists was to be Menno Simons (1496–1561) from Witmarsum in Friesland, who managed to steer the movement into calmer water. Despite their past and despite persecution, the Mennonites increased in number. Many different congregations were formed; the three most important were the Waterlanders, the Frisians and the Flemings. Congregations existed in almost all the towns of Holland. The number of baptists in Friesland *c.* 1600, for example, is estimated at about 25 per cent of the population. The baptists demanded an absolute separation of church and state. They refused to bear arms and to swear oaths. The emphasis that the baptists laid on the formation of a community without spot or stain meant that in some places, a number of different baptist congregations arose. Opponents of the Anabaptists – and they were numerous – spoke of the 'Babel' of the Anabaptists. All the critical voices from Catholics and later from Calvinists about the baptists cannot of course be seen in detachment from the competition that the baptists presented for the Calvinists.

## Calvinists

In 1586 the Calvinist minister Johannes van der Mijle in Delft heard that in distant Appingedam in the province of Groningen, where he had spent some years as preacher, a few pious Christians were still left.[7] He wrote a letter to encourage these reformed Christians. Not only did they want nothing to do with Roman idolatry, but they also shunned the false doctrines of the sects. They visited one another in their houses to read the Word of God and to console and fortify one another with good words. The preacher thanked God that in the scattered church, a seed had been saved which would bear more fruit in good time. The preacher was delighted that the faithful had been able to maintain themselves among the wolves, and that his work therefore had not been in vain. Those members who had heard the word in Appingedam, and later gone into exile, were also conducting themselves as pious Christians in their exile in East Friesland. He hoped that they would persist in the faith until the Second Coming of Christ: this was the prayer of the former preacher of the congregation at Appingedam. For even though they were separated in body and soul, in his heart Van der Mijle was with his congregation every day. If there were people who had some taste of the Word of God and a little spark of knowledge, then the faithful must spare no effort to bring them into the flock. The true believers must arm themselves against the enemies of the Gospel and must read the Bible assiduously. At their meetings they must read the *Hausbuch* of Heinrich Bullinger in which the doctrine of Christianity was summarised. Members of the congregation who had been led astray from the truth by the sects must be led back to the true path, if that were possible. If it were not possible, he would be glad to know who they were, and what were the points in dispute; the preacher would then write to them admonishing them with God's Word.

In this letter we see a preacher who shows more than a mere theological obsession. He writes that the number of members is distressingly small; some of them had fled to East Friesland. The Calvinists had no support for the authorities. The Catholic church and the Anabaptists formed serious rivals. The preacher does not recommend the Institutes of Calvin, but a work of the reformer Bullinger. The doctrine of predestination is not even mentioned. God is a loving Father. There is scarcely any mention of a great organisation. In 1586 the Calvinists were still meeting as small communities in houses, at the risk of their lives.

Now it may be objected that the situation in the Groningen countryside was exceptional. This is partly true. In most of the other provinces, the war situation was less threatening and therefore the reformed could begin to build up their church. Yet we can use this letter to illustrate the most important developments in research into the history of the Reformed Church in the sixteenth-century Netherlands.

The idea of 'Humanism, the Reformation, Anabaptism and Calvinism', as monolithic entities had long been discredited. Calvinism in the Netherlands as elsewhere was varied and took many forms. There were intolerant and irenic Calvinists, 'moderates' and the 'strictly orthodox', members and supporters, while Calvinists also held differing views on baptism, communion, church and state, predestination, eschatology and christology.[8]

Some historians have asserted that the Netherlands were 'protestantised' in rapid tempo, and that the state tried in all possible ways to give the Reformed Church a privileged position, if not to impose the new faith on the population. The authorities are said to have systematically imposed Calvinism on the population, to have opened public offices exclusively to members of the Reformed Church; the charitable funds and the revenues of church property are supposed to have been as bait for non-members, and the authorities are alleged to have tried every possible means of fending off Catholicism. This is the so called 'protestantisation' thesis which was launched by the historian Pieter Geyl and later elaborated by the Catholic historian L. J. Rogier.[9] In the partly apologetic phraseology of Rogier: 'Fanatical and absolute, [Calvinism] conspires purposefully and methodically until the moment is ripe for the coup d'etat, which will give the opportunity for a small minority to impose its theocracy on the Genevan model, its dictatorship, on an overwhelming majority.'[10] Now it cannot be denied that numerous examples can be found of edicts against the Catholics and of government support for the public church. But thanks to recent research it has become clear that the cooperation of church and state differed widely from province to province and city to city. Moreover, Rogier starts from the idea that Protestantism could not have exercised any attraction for people or have had any power to win new recruits on its own. A. Th. van Deursen shrewdly punctured this theory: 'In Rogier, one almost has the impression that man is regarded as by nature Catholic, so that his conversion to Protestantism always requires a special explanation.'[11] Van der Mijle's loving letter makes it clear that Calvinism was not exclusively a matter of compulsion and violence, but that many of the inhabitants of the Low Countries felt a deep inner involvement with Calvinism.

Van der Mijle's remark on the small number of members is not the lament of a complaining Calvinist. His sighs are another indication of the inaccuracy of the protestantisation thesis. In the sixteenth and the first half of the seventeenth century, the number of members of the Reformed Church grew only slowly. Calvinism for example only took root in the countryside of Utrecht with difficulty. Around 1600, only 20 per cent of the inhabitants of

Den Briel were members of the Reformed Church, in Enkhuizen 3000 of the 21,000 inhabitants were members and on the basis of my own research I can show that in Friesland also, the number of members remained low for many years.[12] Haarlem is an even more eloquent example. By 1620 about half of the population had made its choice: 20 per cent were reformed, 12½ per cent Catholic, 14 per cent baptist, 1 per cent Lutheran and about 1 per cent belonged to the Walloon church.[13] We do not know what sort of ideas were held by the rest of the population. Some were atheists, others perhaps supporters of Calvinism and others again may have had no interest in any variant of Christianity. All these figures deprive the protestantisation thesis of its force. But writing history is more than forming theories, so let us return to the Calvinists themselves.

The first Calvinist impulses reached the southern Netherlands from France and Geneva. Like the baptists, the Calvinists were at first severely persecuted. If the centre of gravity of the Calvinists was at first in the south, where they organised clandestine communities under the cross, during the century it shifted to the north. In 1572 the Calvinists in Holland and Zeeland were able to make a start on the building up of the new reformed church; in the other provinces this was only possible in or after 1578. The Calvinist church organisation was anti-hierarchical. In a local congregation, a church council was formed, consisting of a preacher, elder and deacons. A number of congregations formed a classis. From these classes, representatives were sent to the particular and national synods. The constituent assembly was held at the Synod of Emden in 1571, where an organisational model was worked out which was to be introduced with great differences from place to place, in the different provinces.

Those who are familiar with the minutes of church councils or read through the proceedings of the classical assemblies, are brought into contact with the daily life of often exceptional members. We continually read of drunkenness, whoring, witchcraft, adultery, playing and dancing on Sunday, lack of interest in the Word of God, absenteeism, of fines paid by members unwilling to accept an office, of exorcists, in short of sinners who fell under ecclesiastical discipline and were confronted with the exercise of ecclesiastical discipline in its severe Calvinist form. This discipline leads us to the doctrine of the Calvinists.

For Calvinists as for others, the redemption of mankind was central. Each individual stands alone before God. A human being cannot have any effect on his or her own salvation, for God has predestined all men and women to election or damnation. Calvin's harsh doctrine of predestination was central for the Calvinists of the sixteenth century, to whom it offered a greater certainty of salvation. A Calvinist had to acquire knowledge of the true doctrine from the Bible. Teaching at school and in church, through catechisation and sermons, offered that possibility. The celebration of holy communion was a high point of church life. But a sinner could not possibly take part in this sacrament. Hence it was necessary to let the 'old Adam' die out. A member who had committed adultery had to appear before the church council. In a very extensive and time-consuming procedure, a member could confess his or her sin and thus avoid ultimate excommunication. Whoever became a member of the new church had to realise that faith was not without obligations; high demands were made on his or her morals.

For many inhabitants of the Low Countries, church discipline was prohibitive for membership of the Reformed Church. In Frisian sources, it is sometimes said that the church was full, and yet only seven people were members. The others were the so-called 'sympathisers' (*liefhebbers*) of the reformed religions. They were sympathisers, they went to church, had their children baptised, took part in the life of the church, but they could not attend holy communion. Thus they did not fall under ecclesiastical discipline. Of course it is not possible to determine how many of these sympathisers there were, but there are indications that until well into the seventeenth century, the number of those who wished to remain sympathisers was great. In Friesland in 1647, it was complained that the rights of presentation to parish incumbencies was still in the hands of the sympathisers, among them many Catholics, atheists and Mennonites.

The two categories of churchgoers illustrate the ambivalent character of Dutch Calvinism. On the one hand the reformed church was the privileged and public church where even the supporters could find a place, and on the other hand the members formed the hard core of the Reformed Church. In many places, this ambivalence between a 'purified church' and a larger group of more loosely attached supporters led to serious tensions. Nevertheless it is clear that the conclusion drawn for England also applied to the situation in the Netherlands: 'the religion of Protestants was never popular in the plain and ordinary sense'.[14]

## Conclusion

Reformation and revolution cannot be thought of as entirely separate entities in the sixteenth-century Netherlands. At the beginning of the sixteenth century, the seventeen provinces of the Low Countries formed a part of the Burgundian-Habsburg Empire, and the Catholic Church was the only church in town and countryside. In 1600, a republic had emerged in the North, which gave a privileged position to the Reformed Church. The South remained a politically multiform area, and at the same time predominantly Catholic. Two great variants of Christianity were tolerated, the

Catholic and the baptist. The Catholics managed to maintain themselves in large numbers in a number of places. Those who rely on the edicts against the Catholics could gain the impression that they hardly had any room to manoeuvre but in practice they could do a great deal.

The number of Lutheran congregations was limited. There were also many, sometimes small, esoteric groups of believers who found their inspiration in Sebastian Franck, Hendrik Niclaes, Caspar Schwenckfeld and others who were among the so-called radical reformers. They included spiritualists who wished to read the Bible in a spiritual sense, and sometimes took a great interest in arcane knowledge, hermetic writings and Paracelsism, and were often strongly eschatological in attitude.

We have scarcely any statistical data for the sixteenth century, yet it is clear that many sixteenth century men and women were unable or unwilling to make a choice of one of the larger religious tendencies. They formed the middle group of people who did not make such a choice, the so-called neutralists. There are also indications that some in the sixteenth century were unwilling to make a choice. In 1582 complaints were made of the great masses of atheists and libertines who openly mocked religion and called worship a fable. The unfrocked preacher Caspar Collhaes was the target of frequent complaint from his former colleagues: he had joined the group of those who were most numerous of all, those who wished to found a new general Catholic church and were not eager to trust any definite form of worship. They included those who stood still, speculators and spectators, who were always seeking and never finding. These uncommitted observers, according to the preachers formed an 'innumerable multitude' of people who were unwilling to choose.[15] Of course, a preacher who complains of the lack of religious enthusiasm of his fellow villagers or townsfolk is not exceptional, but there is certainly a kernel of truth in this complaint, as research into the history of Haarlem has shown.

In two respects the Dutch Republic differed from the other countries of Europe. In the first place the Dutch Republic had no state church and no religious homogeneity. In other countries with established state churches, for example in Scandinavia, Catholics were reduced to a minimum. In countries where the Counter-Reformation succeeded, for example, in Spain and Italy, the Protestants all but disappeared. The Dutch Republic had no state church, because the Reformation had not been imposed from above, but had on the contrary arisen in spite of persecution. The absence of a state church implied among other things, that preachers were not in the service of the state and that doctrinal teachings were not under the official influence of the authorities, as for example in the Anglican church or the Lutheran state churches of Scandinavia. In the Dutch Republic, for example, it was possible to have a marriage confirmed in church or by the local authority.

Moreover, membership of the Reformed Church was not *de jure* a precondition of office, although the practice was sometimes different. Indeed, the law forbade consciences to be forced.

In the second place we can see in the Dutch Republic the beginnings of a *longue durée* in its great degree of religious pluriformity. Nowadays we recognise religious pluriformity as an important expression of tolerance. The sixteenth century was the 'Zeitalter der Glaubensspaltung', and not a period of ecumenism, dialogue or mutual understanding. Calvinists regarded the toleration of those who thought differently as an attack on God's honour and a threat to the true church. What we now regard as contemptible intolerance was a question of vital importance for Calvinists. Those who did not belong to the true Calvinist church were not only lost, but played into the hands of Satan. A great champion of tolerance and opponent of the execution of heretics, D. V. Coornhert (1522–90), who urged a series of arguments against the execution of heretics, was rather an isolated case in the sixteenth century.

The absence of a state church in the Dutch Republic brought tolerance in its wake. In spite of all the polemics, mutual suspicions, calls by preachers for persecution of those who thought otherwise, religious fanaticism and mutual misunderstanding, in a European perspective the republic was an exceptionally tolerant country and not only for commercial reasons. Contemporaries repeatedly wrote of the great degree of religious freedom in the marvellous republic. L. J. Rogier once wrote with justice, that the Republic of the United Netherlands was no paradise 'where the wolf sported with the lamb and the fox left the chickens in peace, but it was the most tolerant state of the Ancien Regime'.[16] Only in the Dutch Republic was it possible for the Swiss delegate to the Synod of Dordrecht to lodge with a family in which the father and son belonged to the old mother church, the mother and daughter were reformed, the mother-in-law was a baptist and the father's brother a Jesuit.[17]

*English translation by J. C. Grayson*

NOTES

1 W. Bergsma and E. H. Waterbolk, *Kroniekje van een Ommelander boer in de zestiende eeuw*, (Groningen, 1986), pp. 74ff.

2 Cited by Guido Marnef, 'Antwerpen in Reformatietijd. Ondergronds Protestantisme in een internationale handelsmetropool, 1550–1577' (Ph.D. dissertation, University of Louvain, 1991), vol. I, p. 3. The English edition of this unpublished thesis is forthcoming.

3 A part of this essay was originally published in M. Gijswijt-Hofstra, *Een schijn van verdraagzaamheid. Afwijking en tolerantie in Nederland van de zestiende eeuw tot heden.* (Hilversum, 1989), pp. 69–84. The notes have been kept to a

minimum, since almost all the literature can be found in the books named below. The four most important historical publications on the Reformation in the Netherlands in recent decades are three dissertations and a monograph. J. J. Woltjer, *Friesland in Hervormingstijd* (Leiden, 1962) describes only one province, but his conclusions with regard to the middle groups in church and politics can be applied to the Netherlands as a whole. An excellent description and analysis of the religious situation in the early years of the Republic, to which I fully subscribe, is J. J. Woltjer, 'De religieuze situatie in de eerste jaren van de Republiek', in *Ketters en papen in de Republiek* (Utrecht, 1986), pp. 31–43. A. Th. van Deursen published a finely written book on the reformed church in Holland, *Bavianen en Slijkgeuzen. Kerk en kerkvolk ten tijde van Maurits en Oldenbarnevelt* (Assen, 1974). The studies of Alastair Duke are fundamental and have been published under the title *Reformation and Revolt in the Low Countries* (London, 1990). I follow Duke in essentials, although I have chosen my examples from other regions. The thesis mentioned in note 2 is impressive.

4 For the beginning of reformation tendencies in the Netherlands, see the article by C. Augustijn, 'Sacramentariers en Doopsgezinden', in *Doopsgezinde Bijdragen*, 15 (1989), pp. 121ff. and the commentaries on this article.

5 W. O. Packull, J. M. Stayer, K. Deppermann, 'From Monogenesis to Polygenesis. The Historical Discussions of Anabaptist Origins', in *Mennonite Quarterly Review*, 49 (1975), pp. 83–122.

6 Numbers mentioned in Duke, *Reformation*, p. 71.

7 The letter is published in Abel Eppens tho Equart, *Der Vresen Chronicon, Werken van het Historische Genootschap*, vols. 26–7, ed. J. A. Feith and H. Brugmans (Amsterdam, 1911), vol. II, pp. 351ff.

8 W. Nijenhuis, 'Variants within Dutch Calvinism in the Sixteenth Century', in *Low Countries History Yearbook*, 1979, pp. 48–65.

9 On 'Protestantisation' see Duke's article 'The Ambivalent Face of Calvinism in the Netherlands, 1561–1618', in *Reformation*, pp. 271ff.

10 L. J. Rogier, *Geschiedenis van het katholicisme in Noord-Nederland in de zestiende en zeventiende eeuw*, 3 vols. (Amsterdam, 1947), vol. I, p. 159.

11 Van Deursen, *Bavianen en Slijkgeuzen*, p. 145.

12 Wiebe Bergsma, 'Calvinismus in Friesland um 1600 am Beispiel der Stadt Sneek', *Archiv für Reformationsgeschichte*, 80 (1989), pp. 252–285.

13 J. W. Spaans, 'Haarlem na de Reformatie. Stedelijke cultuur en kerkelijk leven, 1577–1620' (Ph.D. dissertation, University of Leiden, 1989), p. 104.

14 Patrick Collinson, *The Religion of Protestants. The Church in English Society (1559–1625)* (Oxford, 1982), p. 191.

15 Cf. Woltjer, 'Religieuze situatie', p. 104.

16 L. J. Rogier, 'De tolerantie in de Statenbond der Verenigde Nederlanden', in *Terugblik en uitzicht. Verspreide opstellen van L. J. Rogier*, vol. I (Hilversum-Antwerpen, 1964), p. 108.

17 Quoted in H. A. Enno van Gelder, *Getemperde Vrijheid. Een verhandeling over de verhouding van Kerk en Staat in de Republiek der Verenigde Nederlanden en de vrijheid van meningsuiting in zake godsdienst, drukpers en onderwijs, gedurende de 17e eeuw* (Groningen, 1972), p. 3 note 5.

# 5  England

*Patrick Collinson*

Someone has recently written an essay on 'The Myth of the English Reformation', a title easily misunderstood until one reads the first sentence: 'The myth of the English Reformation is that it did not happen.' The author is sure that on the contrary it did.[1] But what was 'it'? No small thing. As the major disjunction in the civilisation of a nation which lives by a virtuous myth of continuity, the scope of the Reformation is daunting, too vast a subject to be neatly packaged in the many books called 'The English Reformation',[2] still less in a modest essay. 'It' redefined the law and the constitution, altered doctrine, liturgy, church architecture and religious aesthetics, affected morality, virtually invented (according to some) the modern family, redistributed landed property, adjusted the social structure which the land supported, modified economic and social policy (including interest rates and social security), and radically transformed both elite and popular culture. There were further implications for language, notions of time and space, perceptions of national identity and destiny. Unlike some more recent revolutions, not much of this was planned in advance. 'The Reformation' has been invented by historians, looking backwards. Some of the topics have been faithfully attended to in the literature: the great Henrician constitutional measures, the dissolution of the monasteries, Thomas Cranmer and his Book of Common Prayer. But there is no history of English Protestantism, not a single book claiming to deal with that subject, indeed no consensus that such a subject even exists.

And when was 'it'? The English Reformation was not an event, not even a series of events, but a protracted process. If narrowly defined as certain legally enacted changes in the status and internal and external relations of the English Church and in its doctrine and worship, then 1529 and 1559 are its confining dates: 1529 when Henry VIII responded to his marital and dynastic problem by summoning the parliament which would break all ties with Rome; 1559, the year of the definitive Protestant settlement made by the child of that schism, Elizabeth I. Within these thirty years, the religion of England altered as often as governments and their policies in a modern democracy, so that some historians now pluralise the concept and speak of a succession of 'reformations', not excluding the counter-reformation under Mary Tudor and extending to the fluctuations in religious policy occasioned by later, seventeenth-century regimes.[3] If we are to define the Reformation more generously as the entire cultural epoch from the date when Catholicism was first significantly challenged to the *coup de grace* which extinguished its political hopes for ever, then we must assign to it not three decades but the three centuries from 1378 (when the ideas of John Wyclif were declared heretical) to 1688 (the deposition of James II). Somewhere along that time-scale, well before 1688 but perhaps not long before 1600, England may be said to have become a predominantly Protestant rather than Catholic country, its national celebrations, ringing of bells and lighting of bonfires, Protestant, or at least anti-catholic occasions.[4] Most people no longer crossed themselves when they sneezed and no longer swore 'by the mass'. Their very identity as Englishmen, an insular and proto-imperial identity at once confronting and turning away from a mostly Catholic continent, was articulated in anti-catholic slogans: 'No Popery!'

The Reformation was protracted because it was contested, not only at the top, at the level of high politics, but throughout the deep fabric of society, with consequences which were simultaneously divisive and unitive. Unitive aspirations were partially fulfilled, yet the end-product was not the all-inclusive church occupying the same space as the commonwealth which for the late Elizabethan divine Richard Hooker was a fundamental constitutional principle.[5] The established Church itself was run through with internal fracture lines, already visible when Hooker wrote, indeed constituting the reason why he wrote. In many fundamental respects a Reformed Church, it retained unusual Catholic features and so a potential for the internal conflicts which would dictate so much of its history in the seventeenth century, as indeed into our own century. And the establishment contended for its place in the sun with both Catholic and Protestant dissenting minorities, excluded or excluding themselves, created paradoxically not so much out of the desire to secede as of the consequence of defeats in the Reformation struggle to control the destiny of the national Church.

If the English Reformation was a contested process in history, it has been no less contested in its historiography, and for reasons which are not unconnected. As late as the last decade of the twentieth century, it is not hard to distinguish between accounts of the subject whose understanding is sympathetically Catholic (whether Roman or Anglo-), and others whose perceptions if not overtly Protestant derive from Protestantism in that secularised form which is vulgarly known as 'Whiggish', which is to say that the Reformation is regarded as 'a good thing'. Accounts of the English Reformation in the first of these traditions still present it in terms of the strange death of Catholic England, a negative, political and unpopular process. 'On the whole, English men and women did not want the Reformation, and most of them were slow to accept it when it came.'[6] The contrary school believes that Protestantism was an idea whose time had come, so that a mid-Tudor Yorkshire cleric of an orthodox catholic outlook becomes 'The Last Medieval Englishman'.[7] These historians call the brief return to Catholicism under Mary 'the Marian Reaction'.

There is also a new 'revisionism' applied to the subject, not necessarily confessional in motivation. Whereas Catholic historians know that the Reformation happened, and deeply regret it, Christopher Haigh, the leading revisionist, almost suggests that it was a non-event. He is so far persuaded (by his sources rather than his prejudices) of the strength and resilience of traditional religion as to doubt whether it was possible to replace it in hearts and minds with the new and mostly unpopular Protestant faith. So the Reformation was stillborn or, at best, a somewhat 'sickly child'.[8]

To insist that the Reformation did happen, as I think we must, is to leave ample scope for debate not only about its nature and scope but about its timing, and modalities, whether it was brought about by political imposition from above ('an act of state' as an earlier historian wrote) or from below, as a spontaneous and voluntary shift in religious sentiment. Haigh has shown how a vast amount of disorderly evidence can be brought under control within the ideal–typical matrices of early and late, from above and from below. In principle, the Reformation could have been secured at the time where historians have usually placed it, in the reigns of Henry VIII and Edward VI, and by means of the legislation and other governmental instruments traditionally emphasised; or with equal rapidity, but in response to grass-roots social and spiritual forces. Or perhaps it was a long haul, lasting at least into Elizabeth's reign, with the eventual success of Protestantism retarded either by the effectiveness of local resistance to the religious policies of the state or by the relatively slow momentum gathered by a more voluntaristic evangelistic bandwagon, slow reformation from above, or from below.[9] None of these scenarios is likely to correspond to the whole truth and it is not clear that any historian thinks so. A. G. Dickens, author of a standard book on *The English Reformation* (1964, revised 1989), has been identified by the revisionists as a champion of early reformation from below, but this he repudiates. There are no pure proponents of either 'from above' or 'from below'. Any competent student of early modern England knows that its history was made in negotiations between the upper and lower levels of the social and political hierarchy, and between centre and locality. Those who physically implemented religious change in the parish churches were the church wardens, literally middle men and simultaneously answerable to higher authority and to their neighbours.

Differences over 'early' and 'late' are harder to reconcile. Geoffrey Elton has written that by 1553 the English nation was closer to being Protestant than anything else, while Dickens believes that the religious failure of Mary's reign, which began in that year, was 'likely to have become more monumental with every succeeding year'.[10] These are great authorities. Yet believers in late reformation appear to be winning the argument. We can hardly talk of a Protestant church without Protestant preachers proclaiming the Protestant Gospel on a regular basis, for such preaching in the under-standing of Protestants themselves was 'the ordinary means of salvation', the very essence of the Church's organised and active existence. It was not before the 1570s and 1580s that a 'godly preaching ministry' was widely and securely established in the towns and villages of southern and eastern England, and as late as the 1620s before it materialised on a comparable scale in much of the north, or even in a county like Somerset.[11]

Underlying this debate is some continuing uncertainty about how to define and evaluate the Protestantism of a Protestant church and nation, as well as the basic arithmetical calculus of majority and minority which has to be brought into assessing the fortunes of any religion which is in a state of contentious growth, and especially of a religion like Protestantism which requires a high level of personal commitment from its converts and adher-ents. In that the first Protestants took to the new religion in ones and twos and small groups, they must have been exceptional people, or at least their singular religious opinions would have made them so. Yet it was recorded as a piece of proverbial wisdom towards the end of the sixteenth century that 'it is safer to doe in religion as most doe.'[12] Not only safer, we may add, but more charitable, more public-spirited. To do as most do not do was not popular, least of all in the kind of face-to-face society which we suppose much of early modern England to have been. Even in Chaucer's day the parson's excessive religious zeal moved the host to remark that while we all believe in God, this man would cause some 'difficulty'. Yet there pre-sumably came a point when that safer thing, the thing that most did, looked more like Protestantism than Catholicism.

But when did that 'point' occur, and how? When does the insomniac historian begin to count a minority of Catholics rather than Protestants in his effort to get some sleep? Psychologically, Protestantism, like all self-selecting and prodigious religious minorities, found it hard to make the transition to majority status, so far so that some never made it. It appears that when conformists became Protestants, Protestants became non-conformists, changing their name to Puritans. It has been said that Prot-estantism was not the best of ideologies with which to build a comprehen-sive, national church.[13]

Historians who believe in reformation from below measure its progress by counting heads, even while they know that not all heads were of the same size or significance, Archbishop Cranmer or the duke of Northumberland counting for rather more than the teenage Brentwood apprentice William Hunter or Rawlins White, the poor Cardiff fisherman who was one of the very few Welsh Protestant martyrs to join Hunter in the pages of John Foxe. Or, to change the metaphor, they stick pins into the map. A biographical database of early Protestants has been compiled, mostly from the records of criminal proceedings in cases of heresy, which provides us with some 3,000 pins.[14] Many more have been produced in the course of investigating the beginnings of the Reformation in a variety of urban and rural localities, so that by the time Dickens has drawn much of this grass-roots research together the map fairly bristles with pins.[15] Since the courts were sometimes less than energetic and their surviving records patchy, and since it was human nature in such circumstances not to stand up and be counted, Dickens believes that some kind of multiplier must be employed to arrive at a realistic assessment of the true size and strength of Protestantism, especially in Edwardian England. 'By 1553 Protestantism had already become a formidable and seemingly ineradicable phenomenon in fairly large and very populous areas of marked political importance.' A broad swathe of eastern and south-eastern England, running from Norfolk to East Sussex, was 'the heartland of the England Reformation'.

But, to persist in the mixing of metaphors, it is a question how many swallows it takes to make a summer. Most of this evidence tells us about what are best described as cells or pockets of Protestantism. They were local in the sense of having had a location, but they were not necessarily localised, since they were connected with a wider network by the same texts (and especially the English New Testament translated by William Tyndale and coming into circulation from the later 1520s), the same teachers and preachers, the same doctrines. The heretical profession of faith made in his will by the Gloucestershire gentleman William Tracey, an early swallow in a region which would remain conservative in religion for decades to come, was printed (by the same Tyndale) as Protestant propaganda and was soon being copied into other wills a hundred and two hundred miles away.[16]

But while national in scope, early Protestantism was cellular in distribution and structure, even in the most important of all localities, if we may call it a locality. Susan Brigden's exhaustive study of the Reformation in London[17] suggests that if we are to name the names and to count the heads which made up the identifiable Protestant community in the pre-Elizabethan capital, those taken into custody in the religious reaction of 1540, those coming under suspicion in Mary's reign, those making unmistakably reformist wills, we are talking about no more than 1 or 2 per cent of the total population, as it happens a socially very mixed group, belonging to no single class, gender or age-group. Brigden can write of 'the evangelical wedding of the year', since this self-selecting minority was evidently inclined, and perhaps even obliged, to marry within itself.[18] But what about the little towns of Tudor England and especially the centres of cloth manufacture, Hadleigh in Suffolk for example? Even the precocity of Hadleigh, which the martyrologist Foxe compared to a kind of bible-reading Open University, proves to be something of a myth, as a testimonial for the bulk of its inhabitants. Its supposedly faithful pastor, the larger-than-life Rowland Taylor whose martyrdom in his own parish provided one of Foxe's most famous set-pieces, proves to have played the part of a national figure under the Edwardian regime, as a civil lawyer a kind of troubleshooter much in demand and rarely in his parish, where his flock was by no means universally inclined to the new learning.[19]

There is no intention here to undervalue England's early Protestants. No reader of Foxe's sprawling and brilliant narrative with its well-chosen original sources and vivid eyewitness accounts can fail to be impressed. A majority of the three hundred or so martyred in the 1550s were common men and women, illiterate or semi-literate, inhabitants of Hadleigh and places like it. Their biblical learning was so prodigious that their letters and other utterances consist of little more than elaborate mosaics of apt and accurate biblical quotations, effortlessly cross-referenced.

The source of that knowledge, and of so much self-punitive zeal, is an important subject in its own right, whether or not it explains the English Reformation. At least part of the explanation for the precocity must be sought in that pre-history of English Protestantism which was Lollardy, a bible-reading and reciting, heretical, above all lay religious tendency which appears intermittently but persistently in the records for a century and a half before we can begin to speak of the Reformation, a tradition deriving, if indirectly, from the radical, philosophically grounded theology of the impatient fourteenth-century Oxford don, John Wyclif. Lollardy bore such a close resemblance to later Protestantism, especially in its denial of such features of traditional Catholicism as the mass, sacred images and pilgrimage, that the leading modern authority on the subject writes boldly of *The Premature Reformation*, and admiringly of the doctrinal coherence and consistency of the Lollards.[20] It was Foxe's strategy as the first historian of the Reformation to recruit the Lollards to his great theme as a 'secret multitude of true professors', so providing English Protestantism with an ancestry which both rivalled and parodied the Catholic claim to antiquity and tradition. The Catholic bishops, for their part, found it difficult and perhaps unnecessary to distinguish between old Lollards and new Protestants and continued to burn both kinds of heretics for the selfsame beliefs (above all denial of the miracle of transubstantiation in the sacrament of the altar) which Lollards had held long before Martin Luther invented Protestantism. Amidst so much blurring of important distinctions, the extent to which the later Lollards were progressively absorbed into something we can call English Protestantism, becoming amenable to the tutelage of the new Protestant clerics and intellectuals, exchanging their tattered Wycliffite manuscripts for the greater authority of print, remains problematical.[21]

We know of English 'Anabaptists', so-called, who rejected that tutelage together with the new theology and all 'clerkly eloquence', even while they shared the same prisons and went to the same stakes. One of these 'free will men' (they rejected predestination) was given to saying that 'all errors were brought in by learned men'. We may suspect that both they and, a little later, the English adherents of the radical Dutch sect known as the Family of Love were nothing but old Lollards under new names.[22] But we cannot be sure. Even the nature of 'orthodox' 'mainstream' Protestant doctrine is not as well understood as it might be, since a competent history of the first hundred years of English Protestant theology remains to be written. A point still at issue is whether or to what extent such English divines as William Tyndale, Robert Barnes, John Frith and, indeed, Thomas Cranmer constructed a distinctively English Protestantism rather than incorporating or eclectically borrowing from German and Swiss doctrine. Meanwhile a caustic and perhaps unfair comment has been made about 'the theological mediocrity of the movement'.[23]

But since none of these names, not even Cranmer's, carries the clout of a Luther or a Zwingli or a Calvin, it may be a fair comment to say that the English Reformation, which created no personalised 'isms', put in the place of any single leader the text of the Bible in English, and the autodidactic authority of the bible-reading layman and woman. When a great nineteenth-century historian, J. R. Green, wrote famously of the English of Shakespeare's generation as becoming the people of a book 'and that book was the Bible', he depended upon little more than sound instinct. Now another Dr Green is establishing this claim statistically. Apparently it really is the case that, up to the mid-seventeenth century, proportionately more bibles were printed in England than in any other Protestant country, in the 1630s ten times as many as had been published in the 1570s, further evidence of late reformation.[24]

We return to the calculus of majorities and minorities, and to the question whether we can infer the changing religious outlook of majority populations, whole communities, from the presence of minority cells. Those who believe that this is where the essential history of the English Reformation is to be found are bound to try. Dickens believes that we are indeed looking at the 'visible tip of a very large iceberg'. It used to be thought that the submerged bulk of the iceberg, if not actually Protestant, had built into its frozen mass an antipathy to the priesthood, conventionally if dubiously labelled with a term borrowed from late nineteenth-century French political culture as 'anticlericalism', a sentiment so strong and so rife as to bring the Church and much of the religion which the clergy personified into disrepute. This is doubtful. We do not have to believe that relations between the laity and the clergy, those paying and those in receipt of tithe, were always cosy, either before or after the Reformation, to discount 'anticlericism' as the principal motor force of a popular Reformation, popular that is with 'most people'.[25]

Is there no evidence for most people's views, indeed that they had views of their own on the matters at issue, and especially views sympathetic to religious change? Dickens was almost the first of many historians to discover an evidential bridge apparently connecting minority Protestantism to the more elusive opinions of the majority. This bridge consists of the last wills and testaments left behind by those whose lives were bisected by the Reformation and which survive in their many thousands for many counties and dioceses. Wills by convention opened with a religious affirmation couched in words which, with religion in a state of flux, might be indicative of traditional or alternatively non-traditional belief. Moreover, the presence or absence of pious bequests, such as the endowment of intercessory masses or other prayers for the soul, or alms-deeds and offerings to saints, should equally enable the historian to register changes in religious sentiment on a sufficiently large scale to convert into statistics possessed of some demonstrative and even explanatory power. But we have learned that most will preambles were formulaic, owing as much to their scribes as to those for whom they ostensibly spoke; that cautiously laconic doctrinal statements, sometimes described as 'neutral' or even 'reformist' (no mention of the saints), are more likely to have concealed than frankly expressed the true beliefs of those making them and to have been designed to do so; while the disappearance of pious bequests at a time when such things were coming into question if not already declared illegal may equally indicate confessional discretion, as well as an understandable reluctance to throw good money after bad. Only if religiously significant changes in the content of very considerable numbers of wills can be shown to have run well ahead of legislation, anticipating as it were by public demand policy changes still to be announced and implemented, would this evidence serve the purpose of the mass observation of public opinion. It appears that this is not the case.[26]

The significance of will evidence, therefore, is not of spontaneity and voluntarism, except among committed minorities such as William Tracey of Gloucestershire and his plagiarists, but rather of the implementation, negotiation and internalisation of religious changes initially made above the heads and consciences of ordinary testators and parishioners. So wills must sit alongside those other sources much favoured by revisionist historians, the annual accounts of income and expenditure made by the church wardens, recording alterations to church fabrics and furnishings and other actions called for by the reformations of Henry, Edward and Elizabeth, and by Mary's counter-reformation.

'Implementation', 'negotiation' and 'internalisation' are words chosen carefully, in preference to 'imposition' or 'enforcement', although enforcement was certainly a significant part of this complex process. For to comprehend the dynamic processes making up the English Reformation must be to understand how it was that drastic and widely unpopular changes in traditional religious practice and the underlying theology were executed by the clergy and parishioners themselves, and mostly by the church wardens, promptly, subject to a surveillance which was rarely close at hand, and without sustained resistance, in spite of a good deal of 'murmuring' and unhappiness. When Henry VIII required lights before images to be extinguished, the lights went out. Images were associated with discredited cults and soon virtually all sculpted images were removed. Certain holy days ceased to be holidays. When under Edward as later under Elizabeth there were injunctions to remove stone altars, which was as much in itself as to abolish the mass as the Church had known it (which Henry VIII had resolutely defended), together with the great 'rood' or image of the crucified Christ with its accompanying life-size images of Mary and John, a focal point of devotion in every church, the orders were eventually obeyed almost everywhere. Virtually none of this imagery now survives, in the Victoria and Albert Museum or anywhere else. That tells us a great deal not only about the English Reformation but about Tudor government and its power to persuade, especially in the more 'civil' shires south of the Trent and east of Exeter; perhaps simply about its power.[27]

But it all remains more than a little mysterious, for these onslaughts on time-out-of-mind religion were not trivial. Rather they amounted to radical surgery performed on the soul and on collective, communal consciousness. What happened in the minds and consciences of the couple, let us regard them as two representatives of 'most people', who believed in one year that by paying for masses they could shorten the time in Purgatory of a dead parent or child, only to be told in the next that this was a superstitious practice for which there was no justification and which would no longer be tolerated? How should we react to the forcible closure of all hospices for the terminally ill? But we live in a kind of democracy.

It is not likely that the theological rationale for these upsetting changes was immediately or widely understood. There is testimony from both Essex and Kent, counties normally associated with precocious reformation, that towards the end of the century there was still much ignorance of such fundamental Protestant doctrines as the relation of faith to works in the economy of salvation. People are said to have hung on to the basic, moralistic notion that Heaven can be earned by fulfilling Christ's summary of the Commandments, love of God and neighbour. It was said that such ignorance prevailed particularly in places where there were no regular sermons, no godly preaching ministry,[28] so perhaps it was presently dispelled; Haigh would say, probably not. The public homilies were quite clear about these matters, and by 1600 they had been read in those parishes for forty years.

There now seems little remaining doubt that the history of the Reformation as a religious transformation capable of permeating whole communities, even the entire nation, belongs to the second half of the sixteenth century and even, especially in the north, to the first half of the seventeenth: which is as much as to say that it takes off where most books on the subject, including (but for postscript) Dickens, end. The 1570s were crucial even in what for Dickens was already the heartland of the Reformation thirty years earlier, in marking the ascendancy of a zealous Protestant county magistracy. We can say with some precision that this happened in Suffolk in the summer of 1578, with consequences which were to endure for a century.[29]

It is also in the late 1570s that we begin to pick up signs of a kind of Protestant cultural revolution, to be understood either as a second reformation (more or less equivalent to what some historians have called the rise of Puritanism) or a fuller internalisation of the first.[30] Early Protestant publicists and propagandists had freely adapted the cultural media of the age, still a Catholic age, for their own purposes: biblical, moral and satirical drama, popular music set to so-called 'scripture songs' (which we may call protest songs), printed pictures, both polemical and prescriptive. This resembled on a more modest scale the exploitation in the German Reformation of the non-verbalised propaganda which has been described by Bob Scribner. Seeing was still believing, but a way of believing evangelical truth rather than popish error.

But by 1580 or so, English Protestants, leaning, as they now increasingly did, to Calvinism, were more likely to insist, with St Paul, that faith cometh by hearing and hearing by the Word of God, and by no other means. A profound reaction set in against stage-plays, especially plays presenting scriptural and moral themes. Ballads and their tunes were no longer thought compatible with psalms. And the Protestant dread of the graven image extended increasingly to the two-dimensional picture. The eye, even the mind's eye, was an idolatrous organ. It would be absurd to suggest that a society as soaked in music, addicted to the theatre, and visually vivid as late Elizabethan England simply succumbed to this wave of iconophobia. But there was now acute tension between increasingly rampant religious values and the aesthetic sense. Even some of the great poets of this and the succeeding age were aware of it, even Donne and, of course, Milton.

The decades between 1580 and 1630 also witnessed a whole succession of conflicts in scores of market towns and many rural parishes all over England, which were simultaneously political, moral, cultural and religious, street wars which were overtures for the Civil War itself.[31] These involved a struggle for the upper hand between factions, one of which invariably made its platform the suppression of popular pastimes, the reformation of manners and the enforcement of strict sabbatarianism. These concerns are much discussed under the category of 'Puritanism', but since so-called Puritans were Protestants under another name and in particular contested circumstances these events too should be seen as the coming to a kind of fruition of the English Reformation process.

The neglect of these Elizabethan and Jacobean chapters is consequently regrettable. It is doubtless the publishing industry, not the facts of the case, which has determined that the subject of the Reformation be wound up by, or soon after, 1559. But it would be absurd to begin the story where so many others end it. It remains true that it was decisions taken, doctrines and liturgies formulated, and other things written, before 1553, of which there is no equivalent after 1559, which were determinative of the course which the English Reformation and, indeed, the English Church would subsequently take. (Foxe's Book of Martyrs is the exception to prove the rule, but this Elizabethan book was a product of the pre-1559 Marian persecution and Marian exile.) It was owing to these formulations that the English Reformation was a very Protestant Reformation, profoundly iconoclastic; but equally that its Protestantism was tempered to an extent which created room for the secondary growth of Puritanism as a church within the Church, and encouraged the eventual growth of a conviction, in contradistinction to Puritanism, that the religion of the Church of England was not Protestant at all but something called Anglicanism.

In conclusion, we may remind ourselves of four of the most perdurable decisions and formulations of the pre-Elizabethan Reformation:

1 In the mid-1530s, Henry VIII (or Thomas Cromwell), having transferred the powers of the pope to the monarch, decided that spiritual government under the royal supremacy should remain in the hands of the bishops and should be exercised in accordance with established practice, through their courts. That ensured that the English Church retained a quasi-catholic episcopal hierarchy, with much of the attendant structures. A further consequence was that the church courts in their oversight of marriage, morals and many other matters continued to administer the old, Roman canon law. In this forum, which touched most English men and

women sooner or later, it could indeed be said that the Reformation did not happen to any marked extent.[32]

2 A little later, Henry VIII signalled his intention to preserve the English cathedrals by creating several new ones out of former monastic churches, the seats of new bishops. The non-dissolution of the cathedrals is a less familiar topic than the dissolution of the monasteries, but its consequences were just as great, mainly in the mitigation of Protestantism which otherwise tended to Puritanism. Puritans hated cathedrals, which had no obvious function beyond the staging of elaborate musical services, which were and are the glory of the Church of England.[33]

3 William Tyndale rendered the New Testament and much of the Old Testament into an authentic vernacular which for ever after was the true voice of English Christianity, and a very Protestant voice. The work of an alienated exile, it was reconciled, as its author was not, to the official Church of Henry VIII and assimilated into successive versions of the Bible which enjoyed royal patronage. Almost a century later, the Authorised Version translators succeeded in making Tyndale a little more stately and even archaic, but they were still careful to retain as much as 80 per cent of his language.[34]

4 Thomas Cranmer's Prayer Book, which in its second, 1552 version was re-enacted with only minor changes in 1559, was a comparable but also very different achievement. Nothing in its prayers or its communion service conflicted with Cranmer's essentially Protestant understanding of the Christian religion. (For a fuller statement of that understanding, the Church was to refer to other authoritative statements, the Homilies and the Forty-Two Articles, revised under Elizabeth as the Thirty-Nine Articles of Religion.) And yet Cranmer's prayers were traditional in their sources, length, shape and above all tone. No other Protestant liturgy kept more closely in touch with the pre-Reformation past. Cranmer even retained the great eucharistic prayer in the Communion Service which spoke of sacrifice, albeit this was now a sacrifice not of Christ's body but of praise and thanksgiving, and of the souls and bodies of the worshippers themselves. This was how the English people could become Protestants as it were effortlessly and osmotically, how it was that 90 per cent of the many thousands of parishioners in the teeming London suburb of Southwark were content round about 1600 to make their Easter communion as the Prayer Book prescribed.[35] For Cranmer made the Protestant religion, even, we may say, Protestantism, a cradle-to-grave thing, a matter of lifelong habit. Noting the churchgoing habits of his parishioners, who came and went and said their prayers without any apparent feeling, a Jacobean curate of Derby told them, politely: 'I can tell you what religion is fittest for you. Even that which we call the old religion.'[36] So did the English Reformation happen?

## NOTES

1 Diarmaid MacCulloch, 'The Myth of the English Reformation', *Journal of British Studies*, 30 (1991), pp. 1–19.

2 Rosemary O'Day, *The Debate on the English Reformation* (London, 1986); and, more recently, W. J. Sheils, *The English Reformation 1530–1570* (London, 1989), A. G. Dickens, *The English Reformation* (2nd edn, London, 1989), Diarmaid MacCulloch, *The Later Reformation in England, 1547–1603* (London, 1990), Diarmaid MacCulloch, *Building a Godly Realm. The Establishment of English Protestantism 1558–1603*, Historical Association 'New Appreciations in History' no. 27 (London, 1992), Diarmaid MacCulloch, 'England', in Andrew Pettegree, ed., *The Early Reformation in Europe* (Cambridge, 1992), David Loades, *Revolution in Religion. The English Reformation 1530–1570* (London, 1992).

3 See a major forthcoming study by Christopher Haigh; and Ronald Hutton, 'The Local Impact of the Tudor Reformations', in C. Haigh ed., *The English Reformation Revised* (Cambridge, 1987).

4 David Cressy, *Bonfires and Bells. National Memory and the Protestant Calendar in Elizabethan and Stuart England* (London, 1989).

5 *The Works of Richard Hooker*, ed. J. Keble (Oxford, 1874), vol. III, p. 330.

6 J. J. Scarisbrick, *The Reformation and the English People* (London, 1984), p. 1. And see *a fortiori* Eamon Duffy, *The Stripping of the Altars. Traditional Religion in England 1400–1580* (New Haven, 1992).

7 'The Last Medieval Englishman' is the title of an essay by A. G. Dickens on Robert Parkyn, curate of Adwick-le-Street near Doncaster in his *Reformation Studies* (London, 1982), pp. 245–83; where it is followed by Dickens's edition of 'Robert Parkyn's Narrative of the Reformation', pp. 287–312.

8 Christopher Haigh, 'The English Reformation. A Premature Birth, a Difficult Labour and a Sickly Child', *Historical Journal*, 33 (1990), 449–59.

9 'The Recent Historiography of the English Reformation', in *The English Reformation Revised*.

10 G. R. Elton, *Reform and Reformation* (London, 1977), p. 371; A. G. Dickens, 'The Early Expansion of Protestantism in England 1520–1558', *Archiv für Reformationsgeschichte*, 78 (1987), p. 220.

11 Claire Cross, *Urban Magistrates and Ministers. Religion in Hull and Leeds from the Reformation to the Civil War*, University of York Borthwick Papers, 67 (York, 1985); Patrick Collinson, *The Religion of Protestants. The Church in English Society 1559–1625* (Oxford, 1982).

12 William Perkins, 'To All Ignorant People', a list of thirty-two 'common opinions' prefacing *The Foundations of Christian Religion Gathered in Six Principles* in *Workes*, I (Cambridge, 1612), Sig. A5$^r$.

13 P. Lake and M. Dowling eds., *Protestantism and the National Church in Sixteenth-Century England* (London, 1987).

14 John Fines, *Biographical Register of Early English Protestants c.1525–1558* (A–C, Appleford 1980, D–Z, West Sussex Institute of Higher Education).

15 Dickens, 'The Early Expansion of Protestantism' and *The English Reformation*, pp. 325–34.

16 The story is told by John Craig and Caroline Litzenberger in a forthcoming article in the *Journal of Ecclesiastical History*.

17 Susan Brigden, *The Reformation in London* (Oxford, 1990).
18 *Ibid.* p. 419.
19 *The Acts and Monuments of John Foxe*, ed. S. R. Cattley, VI (1837), pp. 676–703; Dickens, *The English Reformation*, pp. 298–9; a forthcoming study of the Reformation in Hadleigh by John Craig.
20 Ann Hudson, *The Premature Reformation. Wycliffite Texts and Lollard History* (Oxford, 1988).
21 A. G. Dickens, *Lollards and Protestants in the Diocese of York 1509–1558* (London, 1959); Dickens, *Reformation Studies*, pp. 363–82; J. F. Davis, *Heresy and the Reformation in the South East of England 1520–1559* (London, 1983).
22 J. W. Martin, *Religious Radicals in Tudor England* (London, 1989); Christopher Marsh, 'The Family of Love in English Society, 1550–1630', unpublished Ph.D. thesis, University of Cambridge, 1992. I quote from Henry Hart, *A Godly Newe Short Treatyse* (1548) and John Champneys, *The Harvest is at Hand* (1548).
23 Alister McGrath, *Iustitia Dei*, vol. II (Cambridge, 1986), W. A. Clebsch, *England's Earliest Protestants* (London, 1964) and Peter White, *Predestination, Policy and Polemic* (Cambridge, 1992) suggest in their several ways the need for a truly magisterial account of English Protestant theology.
24 I refer to a major forthcoming publication by Ian Green of the Queen's University, Belfast.
25 C. Haigh, 'Anticlericalism and the English Reformation', in *The English Reformation Revised*; A. G. Dickens, 'The Shape of Anticlericalism and the English Reformation', in E. I. Kouri and T. Scott, eds., *Politics and Society in Reformation Europe* (London, 1987); Dickens, *The English Reformation*, pp. 316–25.
26 The specialist literature on will evidence is now extensive. The most penetratingly critical analysis will be found in Duffy, *The Stripping of the Altars*.
27 Hutton, 'The Local Impact of the Tudor Reformations'; Duffy, *The Stripping of the Altars*; Margaret Aston, *England's Iconoclasts*, I. *Laws Against Images* (Oxford, 1988).
28 Collinson, *Religion of Protestants*, p. 202.
29 Diarmaid MacCulloch, *Suffolk and the Tudors* (Oxford, 1986), pp. 195–7.
30 Patrick Collinson, *From Iconoclasm to Iconophobia. The Cultural Impact of the Second English Reformation* (Reading, 1985); Patrick Collinson, *The Birthpangs of Protestant England. Religious and Cultural Change in the Sixteenth and Seventeenth Centuries* (London, 1988), pp. 94–126.
31 Collinson, *Birthpangs*, pp. 136–9; David Underdown, *Revel, Riot and Popular Politics and Culture in England 1603–1660* (Oxford, 1985).
32 Margaret Bowker, 'The Supremacy and the Episcopate. The Struggle for Control, 1534–1540', *Historical Journal*, 18 (1975) pp. 227–43; R. H. Helmholz, *Roman Canon Law in Reformation England* (Cambridge, 1990).
33 Stanford E. Lehmberg, *The Reformation of Cathedrals. Cathedrals in English Society, 1485–1603* (Princeton, 1988); MacCulloch, 'The Myth of the English Reformation', p. 8.
34 *The Work of William Tindale*, ed. S. L. Greensdale (London, 1938).
35 Jeremy Boulton, 'The Limits of Formal Religion. Administration of the Holy Communion in Late Elizabethan and Early Stuart London', *London Journal*, 10 (1984), pp. 135–54.
36 Richard Kilby, *Hallelu-iah. Praise ye the Lord for the Unburthening of a Loaden Conscience* (Cambridge, 1618), pp. 29–30.

## FURTHER READING

Christopher Harper-Hill, *The Pre-Reformation Church in England 1400–1530* (London, 1989) and W. J. Sheils, *The English Reformation 1530–1570* (London, 1989), both in Longman's Seminar Studies in History, both contain ample, up-to-date bibliographies, as does Diarmaid MacCulloch, *The Later Reformation in England, 1547–1603* (London, 1990). On the Reformation as the strange (and for him sad) death of Catholic England, Eamon Duffy, *The Stripping of the Altars* (New Haven, 1992) supersedes all earlier accounts. In addition to the titles mentioned in the endnotes, the following are recommended:

P. N. Brooks, *Thomas Cranmer's Doctrine of the Eucharist* (2nd edn, London, 1992).

Tessa Watt, *Cheap Print and Popular Piety, 1550–1640* (Cambridge, 1991).

R. Whiting, *The Blind Devotion of the People. Popular Religion and the English Reformation* (Cambridge, 1989). (The subject of this book is the Reformation in Devon and Cornwall.)

S. Wright, ed., *Parish, Church and People. Local Studies in Lay Religion 1350–1750* (Leicester, 1988).

The reader should be on the alert for a forthcoming study of the Henrician Reformation by Richard Rex, for Christopher Haigh's imminent *magnum opus* on the sixteenth- and seventeenth-century reformations, and for Margaret Aston, *The King's Bedpost*, which finds a large and important slice of English Reformation history in a single picture.

Keith Thomas, *Religion and the Decline of Magic* (London, 1971) covers a canvas even wider than that occupied by the English Reformation and remains essential reading.

# 6    Scotland

*Julian Goodare*

The year 1543 would have been a natural moment for the Reformation in Scotland. The death of the orthodox James V in December 1542 had brought the earl of Arran to power as regent for the infant Queen Mary: he moved rapidly towards rapprochement with an England which had rejected the pope and was willing to countenance reforming ideas. The New Testament in English was legalised in the teeth of opposition from the bishops; Arran criticised the pope and denied belief in purgatory. A treaty was negotiated with England, and with the English negotiators came the preacher George Wishart, a charismatic Zwinglian who had fled from Scotland in 1538.[1] He and other Protestants began to preach confidently; Protestant activists led attacks on friaries.

But Arran's 'godly fit', as it became known, lasted less than a year. Scottish politics were deeply divided; a conservative, pro-French faction regained power, repudiated the treaty and had Wishart executed. War with England followed; several destructive English raids culminated in a catastrophic Scottish defeat at Pinkie (1547). The Scots were forced to seek French assistance: in return for sending the young queen to France, a French army arrived in 1548 and by 1550 succeeded in ejecting the English.

Obliged to collaborate with the English invaders, the Protestant party lost credibility. Its doctrines could be referred to in 1549 simply as the 'faith and opinion of England'.[2] Its noble leaders were reconciled or forfeited, its best preachers exiled. By 1552, a general council of the church was satisfied that the danger was past:

Many frightful heresies have, within the last few years, run riot in many diverse parts of this realm, but have now at last been checked by the providence of All-good and Almighty God, the singular goodwill of princes, and the vigilance and zeal of prelates for the Catholic faith, and seem almost extinguished.[3]

## Towards Reformation

Traditional accounts of the Scottish Reformation stressed 'corruption' and 'abuses' prevalent in the old church. But generally the church was functioning as well as it ever had done. At parish level, the main problem was the 'appropriation' of the revenues of 86 per cent of parishes to higher institutions, mostly bishoprics and monasteries, leaving ill-paid curates to serve the parishes. This was an abuse; but was it a cause of the Reformation that came in 1560? Most appropriations were centuries old. Those made in the early sixteenth century were largely for the benefit of universities, which the reformers themselves endorsed. Few criticisms of appropriations were made at the time.[4]

The most entertaining and (since it was performed at court in 1540 and 1554) most influential critique of 'abuses' in the church was Sir David Lindsay's play 'Ane Satyre of the Thrie Estaitis', portraying churchmen at all levels as ignorant and corrupt:

> Parson:
> Ire, hardiness and gluttony
> Is nothing else but life's food.
> The natural sin of lechery
> Is but true love.    All these are good.[5]

His 'Poor Man' attacked the lengthy Latin procedure of the church courts:

> Within a month I got ad opponendum,
> In half a year I got interloquendum,
> And syne I got, how call ye it? ad replicandum,
> But I could never a word yet understand him.[6]

This was good satire, but in fact the church courts were widely accepted as performing a useful function.[7] Lindsay's resort to wholly imaginary grievances like pardoners (of whom only one ever visited Scotland, in 1496) suggests that the supply of 'abuses' was limited.[8]

In fact, however, the church did suffer from real weakness – not through 'abuses' but through economic decline. In a feudal kingdom with little centralised authority, the bishoprics and monasteries were important because of their lands – their status as units of territorial lordship. In the half-century or so after the 1530s, these units of lordship gradually disintegrated.

During the English break with Rome in the 1530s, James V pursued an ostentatiously orthodox doctrinal line. But his church policies otherwise had many parallels with those of his uncle Henry VIII. He too attacked the church with the aim of gaining its revenues – in his case not through expropriation, but through ruinous taxation. He treated the papacy in just as cavalier a way, though the popes' desperate need to retain Scotland's formal allegiance made frontal attacks unnecessary. He also showed a similar willingness to play with and exploit the demand for 'reform' (whether Catholic or Protestant): after the court performance of Lindsay's

'Satyre', James called on the bishops 'to reform their fashions and manners of living, saying that unless they so did he would send six of the proudest of them unto his uncle of England'.[9] This put pressure on the church, but hardly gave reform itself a helping hand.

James's taxation forced bishops and monasteries to raise cash by alienating land through 'feuing'. This was a device by which the existing tenant farmers (or, more often, third parties) could purchase the heritable right to the lands, leaving the benefice-holder with only the right to collect feudal dues fixed in perpetuity.[10] With the heavy inflation of the sixteenth century, the benefice-holders were left with ever-diminishing long-term revenues. Moreover, from the 1530s, nobles and crown imposed their kinsmen as commendators of monasteries: secular heads who drew the revenues without taking monastic vows.[11] The monks were powerless to resist feuing and creeping secularisation. There was no 'dissolution' of the Scottish monasteries after 1560: they just faded away. The feuing movement revolutionised land tenure, helping to launch a new class of small (and not so small) independent proprietors. If any social group made the Reformation, it was the lairds.

The sixteenth century saw the expansion of literacy and formal education among the ruling class, where previously few but the higher clergy had needed it.[12] Key literacy-oriented groups were also expanding: lairds, merchants, lawyers. The first books were printed in Scotland in 1507; from the 1540s the number of known titles expands steadily. The full ramifications of the expansion of learning cannot be discussed here; but humanism, as an intellectual movement seeking to abandon tradition and recover a fresh understanding of ancient texts, detonated with seismic force in the field of theology.[13] Conceptions of what the church should do were transformed. Instead of quasi-magical ritual which all could appreciate, it should respond to the educated classes' demand for intellectually satisfying religion based on the primary text of Christianity – the Bible. Instead of celebrating mass, it should preach.

> Spirituality [the bishop]:
> Friend, where find ye that we should preachers be?
> Good Counsel [the councillor]:
> Look what Saint Paul writes unto Timothy.
> Take there the Book: let see if ye can spell.
> Spirituality:
> I never read that, therefore read it yoursel.[14]

The demand for preaching – not in itself a Protestant demand, though Catholics were not yet able to compete effectively with Protestant preachers sustained by continental literature – threw the church into disarray. It was not yet simply a question of 'Catholics' versus 'Protestants': there were already various brands of Protestantism, and Catholicism lacked definition until the Council of Trent completed its work in 1563. In the meantime, all agreed that changes were necessary – but what changes? The church council of 1552, quoted above, authorised a vernacular catechism that made one or two concessions to Lutheranism and failed to mention the pope. It also made efforts to endow preachers. It was not clear how far this kind of thing would go: where should the line be drawn? Those who went too far were intermittently persecuted, but this caused further dissension within the church; the *Complaynt of Scotland* (1550), though doctrinally conservative, demanded 'reform' and opposed persecution.[15]

It is time to take up the story of the Protestant movement once more. In the mid-1550s, it was in the doldrums. John Knox, the exiled disciple of Wishart, returned in 1555–6 to conduct a semi-clandestine tour of the few remaining active Protestant cells, which had been forced underground.[16] Wishart, ten years earlier, had been able to hold public mass meetings. Clearly the movement was no longer able to mount an effective challenge to the regime, nor had it a viable strategy for doing so. Knox encouraged it to take the only direction left to it: to become an elite separatist group, refusing to participate in Catholic sacraments. Back in Geneva, he and other Scottish exiles kept the movement alive as active participants in the well-organised English network of Protestants who had fled to the Continent after the accession of Mary Tudor in 1553. The Calvinism which became such a distinctive feature of Scottish Protestantism first took root among these communities of Marian exiles.

Scotland's Protestant movement in the late 1550s closely resembled the burgeoning French reforming party (for which Geneva was also the nerve centre), in that it was by now Calvinist; it had gained a few conversions among the nobility and royal family (notably Lord James Stewart, the queen's half-brother); and it was excluded from a hostile establishment.[17] The French movement was arguably more influential and better organised: it could stage mass assemblies in 1557–8. But unless there was a revolution, both movements were bound to remain in the wilderness, self-excluded from power.

However, at this point, revolution in Scotland began to be a possibility. The regent since 1554 had been James V's French widow, Mary of Guise. In April 1558, her daughter was married to the Dauphin Francis, leading to the prospect of union of the Scottish and French crowns. Scotland's dependence on France took an increasingly unwelcome turn when Frenchmen began to take over offices of state and showed a blatant desire to embroil Scotland in wars with England. An opposition movement began to gather momentum; as in 1543, its core was the anglophile lords, who began to call themselves the 'Lords of the Congregation' and to make Protestant demands in the hope of gaining English support – for in November 1558, the Catholic Mary Tudor was succeeded in England by the Protestant Elizabeth.

Where were the Protestant radicals? They were nowhere in a majority: in most places they were not even a majority among the influential and spiritually committed. When the regent offered Edinburgh a religious referendum, the Protestant party refused to allow religion to be 'subject to the voting of men . . . the most part of men has ever been against God and his truth'.[18] The seven 'privy kirks' (Protestant cells) in key towns hardly made a mass movement, but they were well-placed to become a convincing-looking stage army.[19] Together with the Lords of the Congregation, they were able to form a credible vanguard which would capture the regime from outside rather than (as in the 1540s) permeating it from within. They developed an ideology providing an explicit legitimation for rebellion (making it the duty of nobles, and even of the common people, to resist tyranny), at a time when rebellion was increasingly attractive in practice.

But it was not enough to prove rebellion legitimate: it also had to be made widely popular, something that Protestantism alone could not achieve. The party of revolution still claimed in August 1559 'to promote and set forth the glory of God', but this line of propaganda was abandoned. By September they were urging waverers:

If religion be not persuaded unto you, yet cast ye not away the care ye ought to have over your commonweal, which ye see manifestly and violently ruined before your eyes. If this will not move you, remember your dear wives, children, and posterity, your ancient heritages and houses.[20]

It was a powerful appeal; but many similar revolutionary appeals have been met with stony indifference even when articulating genuine grievances. The radical party of Knox and Lord James, however, succeeded in its appeal to the 'commonweal', achieving such broad support that it could even appear as a conservative revolt against French innovation.

This achievement in uniting the political nation was still not enough to overcome the professional French army. But in early 1560 the Scots gained English military assistance; the wheel had come full circle since 1548. What became known as 'amity' with England now appeared in a positive light, marking the final triumph of the pro-English party. The English ambassador was constantly in the corridors of power when the parliament of August 1560 enacted a new, Calvinist confession of faith, repealed anti-heresy laws, and repudiated the mass and papal authority. The English intervention was so decisive that, for the next generation, radical Scottish Protestants would be able to look to England for support whenever their own government showed signs of taking an independent line. Many national reformations were promoted by states for their own benefit; while it is a commonplace that the Scottish Reformation was made in opposition to the domestic authorities, not enough attention has been paid to the fact that it was established for the benefit of the English state.

In January 1561, a 'Book of Discipline' drawn up by a committee of leading ministers was submitted to a convention of the nobility. It outlined a programme for organising a Protestant church, to pay for which the benefices of the old church were to be dissolved and reconstituted as stipends for parish ministers, schoolmasters and universities. The convention approved the Book's programme, but not its financial provisions, thus effectively nullifying it. Dissolving the benefices would have meant dispossessing the current bishops and commendators, of whom some had joined the reformers, and all were far too well-connected to be got rid of. The chaplains, vicars, commendators, bishops and other clerics of the old church continued in possession of their benefices for life – a church in limbo, no longer able to administer its sacraments. Feuing of benefices continued.

So the early Reformation presents a paradox. On the one hand, the political momentum of 1560 carried the new church through its difficult initial years. In despair or apathy, the Catholic clergy gave up the struggle; a papal nuncio visited Scotland in 1562 and was disgusted that only one bishop would even agree to meet him. There was no prospect of Queen Mary (before her deposition in 1567) restoring Catholicism.[21] But on the other hand, committed reformers were rapidly disappointed by the slow progress made, and by the politicians' failure to move towards an all-embracing godly society. Knox had been the spiritual inspiration of the revolution, and Lord James its political lynchpin; by 1563 the two were no longer on speaking terms.

### The Reformation in the parishes

The immediate success of the Reformation may have been contingent on political faction, diplomatic manoeuvres and war; but that does not mean that the Reformation was not bound up with profound changes. Once established in political power, the reformers allied themselves with lay forces in order to extend their power into the parishes. Through discipline, rigid sexual morality and an emphasis on formal education and written culture, and through the new status which it gave to the middle ranks of society, the Reformation developed in fruitful symbiosis with contemporary trends in Scottish culture and society.

The reformers stressed parish ministry. Their new ministers conducted a radically different type of service, based on lengthy sermons (an hour or often more) learnedly expounding biblical texts. The ritual of the mass disappeared; the seven Catholic sacraments were cut down to two, baptism and communion, neither normally administered without a sermon. In assessing the local impact of all this, it has been common to adopt the perspective of the audience for Knox's sermons in Edinburgh. But an equally valid perspective is that of the islanders of St Kilda. In the 1580s, it was reported that 'once in the year a priest or minister comes to them and baptises all the bairns born amongst them since his last being there, and celebrates marriage to the parties desiring, and makes such other minist-ration of the sacraments to them as he thinks good'. Hardly an active preaching ministry. The minister also collected the teinds (tithes), 'which they pay the most thankfully' of any in Scotland.[22] Baptisms and marriages had to be celebrated, and teinds collected; otherwise, organised religion made few demands on the St Kildans.

This was not unusual in the Gaelic-speaking third of Scotland. 'Readers' were appointed in most parishes, qualified to read prayers but not to preach or to administer the sacraments, and after 1567 they had something to read: the *Book of Common Order*, the Genevan service-book adopted in Scotland, was translated as *Foirm na n-Urrnuidheadh*. But there was only ever one edition, compared with the sixty-plus editions of the *Book of Common Order* up to 1644;[23] and its classical Gaelic was further from the vernacular than the English version was from Lowland Scots. This bible-based religion had no Gaelic Bible. Preaching ministers were few and far between. It was common in both Highlands and Lowlands to assign four parishes to one minister, and Highland parishes were enormous: the unfortunate minister of Applecross, Gairloch, Lemlair and Dingwall in the early seventeenth century had duties stretching from coast to coast.[24] The church had at best a missionary character up to the nineteenth century, leaving the lively pattern of folk-belief largely undisturbed.

In the Lowlands, certainly, the church aspired to better things. The church never deviated from the highest standards for ministers, preferring to leave a parish vacant rather than appoint a 'vain shadow' of a minister 'that in no wise can break the bread of life to the fainting and hungry souls [i.e. preach]'.[25] Adherence to this even after the Book of Discipline's financial proposals were rejected meant that most parishes had to make do with a reader, not a minister, for at least a generation. How different these readers were from the old non-preaching parish priests is not clear, especially since old priest and new reader were usually the same person.

The reformers did take care to make sure of the towns. Town councils were purged of practising Catholics, even (or perhaps especially) in the capital, where committed support for the new faith was confined to a small minority.[26] Ministers' stipends became one of the first charges on council revenues. But the most radical reformers were always confronted with a tendency to dilute their ideals. The 160 'faithful brethren of Edinburgh' who subscribed to a new poor hospital exemplify the respectable civic Protestantism of the burgesses: some of the subscribers were closet Catholics.[27]

The government of Regent Morton in the 1570s sought to extend a watered-down ministry into the countryside by assigning ministers to four parishes each, where they could have little involvement with their parishioners outside the pulpit – 'reprehending the dissolute persons and exhorting the godly to continue in the fear of the Lord'.[28] Prioritising the supply of a minimum level of decent Sunday prayers and rites of passage, while acquiescing in the rarity of preachers, was precisely what the reformers argued against.[29]

But the ideal of the godly society survived with its radical cutting edge intact, as we shall see. Partly this was because, as parish benefices fell vacant, many ministers were able to obtain them. Stipends, fixed in grain, surged upwards as agricultural prices rose, while most Lowland parishes gained ministers during the early seventeenth century.[30] Ministers were mostly graduates, and like lawyers (another significant rising group of the period) they developed a cohesive professional ethos: a homogeneous social stratum replaced the socially diverse hierarchy (from magnates to peasants) that had staffed the medieval church.[31] As they prospered, they became local moneylenders – and a few leading ministers became wealthy enough to lend to lords.

Backing up the minister's pastoral and disciplinary work was the characteristic institution of the Scottish Reformation: the kirk session, or parish committee of lay 'elders', comparable with the Huguenot consistory.[32] Calvin had pioneered intensive moral discipline in Geneva, but his system went into terminal decline in the 1570s.[33] Once established in Lowland parishes, Scottish kirk sessions continued to wield disciplinary authority until the late eighteenth century.[34]

Who were elders in kirk sessions? In towns, the session was an adjunct to the town council, and like the council was run by leading merchants, already accustomed to minute regulation of the citizens' lives. But in the countryside, the natural leaders of traditional society – the nobility – stayed aloof from kirk sessions, which were staffed by men of smaller property, lairds and feuars (the new heritable proprietors), with a leavening of larger tenant farmers, who had never before gained such authority in a feudal society.[35]

Kirk-session discipline in theory covered all scriptural offences, but in practice concentrated overwhelmingly on extra-marital sex. It may have been a clerk accustomed to kirk session minutes who in 1563 wrote 'fornication' as a mistake for 'reformation' in the General Assembly minutes.[36] In second place were offences against the sabbath; in third place, drunkenness and other activities (such as dancing) linked with popular festivities. In view of ministers' moneylending proclivities, it is not surprising that usury, for instance, was neglected.

The penalties were severe. For simple fornication, offenders had to appear in church on the 'stool of penitence', wearing sackcloth, for three successive Sundays. A second offence meant six appearances; adultery, twenty-six. A fine of between £5 and £40 was also exacted from each partner if they could afford it. The rich escaped public humiliation, and at worst were fined; the many vagrant poor were also beyond the session's reach. But most ordinary people had little alternative but to submit, however reluctantly, to discipline backed by the sanction of excommunication, followed if necessary by banishment by the secular authorities.

It should not be thought that discipline was universally unpopular. The independent 'middling sort' found it congenial. The leading minister John Davidson preached a major sermon in Edinburgh in 1594 attacking many classes' religious backslidings – the king was a hypocrite, the nobles were bloodthirsty, the 'multitude' were worse – but the middling sort escaped with only an attack on the supporters of a controversial Monday market (which encouraged the sin of travelling on Sunday).[37] Davidson and his like could eventually mobilise sizeable numbers of supporters on the streets of some towns, and they seem not to have been primarily the 'multitude'. The notorious riot of 1596 in Edinburgh, which the king used as an excuse to clamp down on radicalism in the church, included wealthy merchants.[38]

Popular Protestantism was a largely urban affair, despite its considerable attraction for lairds who shared its values, and the Reformation cemented an urban cultural hegemony. The weekly rhythms of sabbatarianism were more meaningful in trade and crafts (where sabbath enforcement could prevent unfair competition) than in agriculture, where seasonal festivals were natural.[39] The values of traditional rural society centred on kinship, for which the reformers had little sympathy: Knox's deference towards his family's lord, the earl of Bothwell, is a noted anachronism in his thinking. With kinship went the self-help justice of the bloodfeud, which reformers vigorously condemned.[40]

The religious ideal of the medieval church had been the rural seclusion of the monk, withdrawn from a corrupt world in order to seek God, performing spiritual exercises and abstaining from worldly luxury; but the ideal of religious poverty was thrown overboard by the reformers. The 'Beggars' Summons' of 1559 called on the friars to quit their 'pretence of poverty' and to hand over their property to the genuinely poor. 'Let him therefore that before has stolen, steal no more; but rather let him work with his hands, that he may be helpful to the poor.'[41] Preachers gradually refined the Calvinist concept of the 'calling' to include not just a general divine calling to a godly life, but a 'particular calling' to a specific occupation or trade. Some singled out urban occupations like that of merchant for special approval. Trade and profit-making, formerly frowned on by theologians, thus received divine sanction.[42]

The peasants, as always, believed what they were told to believe – though they believed other things as well, as we shall see. If they went to church they may have been impressed by the consciously dramatic pulpit performances of the new ministers, though the actual content of sermons was way above their heads. They probably did not welcome the new insistence on rote-learning of catechisms and creeds from an alien, written culture. The old church had adapted itself comfortably – too comfortably, perhaps – to popular magical beliefs and rituals: the new church launched a frontal attack on 'superstition', now separate from the official religion of the educated.[43]

How successful was this? The periodic witch-hunts, beginning in 1591, provide a valuable case-study of the interaction of official and popular belief. The witch-hunts, by driving home the message that all individuals were responsible for their own salvation, were useful adjuncts to catechisms and creeds in inculcating Christian doctrine.[44] However, the lairds and ministers who conducted the witch-hunts in the localities *drew on* popular beliefs rather than attacking them. The correct theological view of witchcraft was that it consisted of selling one's soul to the devil in return for supernatural powers. Black magic and white magic were equally demonic. But to the end of the witch-hunts and after, the peasants accepted white magic, denouncing as witches only those women seen to have used magic to *harm* their neighbours. Moreover, many 'superstitious' folk beliefs were taken up by demonologists (including the king) seeking to refine their theories.[45]

Catholic recusancy was a straightforward problem by comparison. It was not enough to capture parliament in 1560: each burgh council, and indeed each school and craft guild, had to be taken over piecemeal, and a few such local institutions sheltered committed Catholics for some time.[46] But ultimately it came down to a few nobles, mainly in the north-east, strong enough and remote enough to resist central government. This reliance on local power centres was the best that Catholicism could manage; the future, however, belonged not to local institutions, but to the nation-state.

## The Reformation and the state

The Scottish Reformation, born in opposition to the state, retained much of its character as an opposition movement. The church saw 1560 as the beginning of a programme of continuing reform, and regularly denounced the government for failure to promote this. But opposition movements seek power, and the church also sought to build a partnership with the secular authorities in realising its programme for a truly godly state.

This programme began with the demand for the recovery of the largely secularised revenues of the medieval church. With this wealth the reformers aspired to institute a massive scripture-based educational programme, and to pay generous stipends to the elders of kirk sessions as well as to ministers, allowing religious professionalism to be carried into every urban household and every remote farming settlement. The poor would be relieved, and the 'tyranny of the lord and laird' – which threatened to replace the 'papistical tyranny' – suppressed.[47]

The tenacious adherence of the church to this programme was articulated through a new, centralised governing body: the General Assembly of the church. A newly centralised state was also emerging at this time, based on an increasingly powerful parliament, privy council, exchequer and other institutions. The core of the state was in south-east Scotland, and its administrators were urban. Of the elite ministers who gave the General Assembly its driving energy in the 1580s and 1590s, two-thirds were from that same area, and almost all the leaders were likewise urban.[48] Both church and state sought to take power from traditional local institutions; there was plentiful scope for cooperation. There were moments (for instance, when a second revolution deposed Mary in 1567) when it seemed that the government might adopt the church's programme fully. Parliament regularly responded positively when the Assembly lobbied for legislation against Catholicism and in support of kirk-session discipline. But as long as money was not forthcoming in quantity, and as long as the government (as we have seen) tended to favour watered-down civic Protestantism, the reformers were never satisfied and conflict was inevitable.

The struggle took place over two distinct but connected issues. Firstly, how should the church be organised on a regional level? Traditionally, parish clergy were answerable to bishops; but radical ministers denied that episcopacy had scriptural warrant, and developed an alternative in presbyteries – committees of parish ministers and elders. These began to be set up in the early 1580s, provoking conflict with the government which saw them as harder to control than crown-appointed bishops. This led on to the second, and more fundamental, issue: should the state have authority over the church? Yes, said the bishops: 'the king is pope now, and so shall be', said Archbishop John Spottiswoode in 1620.[49]

Polemicists of the early seventeenth century fought a bitter historiographical battle over whether Knox and the early reformed church had been essentially episcopalian or presbyterian[50] – a battle which some historians seem intent on continuing. In fact, Knox's church had no settled polity. Both presbyterianism and episcopalianism, as comprehensive and mutually exclusive systems, were foreign imports of the 1570s: Andrew Melville, the scholar who inspired many second-generation reformers, brought the former from Geneva, while the Regent Morton instituted the latter on an English model. It was the presbyterians who stood more fully in the radical tradition of Knox, not because of presbyterianism as such but because they sought church independence from state control, coupled with a drive to make the church into a powerhouse for continuing reformation in the state. Regent Morton, and later James VI, did their best to use state authority to rein in this tendency.

Both sides naturally assumed that if their view prevailed there would be harmony between church and state. At a local level, many towns demonstrated the potential for fruitful cooperation between town council and kirk session, though in practice ultimate authority lay with the secular power. But if there was disharmony at a national level, how would it be resolved? Many historians have treated this as a theological question, but in practice it was simply an ongoing struggle for political power.

The details of this struggle need not detain us. The presbyterians had the better of it in the late 1580s and early 1590s, but after James succeeded to the English throne in 1603 he threw his weight successfully behind the re-establishment of bishops. These new bishops were very much royal agents. They hoped that presbyteries would wither away when shorn of authority, but a dedicated band of presbyterian ministers kept up a stubborn rearguard action, often with popular support. The mixed polity of these years has sometimes been presented as a sensible and moderate compromise:[51] in fact it was two parties locked in mortal combat. Here is Thomas Hogg, minister of Dysart, hauled before the new prerogative court of High Commission in 1619:

The archbishop said, 'Mr Thomas, it cannot content you to declaim vehemently in your sermons against the estate and course of bishops, but also ye pray ordinarily after sermon against bishops, as belly-gods and hirelings.' Mr Thomas answered, that he prayed ordinarily against belly-gods and hirelings in the ministry, by the warrant of God's word; and alleged that his prayer was conform to the common prayer contained in the Book of Discipline ... The archbishop replied, 'When ye pray against belly-gods and hirelings, the people apply that prayer to us that are bishops.' Mr Thomas answered, that he could not be answerable for the people's application of his prayers.[52]

The General Assembly, bastion of presbyterian independence, was browbeaten by the king, gerrymandered by the bishops, and not allowed to meet after 1618. The presbyterians thus had to learn the techniques of constitutional and legalistic opposition, questioning the king's powers. That they could do this illustrates the decline of habits of deference in both politics and religion. The educated middling sort were more independent than before, less in awe of magnates whether spiritual or temporal. The reformers encouraged people to take personal control of their destiny rather than relying on the church's traditions. There was nobody less deferential than the radical ministers, modelling themselves on Old Testament prophets and denouncing nobles and king by name from the pulpit. Perhaps this was why, after the first decade or two, few nobles gave much support to the ideal of a godly state, although 'godly magistrates' were eagerly sought after.[53] In the 1590s they (and the king) switched support away from the radicals, by now solidly presbyterian, and towards episcopacy. A large minority of nobles went further and turned back to Catholicism.

The conservative offensive in the church (which needs to be seen in the context of attempts to create a more unified British church) led in 1618 to the 'Five Articles', requiring worship to be altered in a ceremonial direction. Many ministers, backed by their congregations, refused to implement the Five Articles, thus spearheading what became an organised resistance movement. Clandestine conventicles sprang up – far more numerous than the privy kirks of the 1550s, but with a similar ethos.[54] They had wide support, particularly in the towns: burgesses' votes, together with those of many lairds, nearly capsized the Five Articles in the parliament of 1621.[55] It was an ominous warning of what would happen when Charles I renewed the conservative programme in the 1630s.

This is where the covenanting ideal comes in. Covenant theology was developed by Calvinist theologians in the late sixteenth century, arguing that God's grace came in the form of a covenant or contract with the individual. In Scotland this belief fused with the indigenous local custom of making 'bonds' – associations to pursue secular ends – to produce the idea of a covenant, not between the individual and God, nor between the local community and God, but between the nation and God.[56] The belief that the nation had made a covenant with God sustained the radicals through many dark days when it seemed that conservative liturgical and constitutional innovations might triumph.

## Conclusions

An important recent interpretation of the Reformation stresses that there was a temporary 'coalition' between reformers and a broad section of influential people.[57] This was a coalition doomed ultimately to break down, as the reformers (like other revolutionaries after them) saw their ideals frustrated and betrayed in the process of becoming an establishment. This certainly happened in Scotland, but in a distinctive way.

The first enduring achievement of the Scottish Reformation was to erect an intensive system of kirk-session discipline. But the early reformers had envisaged a godly society on a far wider basis, with reconstructed social relations to give dignity to all believers and removing secular oppression. Reformers of more limited vision were content to use the local power of the kirk session to wage war on social nonconformity; this was a success in Scotland because of the social changes that were dissolving older forms of local power.

The second enduring achievement followed from this: a revolutionary tradition continued among the most committed reformers. They stressed the failures and betrayals of the years after the Reformation – stemming, as they saw it, from the interference of the crown and its attempt to impose bishops on the church. Within the power-base of many kirk sessions, radical ministers in the early seventeenth century nurtured a tradition of resistance to crown authority, but they also petitioned parliament. They aspired to capture and develop central power, in order to establish a more powerful and truly godly state. The stage was set for the National Covenant of 1638.

## NOTES

This chapter owes many debts to Professor Michael Lynch.

1 M. H. B. Sanderson, *Cardinal of Scotland. David Beaton, c.1494–1546* (Edinburgh, 1986), p. 193.
2 *Register of the Privy Seal of Scotland*, vol. IV, ed. J. Beveridge (Edinburgh, 1952), no. 138.
3 *Statutes of the Scottish Church, 1225–1559*, ed. D. Patrick (Scottish History Society, 1907), p. 143.
4 I. B. Cowan, 'Some Aspects of the Appropriation of Parish Churches in Medieval Scotland', *Records of the Scottish Church History Society*, 13 (1957–9), pp. 203–22.
5 Sir David Lindsay of the Mount, 'Ane Satyre of the Thrie Estaitis', *Works*, vol. II, ed. D. Hamer (Scottish Text Society, 1931), p. 325.
6 Lindsay, 'Satyre', p. 289.
7 S. Ollivant, *The Court of the Official in Pre-Reformation Scotland* (Stair Society, 1982), chapter 9.
8 I. B. Cowan, 'Church and Society', in *Scottish Society in the Fifteenth Century*, ed. J. M. Brown (London, 1977), p. 114.
9 Lindsay, 'Satyre', p. 2.
10 M. H. B. Sanderson, *Scottish Rural Society in the Sixteenth Century* (Edinburgh, 1982), chapters 6–7.
11 M. Dilworth, 'The Commendator System in Scotland', *Innes Review*, 37 (1986), pp. 51–72.
12 R. A. Houston, *Scottish Literacy and the Scottish Identity, 1600–1800* (Cambridge, 1985), pp. 11–12. More study of this topic is needed.
13 E. Cameron, *The European Reformation* (Oxford, 1991), pp. 64–9; J. MacQueen ed., *Humanism in Renaissance Scotland* (Edinburgh, 1990).
14 Lindsay, 'Satyre', p. 275.
15 *The Complaynt of Scotland*, ed. A. M. Stewart (Scottish Text Society, 1979), pp. 126–7.

16 John Knox, *History of the Reformation in Scotland*, vol. I, ed. W. C. Dickinson (Edinburgh, 1949), pp. 119–24.

17 See J. H. M. Salmon, *Society in Crisis. France in the Sixteenth Century* (London, 1975), pp. 117–19.

18 *Extracts from the Records of the Burgh of Edinburgh*, vol. III, ed. J. D. Marwick (Scottish Burgh Records Society, 1875), pp. 46–8.

19 For a restatement of the traditional view of the privy kirks' importance, see J. Kirk, *Patterns of Reform* (Edinburgh, 1989), chapter 1.

20 R. Mason, 'Covenant and Commonweal. The Language of Politics in Reformation Scotland', in *Church, Politics and Society. Scotland, 1408–1929*, ed. N. Macdougall (Edinburgh, 1983), p. 107.

21 For her one abortive attempt to do so, see J. Goodare, 'Queen Mary's Catholic Interlude', in *Mary Stewart. Queen in Three Kingdoms*, ed. M. Lynch (Oxford, 1988).

22 W. F. Skene, *Celtic Scotland*, vol. III (2nd edn, Edinburgh, 1890), p. 432.

23 G. Donaldson, 'Reformation to Covenant', in *Studies in the History of Worship in Scotland*, ed. D. Forrester and D. Murray (Edinburgh, 1984), p. 36.

24 Kirk, *Patterns*, p. 467.

25 *The First Book of Discipline*, ed. J. K. Cameron (Edinburgh, 1972), p. 104.

26 M. Lynch, *Edinburgh and the Reformation* (Edinburgh, 1981), p. 187.

27 M. Lynch, 'The "Faithful Brethren" of Edinburgh. The Acceptable Face of Protestantism', *Bulletin of the Institute of Historical Research*, 51 (1978), pp. 194–9.

28 *The Second Book of Discipline*, ed. J. Kirk (Edinburgh, 1980), p. 185.

29 F. D. Bardgett, 'Four Parische Kirkis to ane Preicheir', *Records of the Scottish Church History Society*, 22 (1985–6), pp. 195–209; cf. the two types of minister discussed in P. Collinson, *The Religion of Protestants* (Oxford, 1982), pp. 104–10.

30 W. R. Foster, *The Church Before the Covenants, 1596–1638* (Edinburgh, 1975), chapter 8.

31 R. Mitchison, 'The Social Impact of the Clergy of the Reformed Kirk of Scotland', *Scotia*, 6 (1982), pp. 1–13.

32 For kirk session discipline generally, see G. Parker, 'The "Kirk by Law Established" and the Origins of "the Taming of Scotland". St Andrews, 1559–1600', in *Perspectives in Scottish Social History*, ed. L. Leneman (Aberdeen, 1988).

33 G. Lewis, 'Calvinism in Geneva in the Time of Calvin and of Beza (1541–1605)', in *International Calvinism, 1541–1715*, ed. M. Prestwich (Oxford, 1985), pp. 52, 57.

34 R. Mitchison and L. Leneman, *Sexuality and Social Control. Scotland, 1660–1780* (Oxford, 1989).

35 W. Makey, *The Church of the Covenant, 1637–1651* (Edinburgh, 1979), chapters 9–10.

36 G. Donaldson, *Scottish Church History* (Edinburgh, 1985), pp. 116–17.

37 David Calderwood, *History of the Kirk of Scotland*, vol. V, ed. T. Thomson (Wodrow Society, 1844), pp. 337–9.

38 R. Pitcairn ed., *Criminal Trials in Scotland*, vol. II, part one (Bannatyne Club, 1833), pp. 33–4.

39 See C. Hill, 'The Uses of Sabbatarianism', *Society and Puritanism in Pre-Revolutionary England* (3rd edn, Harmondsworth, 1986).

40 K. M. Brown, *Bloodfeud in Scotland, 1573–1625* (Edinburgh, 1986), chapter 7.

41  G. Donaldson ed., *Scottish Historical Documents* (Edinburgh, 1974), pp. 117–18.
42  G. Marshall, *Presbyteries and Profits. Calvinism and the Development of Capitalism in Scotland, 1560–1707* (Oxford, 1980), chapter 4.
43  See K. Thomas, *Religion and the Decline of Magic* (London, 1971).
44  C. Larner, *Enemies of God. The Witch-hunt in Scotland* (London, 1981), especially chapter 12.
45  James VI, *Daemonologie* (1597), in *Minor Prose Works of King James VI & I*, ed. J. Craigie (Scottish Text Society, 1982).
46  M. Lynch, 'From Privy Kirk to Burgh Church. An Alternative View of the Process of Protestantisation', in *Church, Politics and Society 1408–1929*, ed. Macdougall (Edinburgh, 1983), p. 94.
47  *First Book of Discipline*, especially pp. 156–7.
48  J. Kirk, 'The Development of the Melvillian Movement in Late Sixteenth Century Scotland' (Ph.D. dissertation, Edinburgh University, 1972), pp. 389–95.
49  Calderwood, *History*, vol. VII, p. 421.
50  D. G. Mullan, *Episcopacy in Scotland, 1560–1638* (Edinburgh, 1986), chapter 8.
51  Foster, *Church Before the Covenants*, chapter 9.
52  Calderwood, *History*, vol. VII, pp. 368–9.
53  K. M. Brown, 'In Search of the Godly Magistrate in Reformation Scotland', *Journal of Ecclesiastical History*, 40 (1989), pp. 553–81.
54  D. Stevenson, 'Conventicles in the Kirk, 1619–37. The Emergence of a Radical Party', *Records of the Scottish Church History Society*, 18 (1972–4), pp. 99–114.
55  J. Goodare, 'The Scottish Parliament of 1821', *Historical Journal*, 37 (1994).
56  S. A. Burrell, 'The Covenant Idea as a Revolutionary Symbol. Scotland, 1596–1637', *Church History*, 27 (1958), pp. 338–50.
57  Cameron, *European Reformation*, part four.

## FURTHER READING

The standard textbook is I. B. Cowan, *The Scottish Reformation* (London, 1982), which lives up to its subtitle *Church and Society in Sixteenth-century Scotland*. Also valuable on the pre-Reformation period is D. McRoberts ed., *Essays on the Scottish Reformation, 1513–1625* (Glasgow, 1962). Among more narrowly focused ecclesiastical histories, the best are G. Donaldson, *The Scottish Reformation* (Cambridge, 1960), W. R. Foster, *The Church Before the Covenants, 1596–1638* (Edinburgh, 1975) and J. Kirk, *Patterns of Reform* (Edinburgh, 1989). For the Reformation in the context of general Scottish history see J. Wormald, *Court, Kirk and Community. Scotland, 1470–1625* (London, 1981).

The Reformation's uneven progress in local society has been charted by M. Lynch, *Edinburgh and the Reformation* (Edinburgh, 1981). For intellectual aspects, see A. Williamson, *Scottish National Consciousness in the Age of James VI* (Edinburgh, 1979) and J. MacQueen ed., *Humanism in Renaissance Scotland* (Edinburgh, 1990), while two major social studies are C. Larner, *Enemies of God. The Witch-hunt in Scotland* (London, 1981) and G. Marshall, *Presbyteries and Profits. Calvinism and the Development of Capitalism in Scotland, 1560–1707* (Oxford, 1980).

# 7 Scandinavia

*Ole Peter Grell*

The considerable differences in the religious, as well as the ecclesiastical outcome of the Danish and the Swedish Reformations were manifest when the two countries came to celebrate the centenary of the Reformation. The Lutheran Church of Denmark chose to acknowledge its Wittenberg roots and adhered to the suggestions laid down by the theologians of Wittenberg and Leipzig in the *Epistola Invitatoria* of September 1617. Under its leading Bishop, Hans Poulsen Resen, the Danish Church followed the Wittenberg pattern for the centenary celebrations – starting on 31 October at the University of Copenhagen with an oration by the leading professor of theology and continuing with a week of festivities in the country's churches and the university. Having got off to a good start, the Lutherans in Denmark seem to have developed a taste for Protestant celebrations, since they not only proceeded to commemorate Luther's day of death, but decided to have an annual celebration of the Reformation at the University of Copenhagen, something which at a much later date, in 1668, inspired the University of Wittenberg to follow suit. As in Wittenberg the centenary in Copenhagen was used to cement Lutheran orthodoxy, even if its Copenhagen version turned out to be considerably less rigid and anti-Melanchthonian than in Wittenberg.[1]

By contrast, the Swedish Church took no steps to commemorate the centenary of the Reformation in 1617. Instead, it waited until 1621, when, on the orders of King Gustavus Adolphus, it celebrated the centenary of what the House of Vasa considered the beginning of the Swedish Reformation. Sweden, in other words, chose not to take part in the international celebrations of the Lutheran Reformation in 1617, preferring to mark a strictly national centenary of undoubtedly greater political than religious significance. 1521 was, after all, the year Gustavus Adolphus's grandfather, Gustav Vasa, had started the rebellion against Danish hegemony in general and the rule of Christian II in particular. By the beginning of the seventeenth century this politically motivated rebellion had also, at least in official Swedish mythology, come to be portrayed as a battle against 'papal darkness' and in defence of 'evangelical light', conveniently glossing over the considerable gap between rebellion and reformation.[2] Where Denmark joined Lutheran Germany in a predominantly religious celebration of the Reformation, Sweden preferred to commemorate a primarily political centenary of the country's re-emergence as an independent state.

As in Germany, the Reformation in the Nordic countries had taken place within a framework of considerable social and political instability. The defeudalisation process of the late middle ages had brought lay and ecclesiastical aristocracy into conflict with peasants, burghers and the Crown. From 1524 to 1542 a succession of peasant rebellions and one major civil war had dominated events in Denmark and Sweden in particular. These revolts were all primarily social and economic in origin, but more often than not they were conditioned by the growing conflict between new and old in the religious domain.

By the beginning of the sixteenth century the Union of the Scandinavian kingdoms which had been created in 1397, was on the verge of collapse. Comprising the kingdoms of Denmark, which then included Scania, Halland and Blekinge (now southern Sweden), Norway, and Sweden, which incorporated Finland, plus the duchies of Schleswig and Holstein, the Union had always been an unwieldy entity. But the often arbitrary attempts of King Christian II to secure further power for the Crown which, among other things, manifested itself in the execution of more than eighty leading members of the Swedish lay and ecclesiastical aristocracy in Stockholm in November 1520, brought about a rebellion in Sweden. It was led by the Swedish nobleman Gustav Vasa, whose father had been among the casualties in Stockholm. A year later he was in total control of Sweden while Christian II was facing mounting difficulties in Denmark. By early 1523 the King's attempts to weaken the political influence of the Danish aristocracy had led to his deposition by the Danish Council (*Rigsrådet*). Rather than confronting the rebels, Christian fled Denmark for the Netherlands, seeking protection and support from his Habsburg relations (he had married Emperor Charles V's sister, Elizabeth, in 1515). In his place the Council elected Christian's uncle, Duke Frederik of Schleswig and Holstein, who had supported the rebellion.

Although deposed, Christian II continued to influence events in Scandinavia for decades to come. His dynastic connection with the house of Habsburg guaranteed that the possibility of an invasion with Habsburg backing remained a constant threat to the Scandinavian kingdoms. From Christian's unsuccessful attempt to raise an army in northern Germany during the autumn of 1523, via his failed military venture in Norway in 1532, which led to his life-long imprisonment in Denmark, till the Peace of Speyer in 1544, his and his daughters' claims to the Scandinavian kingdoms were important factors which could not be ignored. They served to unite the usurping dynasties in Stockholm and Copenhagen. Mutual fear of Habsburg intervention and opposition to Lubeck's continued dominance of trade in the Nordic countries and the Baltic brought about a close, if tenuous, cooperation between Gustav Vasa of Sweden, Frederik I of Denmark and the latter's son, Duke Christian, who became stadtholder over Schleswig–Holstein in 1526.

In spite of this shared social and political context, the Reformation in Schleswig–Holstein, Denmark and Sweden neither proceeded to a common pattern nor succeeded with the same speed.[3] Initially evangelical ideas were introduced into Scandinavia through itinerant German preachers who started preaching during the early 1520s in the major coastal market towns such as Copenhagen, Malmø and Stockholm, which all contained large, resident German merchant populations. In Schleswig–Holstein the first contact with Protestant ideas occurred simultaneously and through the same channels, even if a considerable number of local ministers were active in the early Reformation movement.[4] Initially, the Reformation was most successful in the duchies where the support of the young Duke Christian, who had begun playing an active part in the government of Schleswig–Holstein from 1525, proved essential. In 1528 the Duke was able to introduce the first evangelical Church Ordinance in Scandinavia, in his personal fief, Haderslev–Tønning in Schleswig. With the ordinances of Braunschweig and Saxony from the same year, it was the first Lutheran Church Ordinance to be issued.[5] Most of the towns of Schleswig–Holstein had been won over to the Reformation by that year, primarily through princely initiatives rather than popular support. For political reasons, however, the duchies with their mixed nationality (Holstein was part of the Holy Roman Empire while Schleswig was a fief of the kingdom of Denmark) fell behind the evangelical developments in Sweden in the late 1530s. Thus Denmark received a full Lutheran Church Ordinance in 1537, five years earlier than the duchies.

Similarly, the Reformation in Sweden proved a predominantly princely phenomenon. Here popular support for the new teachings was even less significant than in the duchies. Only the population of Stockholm demonstrated support for the evangelical cause and Sweden accordingly witnessed a princely reformation which, however, often lacked religious cohesion and direction due to the predominantly political concerns of its ruler. Gustav Vasa's Protestantism was, to say the least, questionable. Dynastic and political considerations guaranteed that it was not until 1539–40 that Sweden was on course for a full Reformation, and a further thirty years had to lapse before the Swedish Church received its first Protestant Church Ordinance (1571). Even then the continued success of its Reformation was far from secure.

Denmark, on the other hand, went through the three 'classical' Reformation sequences, beginning with a popular evangelical movement, primarily in its market towns, and then proceeding via the magisterial to the princely stage in its reformation.[6] It will, however, make sense to take a closer look at the Reformation in Schleswig–Holstein first, since the evangelical movement not only made its first real breakthrough here, but also provided inspiration for the Reformation elsewhere in Scandinavia.

Evangelical preaching had already begun in the town of Husum in Schleswig–Holstein in 1522, where the Wittenberg-trained minister, Hermann Tast, had started to spread the Protestant message in Low German. He appears to have generated considerable popular support and was soon joined by other former Catholic colleagues in the town.[7] The Wittenberg connection was to characterise the Reformation in Schleswig–Holstein from the outset. Duke Christian, who had attended the Diet of Worms in 1521, was an early convert to Lutheranism. This was probably more due to the influence of his Lutheran and often Wittenberg-educated councillors than to Luther's impressive performance at the Diet.[8] Christian's Lutheran sympathies, however, appear to have caused him some problems in his early career. Opposition among the lay and ecclesiastical aristocracy appears to have prevented his father, King Frederik I, from making him stadtholder of the duchies before 1526. Meanwhile, in 1525, the Duke had been given the fief of Haderslev–Tønning on which to sharpen his political teeth. By then the tide had already started to turn against the Catholic Church in Schleswig–Holstein. The Diet of Rendsburg in 1525 demonstrated that the traditional solidarity between lay and ecclesiastical aristocracy was disintegrating. Increased taxation to pay for the armaments against the threat from the deposed king, Christian II, caused the lay aristocracy to abandon their colleagues within the Church. They demanded that the clergy pay a greater share of the increased tax-burden. The Diet also intervened in the jurisdiction of the Church, ordering that in future the Gospel should be preached purely and in the vernacular.[9]

With the Catholic Church politically weakened, Duke Christian immediately proceeded to introduce the Reformation in his fief. He commenced by dismissing the dean of the collegiate chapter in Haderslev while clashing with the Bishops of Schleswig and Ribe over everything from tithes to ecclesiastical jurisdiction. In spite of losing some of these early encounters, the duke continued to promote the evangelical cause in Haderslev–Tønning. In 1526 he recruited two German, evangelical theologians, Eberhardt Weidensee and Johann Wenth, to assist him in the reformation of his fief. Both came to play an influential part in the reformation of the duchies, Weidensee in the capacity of superintendent, while the Wittenberg-graduate, Wenth, became one of the authors of the Danish Protestant

Church Ordinance of 1537–39 and the Schleswig–Holstein Church Ordinance of 1542, both produced under the supervision of Johann Bugenhagen.[10]

Christian took advantage of a further political weakening of the Catholic Church after the Diet of Kiel in February 1526 and called a synod of the clergy in and around Haderslev. They were presented with new evangelical articles of faith, written by Weidensee and Wenth, which were probably identical to the later Haderslev Ordinance of 1528. Meanwhile the Duke saw his political position enhanced when he was appointed stadtholder of the duchies on 25 May 1526.[11] By the end of 1527 most of the parish churches in the towns of Schleswig–Holstein had received Protestant ministers, in many cases Wittenberg-educated Germans who had been introduced personally by either King Frederik I or Duke Christian. In Haderslev, Johann Wenth had turned the collegiate chapter-school into the first training academy for Lutheran ministers in Scandinavia.[12] It became a model for similar schools in Denmark which were established in the towns of Malmø and Viborg within a few years. In general the reformation of the towns of Schleswig–Holstein proved a quiet affair with minimal disruption.

The example of Husum demonstrates the considerable degree of continuity between old and new in terms of personnel – fifteen of the original nineteen priests in the town remained. In an agreement between the magistracy and the Catholic Church, the clergy were guaranteed their income for life on condition that they abstained from celebrating mass. From now on only evangelical services were allowed in Husum. The magistracy also took the opportunity to order a survey of all property belonging to the Church and decided that part of it should henceforth be used to pay for a schoolmaster and a parish clerk.[13] The reformers' concern for education was in evidence from the start in the duchies.

When, in 1528, Duke Christian called another synod, this time of all the clergy of Haderslev–Tønning, only the reformation of the villages needed further attention. The village clergy were presented with the Haderslev Church Ordinance, which in its first paragraph stated that it was lack of uniformity in ceremonies and teaching which had necessitated its formulation. The shortage of evangelical ministers obviously argued for a tolerant and positive attitude towards Catholic parish priests whose commitment to Protestantism was at best vague, but who were willing to continue their work, exchanging the pope for the duke as their master. Often the priests would have been tempted to stay on for social and practical reasons alone. The chance of regularising their often illegitimate domestic circumstances through marriage would have been particularly tempting for many. Without this continuity, however, the new Protestant Church would have been unable to serve most local communities. All the evidence for Schleswig–

Holstein indicates that most of the Catholic incumbents stayed on in the countryside, where only a handful of village priests refused to accept the Haderslev Church Ordinance and had to be expelled.[14] The old Catholic priests were, in other words, preferable to no ministers at all, even if this meant that the Gospel was not necessarily purely preached. This, however, was expected to be remedied along the way through teaching and instruction, as laid down in the Ordinance.

The Haderslev Ordinance's dependence on Wittenberg is obvious. All ministers were advised to follow Luther's *Kirchenpostille* in their sermons and warned only to preach the Gospel. Parishes less than a mile from the towns of Haderslev and Ribe were obliged to recruit their parish clerks from the Latin schools in these places, thereby making sure that they at least might benefit from the recent Protestant instruction given to such pupils. The ministers were told to catechise the congregation after each Sunday sermon. Likewise they were obliged to explain the catechism to their congregations in a series of sermons twice a year. A number of rural deans should carry out yearly visitations on the duke's behalf on a par with what Philipp Melanchton had prescribed for Saxony, in order to secure uniformity and good administration.[15] Thus Duke Christian had not only used his *ius reformandi* ('right of reformation') in his fief, but he had also taken over the *cura religionis* ('supervision of religion'): all ministers were bound to lay authority through an oath of loyalty.[16]

It was Duke Christian's concern for the *cura religionis* which caused him to take action against Melchior Hoffman and have this radical reformer expelled from the duchies.[17] He had, however, been encouraged to act against Hoffman by Luther personally, whose letter of 1528 initiated what were to prove life-long close contacts between Christian and the Wittenberg theologians. The Hoffman episode, however, was unique in the quiet progress made by the Reformation in Schleswig–Holstein. But further advances for the Protestant cause in the duchies were to be much slower during the next decade. When Christian succeeded his father as ruler of Schleswig–Holstein at the Diet of Kiel in 1533, it was decided to await further developments in Germany and Denmark before any final decisions about religious and ecclesiastical matters should be taken. This compromise, which allowed Catholic services to continue in the duchies, did not prevent Christian from squeezing further concessions out of the Bishop of Schleswig, who was forced to tolerate Protestant services in his cathedral.[18] But in spite of this, the duchies still had to wait another ten years before a Protestant Church Ordinance covering the whole territory could be introduced.

Christian's victory in the civil war (*Grevens Fejde*) in Denmark and his succession to the Danish throne depended in no small measure on the loyal support of both lay and ecclesiastical aristocracy in Schleswig–Holstein. When he tried to introduce the recently issued Danish Church Ordinance in the duchies, a considerable number of the lay nobility joined hands with the Bishops of Schleswig and Holstein and objected, primarily for constitutional reasons. They wanted to maintain the independence of the duchies while family loyalty and respect for Schleswig's elderly Bishop, Gottschalk Ahlefeldt, may well have played a part too. Furthermore, a significant minority among the lay aristocracy was not yet prepared to abandon their Catholic faith. Christian III must have decided that a confrontation would have had a negative effect in this situation. Instead, he by-passed the diet and called a synod at Gottorp in February 1538, consisting of ministers and local, lay authorities, such as town councillors, to deliberate a new Church Ordinance.[19] Christian evidently attempted to retain the initiative in the religious domain. He used the synod to appoint four inspectors for the towns and areas around Haderslev, Husum, Schleswig and Flensburg. They seem to have started work immediately, as can be seen from Gerhard Slewart's 'Flensburger Propsteibuch' which starts in 1538.[20]

Meanwhile, Christian had commissioned a translation of the Danish Church Ordinance into Low German. With this in hand Christian III hoped to get the diet which met in Flensburg in 1540 to introduce a Lutheran Church Ordinance for the duchies. But once again he failed to convince the conservative minority who wanted to maintain the status quo, and the plans had to be dropped. Instead, the King reverted to his approach of 1538, introducing administrative changes through the back door. The four inspectors were given further authority. They were created superintendents and a reformation of the remaining Catholic monasteries and convents was organised. These institutions were ordered both to appoint and pay for evangelical lecturers who should catechise them in the new teachings and to halt their Catholic activities.[21] Thus when the Bishop of Schleswig, Gottschalk Ahlefeldt, died in January 1541, only the formal introduction of a Church Ordinance for Schleswig–Holstein was still outstanding. With the Bishop's death, the declining conservative faction within the aristocracy lost its standard-bearer and fourteen months later a Lutheran Church Ordinance was formally accepted. It was essentially a direct translation of the Danish Church Ordinance from 1537, which again contained parts of the Haderslev Church Ordinance from 1528 and, like its Danish counterpart, it had been drawn up under Johann Bugenhagen's supervision.[22]

Thus the duchies had finally seen a Lutheran territorial Church established within two decades of Herman Tast having begun preaching the Gospel in Husum in 1522. The popular element of the Reformation in Schleswig–Holstein was, however, never particularly significant. Instead, the success of the Reformation in the duchies depended on the initiative of

Duke Christian. It was his personal commitment to Protestantism which saw most of the changes through well before the diet finally accepted the new Church Ordinance in 1542. Christian, however, in using his *ius reformandi* and his *cura religionis*, depended not only on the advice of Bugenhagen in particular, and the Wittenberg theologians in general, but also on more direct assistance from a considerable number of Wittenberg-educated Germans. The Reformation of Schleswig–Holstein had a distinct Lutheran Melanchthonian flavour from beginning to end. That, of course, does not tell us how fast and to what extent the Reformation succeeded in winning over the population of the duchies. Catholic traditions and practices undoubtedly survived for generations to come, especially in country parishes, but the Protestant emphasis on education and catechism bore fruit within a couple of generations.[23] The fact that the Counter-Reformation only had little effect, and that the Jesuits never made any serious missionary efforts there, is the best proof that little if any Catholicism survived in the duchies towards the end of the sixteenth century. Only with the town of Flensburg do the Jesuits appear to have had reasonable connections. Here they were able to make a few converts, apart from one of two of the more spectacular sort among the Schleswig–Holstein gentry.[24]

Like the duchies, Denmark remained outside the sphere of Counter-Reformation influence. Towards the end of the sixteenth century, when fear had begun spreading among leading Lutheran theologians in the kingdom about the danger constituted by the Jesuits, Catholicism appears to have attracted only a few noblemen and intellectuals. The Jesuit College in Braunsberg, established in 1565, had by the end of the century, become a centre for students from the area around the Baltic. Here the Norwegian Jesuit, Laurentius Nicolai (Laurits Nielsen, also known as Klosterlasse), worked energetically to convert his fellow Scandinavians.[25] Fears of a Jesuit conspiracy were reinforced by the publication of a pamphlet in 1604 by Jonas Henriksen of Ditmarschen in Holstein, which disclosed a sinister Catholic plot against the Nordic countries.[26] Worries about possible Jesuit infiltration, especially within the educational sector, caused the University of Copenhagen to place increased emphasis on religious orthodoxy among its students and teachers. The Jesuit propaganda campaign in Denmark was masterminded from abroad by Laurentius Nicolai, but Jesuit hopes for a positive response from the Danish government were quickly dashed when, in October 1604, anyone who had received training by the Jesuits was forbidden to hold a position in either church or school, in order that they should not bring about 'a great change in Religion'.[27]

Consequently, some schoolmasters were forced to leave their jobs, as in the case of the headmaster of the Latin school in Malmø, Jens Aagesen, who was dismissed in 1605.[28] Why the Jesuit Laurentius Nicolai should have decided personally to try to promote the Catholic cause in Denmark in such negative circumstances is incomprehensible. It can only be explained by a total lack of reliable information available to the Jesuits about conditions in Denmark. Evidently there was a dearth of Catholic sympathisers and believers within the Kingdom on whom they could rely.

Laurentius Nicolai arrived in Copenhagen in 1606 and immediately forwarded his apology for the Catholic Church, *Confessio Christiana*, to leading members of the government including the Lutheran Bishop of Zealand, Hans Poulsen Resen. It brought about a prompt government reaction against Catholicism and Laurentius Nicolai was expelled. The incident guaranteed that no further missionary efforts were undertaken by the Jesuits in Denmark for years to come. Apart from alarming the authorities and alerting them to possible Catholic subversion, nothing had been achieved. If anything, Laurentius Nicolai's misguided missionary visit to Denmark tends to underline the relative success of Protestantism in that kingdom in uprooting and replacing Catholicism in less than sixty years.[29]

Already by the mid-1520s Protestantism had proved its popular appeal in a number of market towns in Denmark. Initially it had been promoted by Christian II who appreciated its potential value for his absolutist plans for the kingdom. For a while the king had surrounded himself with Wittenberg-educated humanists and theologians who were allowed to preach in Copenhagen. Here they may well have found a receptive audience, especially within the university, where humanist and Erasmian interests had been reinforced by the creation of a Carmelite College in 1519. It was from this College that several of the leading figures of the Danish Reformation, such as Peder Laurentsen and Frants Vormordsen, were to emerge in the late 1520s.[30]

When Frederik I succeeded his deposed nephew as king in 1523, his power was severely circumscribed by the conservative lay and ecclesiastical aristocracy represented by the Council (*Rigsrådet*). These internal limitations on Frederik's liberty of action were supplemented by the above-mentioned restrictions dictated by foreign policy. Initially the king was limited to offering only passive support for the Reformation such as royal letters of protection issued to individual evangelical preachers.[31] Among the first to benefit from those were Hans Tausen and Jørgen Jensen Sadolin, both Wittenberg-educated, who had generated considerable popular support for the evangelical cause in Viborg. By 1526 most of the market towns in Jutland appear to have been won over to the Reformation, often, as in the case of Viborg, with strong support from the magistracy.[32]

The parliaments of 1526 and 1527, not only broke the traditional links between the Catholic Church in Denmark and Rome, but they also demonstrated the declining political power of the Catholic bishops. The ecclesiastical aristocracy had been unable to force the king to interfere with the growth of evangelical preaching, while they had experienced the first examples of an increasing willingness among their lay colleagues to turn against the Church if economic gains could be made. The Catholic clergy's inability to force Frederik I to obey his coronation charter in which he had promised to fight Lutheranism can only have encouraged the king to assist the growing evangelism in the market towns further.[33]

By 1528 it was no longer the towns in Jutland, in general, or Viborg, in particular, which were in the vanguard of the evangelical movement in Denmark. By then it was centred in the larger and commercially far more important cities of Copenhagen and Malmø. In Malmø especially, encouraged and assisted by the city's strong and united magistracy, Protestantism blossomed. The commitment to the new teachings of Malmø's mayor, Jørgen Kock, proved particularly important for the evangelical movement. It was he who secured a series of royal privileges for the city which, by 1530, had seen Malmø fully reformed.[34] Malmø's conversion to Protestantism had been greatly facilitated from 1529 by the presence of two of the leading theologians of the Danish Reformation, Frants Vormordsen and Peder Laurentsen. Both were present in Copenhagen in July 1530 when Frederik I had intended to introduce a full reformation on a par with what several of his relations had already done in Germany. However, it all had to be abandoned owing to the threat of an impending invasion from Christian II and only the market towns received a general charter, giving them carte-blanche to introduce evangelical services.[35]

This was how matters stood when Frederik I died in April 1533. The parliament which met in Copenhagen the following summer was dominated by the Catholic and conservative majority led by the bishops. The ecclesiastical aristocracy realised that this meeting constituted their last chance of opposing Protestantism. On no account did they want to elect the Lutheran, Duke Christian. Instead, an interim government of the Council was established until a new parliament would meet the following year. This attempt by the conservative majority to turn the clock back religiously, as well as politically, resulted in a civil war (*Grevens Fejde*). The rebellion of Malmø in May 1534 and its alliance with Copenhagen and Lubeck quickly forced the aristocracy in Jutland and Funen to rescind their plans. In July they were obliged to elect Duke Christian king.[36]

When Copenhagen surrendered two years later, Christian III was the victor of the civil war. Having achieved victory through an army of his own, he was able in an unprecedented way to impose his policies on the kingdom. The aristocracy, especially the bishops, were severely compromised after the parliament of 1533 and the ensuing civil war. On 12 August the King imprisoned all the Catholic bishops. This was to be the single most dramatic act against the old Church and its supporters. The parliament which followed decided to remove the bishops and replace them with other 'Christian bishops and superintendents' and to introduce an evangelical church order. This was achieved in 1537, when the Church Ordinance, produced under Johann Bugenhagen's supervision, received royal confirmation.[37]

Cathedral chapters, monasteries and convents were, however, allowed to continue. As opposed to the dismissed Catholic bishops who seem to have settled down quite happily as feudal landowners and even in some cases to have converted to Lutheranism, these institutions were to constitute the last bastions of the old faith.[38] During the 1540s and 50s the canons in the two most prestigious chapters, those of Roskilde and Lund, fought a rearguard action against the Reformation. The government must have realised the potential for resistance within these chapters and had accordingly taken the precautionary measure of attaching two of the leading Danish reformers, Hans Tausen and Peder Laurentsen, as lecturers to these institutions, thus turning them, together with the rest of the chapters, into what has been termed 'one-man divinity schools'.[39] However, the government still found it necessary to intervene directly during the 1540s when it forced recalcitrant canons to sign the Lutheran confession. Apart from the obstinacy of a handful of canons, most of the Catholic clergy who were incorporated into the new Lutheran Church, appear to have accepted the change without any complaints or attempts at obstruction. Thus only a few examples can be found of village-ministers who were defrocked for false teaching and continued use of Catholic ceremonies.[40]

Dealing with a Catholic residue, however, was not the most crucial problem for the Lutheran Church in Denmark. The new teachings had to be disseminated among the laity, and the Reformation had yet to make an impact in the countryside. A major educational effort was needed to promote the Lutheran faith – a necessity, which had already been acknowledged by the evangelical preachers from as early as 1530.[41]

As in the case of the German territorial churches, the new Lutheran Church in Denmark concentrated most of its efforts on education and social provisions such as hospitals and poor relief. The University of Copenhagen, which had been closed in 1531 to hinder the spread of Protestantism, was reopened in 1537, remodelled on the University of Wittenberg which had recently been reformed by Melanchthon. Lack of finances and the University's inability to attract students guaranteed that it remained a backwater until Christian III's son and successor, Frederik II, provided it with adequate funds in 1570.

The government fared considerably better with regard to schools. Before the death of Christian III in 1559, nearly all towns in the kingdom had been provided with Latin schools. The administration, however, appears to have concentrated its efforts within secondary education and demonstrated only limited interest in providing elementary schooling for the majority of the population. The religious instruction given in the schools and supplemented by that provided by the ministers and the parish clerks in the rural areas was considered essential in bringing the Reformation to the people. The first Protestant bishop of Zealand, Peder Palladius, hoped that the children who benefited from schooling would be able to bring the evangelical message back to their elders – 'the egg had to jump up and teach the hen' was the way he phrased it.[42] For the Lutheran, Christian III, church and school were intimately connected. They represented supplementary avenues along which the Gospel could be spread. The King and his Chancellor, Johan Friis, took great personal interest in education – supporting Danish students in Wittenberg and providing capital for the Latin schools which were established in the market towns. However, most of the major improvements within the educational sector, due to the economic restraints in the wake of the civil war, were not implemented until the reign of Christian's son, Frederik II.[43]

A new ecclesiastical administration was created to monitor the clergy's and laity's adherence to the Protestant faith. The superintendents constantly inspected their dioceses and examined candidates for the ministry. Their visitations were supplemented on the local level by the rural deans who, together with the royal officials, inspected the local clergy, schools and social institutions, not to mention the laity in the parishes. A constant synodal activity, from national via provincial down to local synods, helped secure a measure of uniformity.[44] As can be seen from the detailed provisions laid down for the visitations by Zealand's first Protestant bishop, Peder Palladius, the importance of the evolutionary implementation of the Reformation through education and catechising was paramount to the new Lutheran Church.[45]

The acts of the diocesan synods of Zealand from 1554 to 1569 show the constant preoccupation of the Church with the need to ensure that local churches and ministers had the necessary books, such as the Bible, books of sermons by Luther, Melanchthon, and Brenz, Melanchthon's *Loci communes*, Brenz's and Palladius's Cathecisms, not to mention the Danish Church Ordinance. Much was lacking in the first decades after the Reformation, unqualified and unauthorised ministers were seen as a constant threat by the authorities, while incumbents repeatedly had to be admonished to preach and not to read their sermons from books, and to fulfill their obligation of catechising their congregations every Sunday. If the clergymen were in need of constant admonition, so was the rural population. Peasants were reminded that they were obliged to send their children to school and that continued refusal to comply would lead to punishment by lay authority. That failure to take heed of the ecclesiastical authorities could eventually have dire consequences can be seen from the example of the tenant farmer who, in 1574, lost his farm because he had been excommunicated by his vicar for lack of church attendance for more than six years, during which time he had never taken communion.

Likewise, many Catholic traditions refused to die within a Lutheran Church which permitted most high altars, side altars, images of Saints, and frescos to remain in place. Many rural ministers, who might well have started their careers as Catholic priests, continued to elevate the communion wine and bread while the congregation knelt according to the Catholic custom. Furthermore, the same ministers would, more often than not, follow the Catholic tradition and consume all the remaining communion wine and bread, showing the empty chalice and dish to their congregation. If the clergy found it difficult to adjust fully to the new order, the laity did not find it any easier. As before the Reformation the popular demand for benedictions of food and seed corn around Easter remained strong, while pilgrimages to popular shrines often continued unabated. Thus in Zealand the shrines in Egede dedicated to the Trinity and the 'Holy Blood' in Bistrup continued to attract crowds during the 1560s. Large sums were donated to these shrines, but the strong local opposition to their closure was as much economically as religiously founded, since the donations were by then evenly divided between the local churches, ministers and poor.[46]

However, the extended period of peace and tranquillity which reigned in Denmark from 1536, after Christian III's victory in the civil war, served the new Protestant Church well, and offered it conditions which most territorial Lutheran Churches in Germany would have envied. In spite of a lack of local, detailed studies of how the Lutheran Church functioned in Denmark in the second half of the sixteenth century, we can safely assume that the Danish Reformation proved a lasting success within two generations of its formal introduction, even if it may have succeeded in a rather sterile 'Melanchthonian reductionist' form.[47]

The Reformation in Sweden was a far more protracted affair and remained a half-way house until the turn of the century. It lacked any significant popular support until the 1560s and only the predominantly German population of Stockholm appears to have been attracted to the new evangelical teachings from the outset. Gustav Vasa himself, who had usurped the Swedish throne in 1523, never became a committed Protestant. Instead he was attracted to the political and economical advantages which could be gleaned from a reformation of the Swedish Church. His lack of genuine Protestant belief, coupled with his fear of being deposed, guaranteed a constant change of the Crown's political and religious policies, more often than not in reaction to the social, economic and religious rebellions the King faced between 1527 and 1543.[48]

Gustav Vasa demonstrated his willingness to interfere in ecclesiastical matters from the outset. Most bishoprics were vacant at the time of his accession, owing to the fact that all the incumbents, who had been promoted by Christian II, had fled the country. Gustav made sure that their successors were loyal to him rather than to the Church. In 1524 he personally encouraged the nascent evangelical movement in Sweden by promoting two leading Protestants. The Archdeacon of Strängnäs, Laurentius Andrea, became his Chancellor, while another Strängnäs theologian, Olaus Petri, was made clerk and minister to the town of Stockholm. They spearheaded the evangelical movement under the king's protection until the early 1530s. By then, however, Gustav Vasa, appears to have had second thoughts about the Reformation. Initially, he had done his utmost to help the reformers. Thus he provided them with printworks while closing down the press set up and financed by Hans Brask, the Bishop of Linköping and leader of the Catholic faction. The expulsion of the radical German, itinerant preacher, Melchior Hoffmann, from Stockholm in January 1527 had so far been the only setback for the evangelical movement in Sweden. But by the summer of 1529 the king had decided to suspend further moves towards a reformation.

In spite of the success of the parliament (Riksdag) of Västerås in 1527 in demolishing the economic and political power of the Catholic Church in Sweden, Gustav Vasa had also had to face the first serious peasant rebellion, the Deljunkeren's revolt, in that year. This had served as a reminder to the king of the volatile social and economic situation in the country, caused to a considerable extent by increasing royal taxation to pay for the costs of the war of independence against Christian II. The revolt was fanned by religious disaffection with the new Protestant teachings being introduced from above. However, Gustav Vasa continued to promote Protestantism from 1527 onwards, while the Catholics lost their most dynamic leader when Bishop Hans Brask acknowledged defeat and fled to Danzig in 1527.

The failure of the national synod of Örebro in 1529 to reach a compromise which satisfied the predominantly conservative and Catholic peasantry, as well as the evangelical population of Stockholm, not only led to disturbances in Stockholm, but caused a far more dangerous peasant rebellion in south-west Sweden in April. This time the anti-evangelical overtones to the revolt were much stronger than in 1527 and leadership was provided by members of the local nobility. Only by promising to retain the status quo in religion, emphasising that changes in ceremonies and discipline, such as services in Swedish, had not been ordered by him, did Gustav Vasa manage to contain the danger.[49] Consequently, Laurentius Andreae and Olaus Petri, found themselves out of royal favour. Andreae was removed from the chancellorship in 1531 and Petri, who had initially replaced him, only managed to hold on to the job for two years. Apart from the internal problems caused by the evangelical movement in Sweden, Gustav Vasa's change of heart might well have been encouraged by developments abroad. On the one hand he might have been inspired by the Catholic reaction in Denmark which followed the death of Frederik I in 1533, on the other, he might well have been alarmed by the more social-radical tendencies of the evangelical movement in Germany. Whatever the reasons, the Reformation was put on ice in Sweden until 1536, when a victorious Christian III had turned the Danish Church into a territorial, Lutheran church. That year another national synod introduced significant changes to the order and ceremonies of the Swedish Church. However, it did not manage to resolve the growing controversy between church and state. The Swedish reformers, led by Olaus Petri and Laurentius Andreae wanted a Lutheran territorial church, as independent of civil authority as possible, while Gustav Vasa wanted it under royal supremacy. This dispute was to dominate Swedish church policy well into the seventeenth century.

Continuing protests among the peasantry combined with, what the king considered to be the reformers' unwillingness to preach obedience to secular authority, convinced Gustav Vasa that he had to intervene. During the parliament of Örebro in December 1539, Gustav Vasa finally secured full royal control over the Swedish Church. He had, undoubtedly, been encouraged in this move by his growing number of German advisers, especially Conrad von Pyhy and the Wittenberg-educated theologian, Georg Norman. A new church organisation was introduced in parallel to the episcopal system which it was intended to replace gradually. Thus by 1540 the Swedish Church had finally experienced what amounted to a princely Reformation, even if only in church government. Most of the changes introduced by Norman, however, were short-lived. Another peasant rebellion in 1542, caused as much by increased taxation as by changes in church government – Georg Norman's visitations were especially singled out for complaint – guaranteed that most of the innovations had disappeared by 1545.[50] Gustav Vasa, however, remained firmly in control of the Swedish Church until his death in 1560. But the lack of any firm doctrinal foundation for the new evangelical church was to cause serious and protracted difficulties in decades to come.

Gustav Vasa had provided his sons Erik and Karl with two Calvinist tutors, Dionysius Beurreus and Jan van Herboville. Together with a number of immigrants from East Friesland, they attempted to promote Calvinism in Sweden during the first years of Erik XIV's reign. It all came to an end in 1565 after the Archbishop Laurentius Petri had attacked the Calvinist position, forcing Erik to reverse his father's policy of inviting persecuted Calvinists to settle in Sweden, while at the same time forbidding Calvinist propaganda in his kingdom.[51]

When Johan III succeeded his deposed brother in 1568, the susceptibility of the Swedish Church to outside influence was in further evidence. This time it was affected by the Counter-Reformation. In spite of having finally received a Protestant Church Ordinance in 1571, Sweden proved remarkably fertile ground for Jesuit missionary efforts in the late 1570s. Admittedly, the Church Ordinance was, to say the least, vague about doctrinal questions. It neither accepted nor rejected the Confession of Augsburg and only emphasised that the Word of God, as contained in the Scriptures, should be purely preached. It also retained most of the Catholic ceremonies. In short it created more problems than it solved.

Johan III, who had married a Catholic Polish princess, Katarina, who was allowed her own priests and chapel, was personally attracted to the splendour of the Catholic Church. Theologically, he was heavily influenced by the writings of Georg Cassander, an irenically minded Catholic churchman, as can be seen from the king's amendments to the Church Ordinance – the *Nova Ordinantia* of 1575. The prospects for the Swedish Church's return to the Catholic fold were positively interpreted by the Polish Jesuit, Warzewicki, who had provided spiritual guidance to Queen Katarina since 1574. His reports encouraged Pope Gregory XIII to send the same Norwegian Jesuit, Laurentius Nicolai ('Klosterlasse'), to Sweden, who, as we have seen, travelled to Copenhagen in 1606. He arrived in 1576, this time as an undercover agent for the Curia and proved an immediate success with Johan III, who allowed him to open a theological college in the former Franciscan monastery in Stockholm. Education in Sweden had been in a deplorable state since 1516 when the University of Uppsala had been closed and, in spite of attempts by Erik XIV and Johan III to reinvigorate it, no place existed where the clergy could be educated in Sweden.[52]

Meanwhile an official embassy from Johan to Pope Gregory XIII had encouraged the Pope to send a former secretary-general of the Jesuit Order to Sweden. Antonio Possevino arrived in December 1577 and within the next couple of years his missionary efforts, combined with Nicolai's, seem to have born some fruit among the Swedish aristocracy.

Johan III's introduction in 1577 of a new, more Catholic liturgy – known as the Red Book – was encouraged by clandestine Catholics such as Laurentius Nicolai, but only received the approval of a high-church minority within the Swedish Church. By the evangelical majority it was considered a dangerous move towards Rome. Their fears of popery were confirmed when during 1578 Laurentius Nicolai revealed himself as a Jesuit. The following year fear turned into panic among evangelical churchmen in Sweden, when Possivino, who had returned from Rome in full clerical garb, ordered all

Catholic priests to throw aside their disguises. The strong anti-Catholic reactions which followed, including riots in Stockholm, lost Possivino and Nicolai the Royal support they had enjoyed, and they were forced to leave Sweden. A few Catholic priests were, however, allowed to remain, but by the time Queen Katarina died in 1583 the threat of the Counter-Reformation to the Swedish Church had receded.[53]

If anything, the Jesuit infiltration of Sweden ultimately served only to undermine the reign of Johan's son, the Catholic King Sigismund, who was deposed in 1598 after only six years on the throne. The Protestant opposition to the high-church policies of Johan and Sigismund had been offered considerable encouragement and protection by Duke Karl, Johan's brother. It was from the safe haven of his dukedom that some of the leading Lutheran theologians of the Swedish Church materialised during the 1590s. Karl, who can be classified as a crypto-Calvinist, succeeded Sigismund, but was unable to find any solution to the struggle for control over ecclesiastical matters between church and state. The predominantly Lutheran churchmen he had protected during their years of persecution now turned against him, maintaining the independence of the Church, while attacking him for his heterodox beliefs. He, on the other hand, did his utmost to impose royal supremacy on the Church, but his Lutheran bishops were able to keep him at bay until he died in 1611.[54]

Thus the Swedish Reformation, became by far the slowest and doctrinally most rickety of the Scandinavian Reformations. Initially it not only lacked popular support, but also faced the greatest opposition of any of the Nordic countries towards its teachings from its peasant population. Later it became subject to the predominantly political and economic calculations of Gustav Vasa. The fact that no Church Ordinance was issued until 1571, and then only in a remarkably vague form, did little to cement the evangelical achievements of the preceding decades. The religious heterodoxy of Gustav Vasa's sons guaranteed that the Swedish Church found itself constantly on the defensive throughout the second half of the sixteenth century, keenly defending some sort of Lutheran orthodoxy, while simultaneously guarding the independence of the Church against royal encroachments.

NOTES

1 B. Kornerup, *Biskop Hans Poulsen Resen* 2 vols. (Copenhagen, 1928, 1968), vol. 2, pp. 146–71.
2 For the Swedish centenary of 1621, see C. A. Aurelius, '"Sverige, känn dig själv". En studie av der svenska reformationsjubileet år 1621', *Kyrkahistorisk Årsskrift* (1987), pp. 105–19, especially pp. 105–7.
3 The Reformation in Norway and Finland will not be treated here. In Finland it

was remarkable by being a purely ecclesiastical affair which saw the Finnish Church move gradually from a traditional Catholic position via reformism to Lutheranism and is perhaps most significant for its cultural impact on the Finnish language. Finland's reformer, Mikael Agricola became the founder of the written Finnish language. The Reformation had no similar cultural impact on Norway, which had been incorporated in the Danish kingdom after the victory of Duke Christian (later Christian III) in the Civil War from 1534 to 1536 (Grevens Fejde). Here the Reformation was introduced in the administrative language, Danish. For both these countries see *The New Cambridge Modern History*, vol. II (2nd edn), G. R. Elton ed., *The Reformation 1520–1559* (Cambridge, 1990), pp. 152–4 and 164–7.

4 See O. P. Grell, 'Scandinavia', in A. Pettegree ed., *The Early Reformation in Europe* (Cambridge, 1992), pp. 94–119.

5 H. V. Gregersen, *Reformationen i Sønderjylland* (Aabenraa, 1986), pp. 244–9.

6 For developments in Malmø and Copenhagen, see O. P. Grell. 'The Emergence of Two Cities. The Reformation in Malmø and Copenhagen', in L. Grane and K. Hørby, *Die dänische Reformation vor ihrem internationalen Hintergrund* (Gottingen, 1990), pp. 129–45.

7 Gregersen, *Sønderjylland*, pp. 49–53.

8 For the traditional view of Duke Christian's sudden conversion in Worms, see Gregersen, *Sønderjylland*, p. 56. For a different and more balanced view of the Duke's conversion to Protestantism, see M. Schwarz Lausten, *Christian den 3. og kirken 1537–1559* (Copenhagen, 1987), p. 10.

10 For Weidensee and Wenth, see *Schleswig–Holsteinisches Biographisches Lexikon*, vol. V, pp. 276–77, vol. 299–301.

11 Gregersen, *Sønderjylland*, p. 93.

12 Grell, 'Scandinavia', p. 101.

13 Gregersen, *Sønderjylland*, pp. 116–17.

14 *Ibid.*, pp. 136–43.

15 Weidensee and Wenth probably used Melanchthon's *Unterricht der Visitatoren* (1528) as a model for this section of the Haderslev Ordinance, see Gregersen, *Sønderjylland*, pp. 129–30 and 133.

16 Lausten, *Christian den 3*, pp. 19–20.

17 K. Deppermann, *Melchior Hoffman* (Edinburgh, 1989), pp. 126–37.

18 G. Waitz, *Urkunden und andere Actenstücke* (Quellensammlung der Schleswig–Holsteiner *Landesgesellschaft*, II, 1863), pp. 109–11.

19 Gregersen, *Sønderjylland*, pp. 178–93.

20 Gerhard Slewart's visitation book has been published by W. Jensen in *Schriften des Vereins für Schleswig–Holsteinische Kirchengeschichte*, Second Series, vol. X, 1 (1949), pp. 35–78.

21 For the administrative changes, see Gregersen, *Sønderjylland*, pp. 198–204. For the reformation of the monasteries, see H. F. Rørdam, 'Om Reformationen af Herreklostrene', in *Kirkehistoriske Samlinger*, Second Series, vol. II, pp. 737–54.

22 Gregersen, *Sønderjylland*, pp. 211–14.

23 This emphasis was further enhanced through the School Order of May 1544 which created the conditions for an expansion of the educational facilities, see H. V. Gregersen, *Sleswig og Holsten indtil 1830* (separate volume of *Politikens Danmarks Historie*, ed. S. Ellehøj and K. Glamann) (Copenhagen, 1981), p. 252.

See also H. F. Rørdam, 'En mækelig Forordning for Hertugdømmerne om Kristendomsundervisningen', *Kirkehistoriske Samlinger* III Række, V (1884–6), pp. 153–9.

24 V. Helk, *Laurentius Nicolai Norvegius* (Copenhagen, 1966), pp. 283–4 and 315.

25 *Ibid.*, *passim* and V. Helk, *Dansk-Norske Studierejser fra reformationen til enevælden 1536–1660* (Dense, 1987), pp. 66, 69.

26 See Jonas Henrikesen, *Consilium politicorum de ratione et via regiones septentrionales ad cultum sedis Romanae reducendi* (1604), pp. 1, 46. See also V. Helk, *Laurentius Nicolai*, *passim* and H. F. Rørdam, *Københavns Universitets Historie* vols. I–IV (Copenhagen, 1868–74), vol. III, p. 160.

27 For this Royal proclamation, see H. F. Rørdam, ed., *Danske Kirkelove*, vols. I–III (Copenhagen, 1881–9), vol. III, pp. 16–17.

28 For Jens Aagesen and his Jesuit education, see V. Helk, *Laurentius Nicolai*, pp. 294 and 348–50, and O. Bjurling ed., *Malmö Stads Historia*, I–II (Malmö, 1971–7), II, 80.

29 Helk, *Laurentius Nicolai*, chapters 24 and 25 and B. Kornerup, *Biskop hans Poulsen Resen* (Copenhagen, 1928), vol. I, pp. 241–2. See also T. Dahlerup, 'Sin, Crime, Punishment and Absolution. The Disciplinary System of the Danish Church in the Reformation Century', in *Die dänische Reformation*, p. 287.

30 O. P. Grell, 'The City of Malmø and the Danish Reformation', in *Archiv für Reformationsgeschichte*, 79 (1988), pp. 311–40, and M. Schwarz Lausten, 'Die Universität Kopenhagen und die Reformation', in L. Grane ed., *University and Reformation* (Leiden, 1981), pp. 99–103.

31 See O. P. Grell, 'Herredagan 1527', in *Kirkehistoriske Samlinger* (1978), pp. 69–88.

32 See A. Heise ed., *Skibykrøniken* (Reprint, Copenhagen, 1967), p. 111 and Grell, 'Scandinavia'.

33 Grell, 'The City of Malmø, pp. 311–16.

34 For Malmø and Copenhagen, see Grell, 'The Emergence of Two Cities', pp. 129–45. For Jørgen Kock, see O. P. Grell, 'Jørgen Kock. En studie i religion og politik i reformationstidens Danmark', in S. E. Green-Pedersen *et al.* eds., *Festskrift til Poul Enemark. Profiter i Nordisk Senmiddelalder og Renæssance* (Aarhus, 1983), pp. 113–26.

35 Grell, 'The City of Malmø', pp. 322–5.

36 M. Schwarz Lausten, 'Weltliche Obrigkeit und Kirche bei Konig Christian III, von Dänemark (1536–1559)', in *Die dänische Reformation*, pp. 91–107.

37 Lausten, *Christian den 3*, pp. 20–7 and A. E. Christensen *et al.* eds., *Gyldendals Danmarkshistorie*, vol. II, part one (Copenhagen, 1980), pp. 318–22 and 349–52.

38 H. Koch and B. Kornerup, *Den danske Kirkes Historie*, vol. IV (Copenhagen, 1959), pp. 33–4.

39 *Ibid.*, p. 38 and L. Grane, 'Teaching the People – the Education of the Clergy and the Instruction of the People in the Danish Reformation', in *Die dänische Reformation*, p. 174.

40 Lausten, *Christian den 3*, pp. 55 and 88; see also G. Johannesson, *Den skånska Kyrkan och Reformationen* (Lund, 1947), pp. 316–19.

41 See H. F. Rørdam ed., *Malmøbogen* (Copenhagen, 1868), fols. 50–1.

42 Quoted in M. Schwarz Lausten, *Biskop Peder Palladius og Kirken 1537–1560* (Copenhagen, 1987), p. 171, see also pp. 164–74.

43 Grane, 'Teaching the People', in *Die dänische Reformation*, pp. 171–3 and P. Colding, *Studier i Danmarks politiske Historie. Slutningen af Christian III's og Begyndelsen af Frederik II's Tid* (Copenhagen, 1939), pp. 151–66.
44 Lausten, *Christian den 3*, pp. 73–84.
45 For Palladius's visitation-instructions, see L. Jacobsen ed., *Peder Palladius' Danske Skrifter* (5 vols. Copenhagen, 1911–26), vol. V, pp. 84–95.
46 For the diocesan acts, see H. F. Rørdam, 'Forhandlinger paa Roskilde Lande-mode 1554–1569; *Kirkehistoriske Samlinger*, New Series, II (1860–2), pp. 441–511. For the example of the tenant farmer, see H. F. Rørdam, *Københavns Universitet*, vol. 152–3 and 356–7. See also Troels-Lund, *Dagligt Liv i Norden i det sekstende Århundrede* (Copenhagen, 1969), pp. 313, 342 and 355.
47 I have borrowed this term from Grane, 'Teaching the People', in *Die dänische Reformation*, p. 183.
48 See O. P. Grell, 'Scandinavia', in A. Pettegree, *The early Reformation in Europe* (Cambridge, 1992), p. 117.
49 H. Yrwing, *Gustav Vasa kroningsfragan och Västerås Riksdag* (Lund, 1956) and H. Holmquist and H. Pleijel eds., *Svenska Kyrkans Historia*, 4 vols. (Uppsala, 1933–41), vol. III, pp. 190–8.
50 M. Roberts, *The Early Vasas. A History of Sweden 1523–1611* (Cambridge, 1968), pp. 107–24.
51 See S. Kjöllerström, *Striden kring kalvinismen i Sverige under Erik XIV* (Lund, 1935).
52 See S. Kjöllerström, *Kyrkolagsproblemet i Sverige 1571–1682*, Samlingar och Studier til svenska Kyrkans Historia, no. 11 (Uppsala, 1944), and C. Anner-stedt, *Upsala Universitets Historia*, vol. I (Uppsala, 1877).
53 See V. Helk, *Laurentius Nicolai Norvegius*, and O. Garstein, *Rome and the Counter-Reformation in Scandinavia*, vol. I (Oslo, 1963), vol. II (Copenhagen, 1980), vols. III–IV (Leiden, 1992).
54 See H. Block, *Karl IX som teolog og religiös personlighet* (Uppsala, 1918).

FURTHER READING

N. K. Andersen, *Confessio hafniensis. Den københavnske Bekendelse af 1530* (Copenhagen, 1954).
Carl-Gustav Andred ed., *Reformationen i Norden. Kontinuitet och Fornyelse* (Lund, 1973).
L. Grane and K. Hørby eds. *Die dänische Reformation vor ihrem internationalen Hintergrund* (Göttingen, 1990).
H. V. Gregersen, *Reformationen i Sønderjylland* (Aabenraa, 1986).
O. P. Grell, 'The City of Malmø and the Danish Reformation' *Archiv für Reforma-tionsgeschichte*, 79 (1988), pp. 311–39.
O. P. Grell, 'Scandinavia', in A. Pettegree ed., *The Early Reformation of Europe* (Cambridge, 1992).
G. Johannesson, *Den skånska Kyrkan och Reformationen* (Lund, 1947).
M. Schwarz Lausten, *Christian den 3. og Kirken 1537–1559* (Copenhagen, 1987).
M. Roberts, *The Early Vasas. A History of Sweden 1523–1611* (Cambridge, 1968).
G. Schwaiger, *Die Reformation in den nordischen Ländern* (Munich, 1962).

# 8 Bohemia

*František Kavka*

Reformation – understood as a new approach to the evangelical message, as the rise of a new religious doctrine and of churches independent of the papacy, and involving radical changes in society – occurred at an earlier date in the Czech Kingdom than elsewhere in Europe.[1] The crisis of spiritual and social life accompanied by socio-political shocks, from which the Reformation of the sixteenth century arose, hit the lands of the Czech crown much earlier, indeed in the latter part of the fourteenth century. Similar developments took place in England and Northern Italy, but in the Czech Kingdom the gradual accumulation of various contradictions created favourable conditions for the crisis to result in a real Reformation and in the Hussite revolution (1419–36).[2] The Czech Reformation laid the foundations for this revolution and created its ideology, but it also drew on it in turn for its stimuli.[3] Thanks to the successful revolution neither the Roman Church nor the secular power were able to suppress this first Reformation; they only succeeded in limiting it to the Czech national context, where it developed further, even in the post-revolutionary period, isolated from the rest of the orthodox Catholic world, which held in contempt its followers (that is, the majority of the Czech nation who adhered to its doctrines), calling them schismatics and heretics. Only at the beginning of the sixteenth century did the Czech Reformation encounter another wave of reformation in neighbouring Germany and thus find its historical fulfilment.

The Czech Reformation is older than the teaching of the university don and preacher John Hus (d. 1415), with whose name it is inseparably linked. The 'father of the Czech Reformation' is rightly considered to have been John Milič of Kroměříž (d. 1374), while its theological premises were formulated by Master Matthew of Janov (d. 1393). Their spiritual impact resulted from their recognising the signs of the Last Days, calling attention to the imminent 'end of all time' and pointing out Christianity's unreadiness for the Second Coming of Christ. This eschatological tendency accompanied the Czech Reformation throughout its entire duration until Jan Amos Komenský (Comenius), although its intensity may have varied in certain periods. It had far more important consequences than the contemporaneous zeal for reform of the Church or than the *devotio moderna*, which concentrated on interior spirituality. Incorporating the Church into the context of the eschatological future inevitably relativised its historical existence, revealed its inadequacy as an institution of salvation and urgently addressed the necessity of seeking other ways to achieve salvation.

John Hus's predecessors called for the Gospel to be preached to everyone everywhere. A welcome support in this effort was achieved in the 1370s, a Czech translation of the Bible, further perfected in subsequent editions. It is also necessary to understand Milič's and Janov's concept of eucharistic practice (that is, their demand for frequent communion – in Janov's concept, perhaps even under both kinds) in the original eschatological meaning of a preparation and strengthening for the imminent 'death of all time'. Matthew of Janov's premise that the contemporary Church was ruled by the Antichrist and could therefore no longer fulfil its mission led him to demand the restoration of the Church by a return to its apostolic origins and a consistent observance of the 'Rules of the Old and New Testaments' (this being the title of Janov's extensive and fundamental work). There he set out in detail his programme of discarding all that could not be supported by the evidence of Scripture. Nevertheless, the biblicism of Hus's predecessors was confused by their spiritualism (that is, their belief in an ongoing revelation by the Holy spirit), and it did not lead to the fundamental Reformation principle of *sola scriptura*.[4]

The local origin of the Czech Reformation in its eschatological tendency has only recently been re-evaluated. It has been found even to have influenced the works of John Hus, although these had drawn on other theological sources. Nowadays it seems less important that the main ideas of John Hus were derived from those of the Oxford theologian John Wyclif (d. 1384). Following the episode of Lollardy, Wyclif's ideas owed their widespread social reception to Hus's interpretation of them. Through him these ideas were to be appropriated by the Czech Reformation and were to be realised in the Hussite revolution.[5] The starting point for Wyclifism–Hussitism is the doctrine of the 'law of Christ' (*lex Christi*), which was absolutely self-sufficient and suitable not only for the administration of the church militant, but also as a binding norm for the life and ideas of all people without exception. This law is embodied in Scripture, which is superior to all other sources of faith, especially to the traditions relied on by the Roman Church; by means of Scripture and using our own reason, we can learn God's truth. Other fundamental ideas of John Hus are derived from these principles: the concept of predestination (less strict and less contradictory in Hus than in Wyclif), rejection of indulgences, and especially a revolutionary theory of power and obedience (a powerholder forfeits authority if he or she falls into mortal sin). Consequently everyone had the right, even a duty, to defy orders that were contrary to binding principles of justice, which were to be judged by a person's own reason. Both the principle of *sola scriptura* and the doctrine of predestination were common points of departure of all Reformations, albeit in different formulations or interpretations. In his epochal work *De ecclesia* Hus combined a defence of his defiance of ecclesiastical authority with a Wyclifian analysis of the Church. He then left to the Czech Reformation the task of deducing the theoretical and practical consequences from his discovery that the Roman Church had succumbed under the reign of Constantine to the lure of wealth and power and had betrayed its mission. This task was taken up by the Reformation of the sixteenth century, and is still valid today. On a number of points, however, Hus differed from Wyclif: namely, in his rejection of Wyclif's doctrine of the Eucharist (*remanentia*, that is, that the substance of bread and wine remained after consecration); and in different views formulated during the last period of his life about how reform should be achieved. He did not share Wyclif's belief in the reforming ability of the secular power, namely the king, and increasingly he turned to local traditions such as that of Matthew of Janov. In this tradition salvation was to be brought about by a 'new people' (*novus populus*), a 'simple people' (*populus simplex*), that is by a reform 'from below'. In keeping with the spirit of its eschatological point of departure, this tradition emphasised the model of the early apostolic Church and moved Hus in the direction of the far-reaching Reformation of the election of priests and bishops by the Christian community.[6]

There was a connection between the doctrine of the supreme authority of Scripture, local Czech eschatological tradition and the typical demand of the Czech Reformation for communion in both kinds (*sub utraque specie*) for all Christians, provided they were not in a state of mortal sin. Hus authorised this practice only late in his career, from prison during his trial before the Council of Constance. The chalice was introduced in 1414 and was theologically justified by Hus's university colleague and follower, Master Jakoubek of Stříbo (d. 1429),[7] who became a symbol of the Czech Reformation and of the Hussite revolution, whose followers came to be called 'Utraquists'. In the eyes of even the simplest believers, the Roman Church, which reserved the communion chalice for the officiating priest alone, could not have been more plausibly convicted of despising the Saviour's command at the Last Supper.[8]

The teaching of Wyclif and Hus, further developed by the Masters at the University of Prague to a level capable of sustaining an international intellectual discussion, could only achieve a wider response thanks to a broadly conceived propaganda campaign carried out by a body of priests and preachers. Its success was rooted in the fact that the Czech Reformation had another, popular source in Waldensianism, whose significance, especially for the radical stream of Hussite thought, has become increasingly evident as a result of the research of the past few decades.[9] Waldensianism, mainly in its popular, unlearned form, was spread in the country by channels hitherto undiscovered, but it was also promulgated in its theological form by the so-called Dresden School at the University of Prague (Masters Nicholas and Peter of Dresden). But Waldensianism found a response above all outside Prague, in Tábor, that centre of reformation and revolution. The Hussitism of Tábor went far beyond the framework of Wyclif and Hus. Through Jakoubek of Střibo it followed the legacy handed down to Matthew of Janov, and drew on many Waldensian stimuli (among other things, rejection of purgatory, reduction in the number of the sacraments, simplification of ceremonies, the introduction of the Czech vernacular into the liturgy). It also reflected the impulses of the original Tábor in which the eschatological character of the Czech Reformation culminated. A fundamental change occurred when the movement dissociated itself from chiliasm (belief in the millennium and the imminence of Christ's Second Coming) and the related Pikhartism (denial of any real presence of Christ, whether substantial or sacramental, in the Eucharist). The Tábor movement worked out its own ecclesiology, a social theology and a theory of just war and the right to use violence. It went beyond Hus in criticism of private property, in extending this to secular lords and in refusing to obey legal commands. The movement's decision to dissociate itself from the Roman Church by electing its own bishop (senior) at a synodal assembly in September 1420 can be called epochal. By refusing to consecrate bishops according to the principle of so-called apostolic succession, the Taborite Church also differed from the Hussite Church, which insisted on this principle. The status of bishop was deprived of sacramental content (*potestas ordinis*, i.e. the power to ordain priests). The Taborite bishop was an elected senior with a certain judicial and teaching authority. As with the Waldensians, there was no substantial difference between a lay person and a priest.[10]

The development of Taborite theology reached its climax by the end of the 1430s. The extensive 'Confession' written by the Bishop Nicholas of Pelhřimov (d. after 1452) belongs to the supreme works of the radical wing of the Czech Reformation and assumes a significant place in the history of Protestant dogma. It found a wide response in the Waldensian movement in Germany, Provence and in Italy, where selections were translated into the vernacular. Even more emphatically than Wyclif and Hus, the author formulated the principle of absolute dependence on divine law. The Prague Hussites later wavered on this point and admitted the validity of tradition in the Church. The programme of the Reformation of the sixteenth century was foreshadowed in the reduction of the number of sacraments (only baptism, the Eucharist and matrimony were recognised). Since it was precisely the seven sacraments that bound the world of Catholic believers to the Church, the reduction of the sacraments, and especially the abolition of aural confession, signified a breach in the sacramentalism of the Roman Church. In accordance with Wyclif, the movement rejected the doctrine of transubstantiation, and in the spirit of the Waldensians it simplified the form of divine service, at the same time demanding the use of the vernacular in the liturgy. The rejection of purgatory, of the cult of the saints, and of idols of any kind was also of Waldensian origin.[11] On the whole, Taborite Hussitism anticipated the Reformation of the sixteenth century in the reinstitution of the direct relationship between Christ and the lay person by liberating him or her from the bonds of the institutional church.

The revolution, which prevailed in Bohemia and Moravia under the banner of its conservative noble-burgher wing, also reached a modus vivendi with the Church. At the peace negotiations in Cheb in 1432, the Council of Basel conceded that the basis of an agreement should be the accepted programme of the Czech Reformation, the Four Prague Articles.[12] It also acceded to the principle that the judge in the conflict between the Church and the Hussites was to be 'the law of God, the practices of Christ, the apostles and the early Church, along with the Councils and teachings conforming truly thereto' (*Judex in Egra compactatus*, the so-called 'Cheb Judge'). For the first and last time in history, the Roman Church recognised the principle of an authority higher than itself. This was a great moral victory for the Czech Reformation, one which could not even be diminished by the fact that the result of the negotiations was a compromise, the so-called Compacts of Basel (*Compactata*) of 1436.[13] They were accepted by the Prague Hussite Church and even by the Czech and Moravian representatives as provincial law, and were confirmed by Emperor Sigismund as a condition for his acceptance as the Czech King. The Taborite Church refused to submit to the Compactata and thus outlawed itself. In 1452 Tabor could no longer hold out against armed force and capitulated; consequently the Taborite Church ceased to exist, although its spiritual legacy lived on.

In the Compactata the Roman Church actually acknowledged only one of the Four Prague Articles, namely the chalice for the laity (although not as something necessary for salvation). The other articles were provided with so many amendments that their original meaning seemed virtually negated. The Compactata had been accepted by the Hussites on the condition that negotiations on some of the articles would be resumed later, but this never occurred. The text of the Compactata could, therefore, be interpreted variously. For example, the third Prague Article dealing with the dispossession of church property remained valid, although the text of the Compactata was aimed at its restriction. For political reasons, Sigismund and his successors were obliged to guarantee the secularisation of the Church from which not only the Hussite but also the Catholic nobility had benefited. With some minor exceptions, restitution of church property was not made until after the defeat of the rebellious Estates in 1620. Moreover, the content of the Czech Reformation was broader in scope than the minimal programme of the Four Prague Articles, and therefore it found only partial expression in the Compactata, especially as it affected divine worship. The Prague Hussite movement, under the influence of Tábor, agreed to some simplification of the liturgy and to Czech as the language to be used. The fictitious character of the reconciliation with the Roman Church was further attested by the continual reverence paid to the memory of John Hus, a 'heretic' tried and burned by the Council of Constance. Indeed, the Compactata were never confirmed by the pope and in 1462 Pius II abrogated them, so that the Utraquist Church based on this agreement became schismatic. Nonetheless, the Compactata remained in force as a provincial law which all Czech kings, even Catholic ones, swore to observe until 1567.[14]

The Hussite revolution contributed considerably to the establishment of an Estates monarchy in which the majority of the Estates adhered to the Utraquist church. Even when the kings became Catholic, the natural antagonism between king and nobles developed into a religious one. Thus, even at that early stage, there began the gradual intertwining and eventual identification of political and religious issues. However Estates solidarity bridged even religious differences. The fact that the re-catholicising inclinations of the government could threaten the secularisation of church property, in which both the Utraquists (in the name of revolution) and the Catholics (under the pretext of protecting it) had participated, facilitated the negotiation of a religious peace at Kutná Hora in 1485. The peace agreement guaranteed the status quo and enabled freedom of worship even for those of servile status, something unprecedented in the European history of co-existence and toleration. This was undoubtedly a result of the flexible interpretation of the first Prague Article on the free preaching of the Gospel.[15] The religious peace, renewed in 1512, not only reinforced the binding nature of the Compactata for the royal power, but it also stabilised the position of the Utraquist Church within the Estates, whose majority role guaranteed the Utraquists protection. If the Compactata could be freely interpreted in relation to the Roman Church – by insisting on the redemptive power of the chalice, administration of the Eucharist to children, the continuation of the Czech liturgy and revering the day of Hus's death (6 July 1415) – the same was not true in the case of radical Hussitism. This survived in numerous sects and established numerous contacts with the European Waldensian movement. In the same way as the 'Pikharts' or the 'Waldenses', they were persecuted by both the ruling class and the Utraquist Church, demonstrated by the fact that they were outside the protection of the Compactata. Utraquist orthodoxy resembled the Roman Church in the confrontational stance it took towards the radical stream of the Czech Reformation, especially on the issue of the sacraments and in its insistence on the doctrine of transubstantiation. Even more alarming was the sterility of its ecclesiology, which remained undeveloped and did not even evolve beyond the stimuli given by John Hus.[16]

Although all relations had been severed with the jurisdiction of the Roman Church, the situation was different as concerned the consecration of priests. The Utraquist bishop John Rokycana (d. 1470), elected in 1435 by a committee of the Estates consisting of laymen and priests, was never confirmed by the pope.[17] Since he was not consecrated as a bishop, he did not dare consecrate the priests of his church, nor was there any consecrated bishop among those who administered the church after his death. Since the Utraquists persisted in their demand for a canonically ordained priesthood, which was denied them by the Roman Church, the shortage of priests soon became critical. This brought the Utraquists to the point of breaking with Rome on this issue as well. The idea was voiced by Rokycana's suffragan Martin Lupáč (d. 1468) and even accepted in some of Rokycana's speeches. It had not been forgotten that the early Church had not known bishops in the later sense of the word, that episcopal status in its sum and substance was no higher than that of a priest, and that in case of need any priest could consecrate another man as a priest. The idea also emerged of clinging to the principle of apostolic succession by merging with another church independent of Rome, such as the Byzantine Orthodox Church, and unsuccessful negotiations were conducted in Constantinople in 1452.[18] Inviting into the country Italian bishops who had no fear of the threat of excommunication and who dared to consecrate Utraquist priests in return for a substantial reward, or else sending aspirants to the priesthood to Italy, were really only stop-gap solutions. Moreover, this was morally dubious because of the oath taken by the newly consecrated priests by which they renounced the use of chalice for the laity.

The Czech Reformation, however, chose once again the path of unconditional break with Rome in the Taborite spirit of the Unity of the Brethren. This came into existence in the 1450s, with the tacit approval of Rokycana, as one of many sects that persisted in their efforts to establish a religious life on a higher plane than was allowed by the Utraquist Church of the time. Initially, a small circle of like-minded persons found inspiration in one of the most original spirits of the Czech Reformation, Peter of Chelčice (d. c. 1450). This son of the south Bohemian gentry, a younger contemporary of John Hus living in seclusion, became acquainted with the works of Wyclif, with Waldensian ideas and also with the legacy of Matthew of Janov. He honed his views in polemical discussions with Hus, Jaboubek, Nicholas of Pelhřimov and Rokycana. His works, written exclusively in Czech, breathe a strict biblicism of a Waldensian kind, alongside a critique of Christian society deduced from it reminiscent of Taborite radicalism. But he rejected the theory of the just war and recourse to any kind of violence – a Christian was to restrict his efforts to 'spiritual struggle' alone. Hence the negative attitude Peter of Chelčice took to state power, to any participation in the administration of justice and to the contemporary theory of the 'three estates'.

The adherents of the Unity remained within the framework of the Utraquist Church, yet they differed from it in their doctrine and way of life based on strict discipline and observance of the principles of the Gospel. They rejected transubstantiation, administered the Lord's Supper in ordinary vessels and used bread instead of host-wafers so that outward appearance would not divert attention from the spiritual sense of the sacrament. They believed that a priest in enmity could not consecrate and they rejected the use of oaths, so that they soon came into conflict with both the Utraquist Church and the royal power, and were accused of 'Pikhartism' and 'Waldensianism'. In 1467 they decided to install their own priests and to elect a bishop or senior, following the example of Tábor. This step led to a new wave of repression and to their first martyrs. Only the protection of noble members of the Unity saved them from being banished from the country.[19]

The Czech Reformation entered the sixteenth century in two separate, even ecclesiastically distinct, forms. The conservative wing within the Utraquist church stood out distinctly. It came to be an objective ally of the Catholic ruling power in building a solid bulwark against all the radical trends rooted in Taborite-Waldensian Hussitism. On the other side was a group of 'left Utraquists', as Eberhard has called them, supported by burghers and searching for the broadest interpretation of the Compactata in the sense of the 'Cheb Judge'. Emphasising the redemptive power of the chalice for the laity and its administration to children, this group hindered plans for reconciliation with the Roman Curia and in some ways came close to the legacy of revolutionary Taborite Hussitism. This current also found followers among the Utraquist humanists, graduates of the University of Prague, who with the aid of printing disseminated translations of the patristic authorities in which radical Hussitism found support for its views, as well as authors critical of the Roman Church. Czech literature was thus the first national literature in Europe to be enriched with a translation of Erasmus' *Praise of Folly* (1513). 'Left Utraquism' also strove to moderate the negative attitude hitherto taken towards the Unity of the Brethren.[20]

This second form of the Czech Reformation was capable of still more momentous development. In 1495 it dissociated itself from the ideas of

Peter of Chelčice and led by Lukáš of Prague (d. 1528), the 'second founder of the Unity', embraced the legacy of radical Taborite Hussitism, which developed it yet further. The reform of the Church on the principle of 'the law of Christ' as demanded by Wyclif, Hus and most determinedly by the Taborites, appeared to Lukáš merely as a means, not as an end. Fundamental to his theology was the distinction between things 'substantial' and 'instrumental'. From God's viewpoint, divine mercy, the merits of Christ and the gifts of the Holy Spirit belonged to the 'substantial' things; from the human viewpoint, faith, charity and hope (in a non-traditional order) were necessary for salvation as an inseparable whole. Faith, charity and hope were conceived of as gifts, and unmerited ones at that. According to Lukáš, faith, as the only way to redemption, is required by God more than works. He thus anticipated Luther's teaching by more than a quarter of a century. Unlike Luther, however, Lukáš did not reject works, holding them as the inseparable supplement to faith and its telltale signs. Human control over redemption is, according to him, excluded by a freely given, foreordained divine mercy, which from the human point of view is wholly unconditional. Among the 'instrumental' things were the Gospel, the Church and the sacraments (unlike the Taborites, he always recognised all seven). In his interpretation of the eucharist he followed the Taborite concept of the sacramental presence of Christ, in opposition to the Roman and Utraquist Churches, but also to Luther's notion of consubstantiation. Thus it was not difficult for the Unity to later take over Calvin's teaching on this point. Lukáš ecclesiology went beyond both Wyclif and Hus. He distinguished between a Church understood, like Wyclif and Hus, as the invisible assembly of the elect and outside of which there was no salvation, and a concretely historical Church, whose members also contained the wicked (a *corpus mixtum*) and which was not a redemptive institution. It was conceived of as single and universal, but was divided into many 'unities' (Roman, Utraquist, the Unity of the Brethren, and others). In this way, he deprived the Roman Church of its claims to catholicity, but at the same time transcended the national boundaries of individual churches. Lukáš thus elaborated a truly reformational theological system, which by its teaching on justification could stand alongside Luther's doctrine, while he also anticipated Calvin's theology, both in Christology and in the notion of continual service to Christ the King. The Czech Reformation undoubtedly culminated in Lukáš.[21]

The relations established between the Czech and German Reformations during the first fifteen years after Luther's emergence into public life in 1517 were those of mutuality and continuity. These cannot be challenged by the claim that from the German side the continuity was not conscious and that the connecting links were discovered only retrospectively. It is symptomatic that it was his Catholic opponents who warned Luther that he was treading in the footsteps of the 'heretic Hus'. After initial hesitation, Luther acknowledged Hus's teaching publicly. However, the Czech impulses were not always domesticated by the Reformation of the sixteenth century without some distortion of their original aims, which were of course a response to a different religious and social situation. The Hussite chalice created a precedent for the sixteenth-century reformers which they could not but take into account, especially since radical reformers such as Carlstadt, Müntzer and others zealously acknowledged it. The eucharistic 'Bohemian practice (*consuetudo bohemica*) was taken over by practically all the reformed churches as Hus's legacy. This fact is attested by a frequently recurring iconographic theme of the sixteenth century, which shows Hus administering the chalice to the laity in the presence of other reformers. However, Luther had no understanding for the theology of the Hussite chalice and reduced its original meaning to a purely liturgical usage. In opposition to this, those sixteenth-century reformers who walked in Wyclif's footsteps substituted and burdened the interpretation of the Lord's Supper with ontological thoughts on the theme of remanence (similar to Luther's 'consubstantiation'). These disputes brought about the end of any unity in the reformation movement, beginning with the Marburg Colloquy of 1529.

On the other hand, it was symptomatic that the radical wing of the Czech Reformation accepted the notion of remanence without making it a question of principle. They were not so much interested in metaphysics as in the eschatology of the sacrament, whose shared communion made the believers brothers and sisters, anticipated the coming of Christ the King already present in his blood, and strengthened them for the defence of God's law. The influence of Hus's ecclesiology on the Reformation of the sixteenth century is indisputable. The attention bestowed on his work *De ecclesia*, published in two editions in 1520, attests this fact. This 'pioneering work' (de Vooght) revealed the theological issues of the Church, until then pushed into the background by administrative and judicial problems. Hus's doctrine of predestination became a common point of departure for the whole Reformation, albeit in varying interpretations. In Hus's view, it reinforced and guaranteed the freedom and authoritative character of 'the law of Christ' against the claims of the institutional church, while it enabled the reformers of the sixteenth century to allow Christ's work to be permeated by God's creative initiative, independently of human religious activities, and aiming at the justification and restoration of mankind.[22]

It is understandable that these mutual links between the Czech and German Reformations were more sensitively perceived in a Czech setting, for there they were hailed as a liberation from a century-long isolation and as a source of satisfaction. This fact determined the presentation of Lutheranism and its acceptance in the first two decades. Since the main tasks of the Reformation had already been fulfilled in Bohemia and Moravia a hundred years earlier, the socio-religious motivation from which the German and Swiss Reformations arose was absent here. Czech society, having overcome its own critical moments during the Hussite revolution, was economically stable and content in its dominant social strata of nobles and burghers, although to uneven extent. The dissatisfaction of the poorer classes in the population, especially the peasants, which was at the root of the German Peasants' War and the radical currents of the Reformation in general, had already found a religious vent in sects of the Taborite-Waldensian kind and social pressure, if there was any, no longer threatened to explode. The social driving force of the German Reformation had already been exhausted in Bohemia. Even the corresponding spiritual stimuli were missing. As a result of the usual post-revolutionary fatigue, but also because of the more shallow character of religious life in the Utraquist Church, the society of aristocrats and burghers became insensitive to those distressing questions about whether salvation was assured to which the Reformation of the sixteenth century provided a welcome answer. The nobles and burghers were content to enjoy the cultic activities of the Church within the framework of a kind of 'unconfessional Christianity'. All this forms a sharp contrast to the rapid and widespread reception of Lutheranism in all those places where neither the Czech Reformation nor the Hussite revolution had already asserted itself: among the German population in the so-called minor provinces of the Czech Kingdom (Lusatia, Silesia), and to a lesser extent in the border regions of Bohemia and Moravia populated by Germans and in the predominantly German towns of Moravia.

In the Czech setting those most receptive to the stimuli of Lutheranism proved to be the intellectually and emotionally more receptive burghers, part of the Utraquist clergy and the Taborite-Waldensian sects. The differentiation within the Czech Reformation predetermined the varied character of the response. Supporters of 'left Utraquism' placed Luther on the same level as Hus, whose works acquired in retrospect a new urgency. The constitution of the territorial state church established in Lutheran Saxony was not something completely new, since the Utraquist Church already had the Estates as its head and protector and was actually founded on a Protestant principle. However, Lutheranism provided a possible resolution of the troubled issue of the Utraquist clergy. In his second letter to the citizens of Prague of November 1523, Luther had suggested a solution in the ordination of priests without episcopal consecration. There was also a great response to the simplification of divine worship. In the years 1523–4, the 'left Utraquists' penetrated local administration and prevailed in the Prague town hall. The emergence of a Utraquist-Lutheran Church was imminent. In reaction to this development, all the opponents of reform of any kind joined forces with a group of 'old Utraquists' and in alliance with the Catholics carried out a coup d'etat in Prague in 1524, initiating persecution of any open adherents of Lutheranism. This fatal reverse was carried out without any widespread social reaction, which demonstrates the immaturity of the conditions for a more rapid dissemination of the German Reformation in the Czech context at that time. It is not however without significance that the originality of Lutheran doctrine had been considerably anticipated by the Unity of the Brethren, as we have shown in discussing the teaching of Lukáš, which had attracted those dissatisfied with Utraquism into their ranks. It is symptomatic that membership of the Unity increased at this time, and was also boosted by the somewhat religiously indifferent nobility (1530). It was also the Unity that established active theological contacts with Luther; the moral honesty of their inner life won the Reformer's appreciation.[23]

A more rapid orientation of the Czech lands toward the European Reformation was induced only by the subsequent association of religious issues with a growing political crisis within aristocratic-burgher society that became evident in the middle of the sixteenth century. In 1526 the Czech Estates had elected as their king the Habsburg Ferdinand I (1526–64), brother of Emperor Charles V. An opponent of the Estates system, he consistently aimed to centralise ruling power and subordinated religious issues to this aim. His intention was to enforce a union of the Utraquist Church with the Roman Church, so that the struggle for the liberties of the Estates became identified with that for religious freedom.[24] However, the need for solidarity between the Czech and the German Reformations did not become a political necessity for the Estates until much later. Catholics still represented only a small minority, so that there was little hope of success for Ferdinand's policy of recatholicisation. From the late 1530s, Lutheranism made further progress in the minor provinces of the Czech Kingdom. A number of Silesian princes openly adhered to the Confession of Augsburg and granted protection to the illegal Lutheran churches in their territories. Out of consideration for neighbouring Saxony, Ferdinand could not justify his repressive intentions on religious grounds, but had to make them appear to be measures in defence of law and order allegedly threatened by the violent acts of radically oriented Lutherans. The Silesian Lutherans, in the same way as the lords in the German part of the Empire, demonstrated their loyalty by persecuting Anabaptists and exiling them from the country. Their only place of refuge became Moravia, where the local Estates were the first to understand religious freedom as a rightful privilege. Moravia thus became in the sixteenth century the most tolerant country, and one of the most important centres of the Anabaptist movement in the whole of Europe.[25] In Bohemia Lutheranism also spread vigorously at the foot of the Krušné Mountains, above all among the German population. It even acquired adherents inland and in Prague itself, at the very centre of the Utraquist Church. Historians have labelled these as 'neo-Utraquists'.

The preconditions for a successful defence of the Czech Reformation, that is, establishing closer contacts with the European Reformation and a unity of the local non-Catholic churches, came about only with difficulty. The Unity of the Brethren took initiatives in both directions: in 1535–6 it attempted to reach an understanding with the Utraquists, and at the same time sought support from Lutheran Saxony. The Latin translation of its Confession of Faith in 1538 (it had been published in Czech in 1535) was accompanied by an appreciative foreword by Luther. The Confession demonstrated that the Unity, under the leadership of its bishop John Augusta (d. 1572) was the most suitable basis not just for a mere reception of the German Reformation, but also for a creative dialogue with its fundamental ideas. The Unity accepted the teaching on *sola fide*, but remained faithful to the traditions of its Church by reminding its followers of the importance of good works, even though these were not necessary for salvation. John Augusta, a co-author of the Confession, attempted to demonstrate in another work that salvation derives from God's mercy, not as a result of sacraments administered by the priests, and he related the Lutheran notion of *sola gratia* to the teaching on predestination of John Hus. The attempt to overcome isolation at home was unsuccessful, however, since the Utraquist aristocracy failed to understand the need for unity and opposed it. For the same reasons, there was equal lack of success several years later for the neo-Utraquist project of establishing a national church to include the Unity, a church to be recognised by the ruler but headed by a bishop and subject to non-Catholic Estates. The assembly of Estates agreed in 1542 to the election of a bishop, but this election had to be confirmed by both king and pope. In practice, this meant returning to the idea of a union of Utraquism and the Roman Church in the spirit of a conservative interpretation of the Compactata, and therefore a defeat for the neo-Utraquists. The failure to legalise the Unity led it to the conclusion that it should seek closer ties with Protestants in the rest of Europe. This found expression in the establishment of contacts with the Strassburg reformer Martin Bucer and with John Calvin in Geneva.[26]

The inability of Utraquism to dissociate itself from its traditional image and from national exclusivity led logically to the passive attitude taken up by the Czech Estates towards the Schmalkaldic Wars waged by the Habsburgs against the German Lutherans in 1545–7. Only a minority, mostly noble adherents of the Unity, attempted to establish an active military alliance with Lutheran Saxony, but in vain. The half-heartedness of the first anti-Habsburg uprising of 1547, which was not supported by the Estates of Moravia, consequently led to its tragic defeat. Once subordinated to the king, those burghers who had most actively participated in the Reformation were now excluded from participation in the Estates, while the aristocracy, especially those noble adherents of the Unity, were punished with confiscations. The Unity was faced with such persecution that it had to transfer the seat of its activity to Moravia. The bridging of differences enforced on the non-Catholic camp in this situation was no easy matter. The persecution of the Unity, which the neo-Utraquists could not prevent (and some did wish to do so), led to its renewed isolation and to caution in the political activities of its aristocratic members. John Blahoslav (d. 1571) became spokesman for this current. Moreover, the progress of recatholicisation, which would have speeded up attempts at unity, was slowed by the incapability of local Catholics and the unwillingness of the Utraquists to submit to Rome as Ferdinand I demanded in 1549.[27]

The mid-1560s brought a number of events which considerably accelerated the further development of the Reformation in the Czech Kingdom, both advancing and complicating it. The legislation of Lutheranism in the Empire achieved by the Treaty of Augsburg, along with the recognition of the right of rulers to determine the religion of their subjects, brought about a new wave of Lutheran expansion in the Czech lands, in the hope that it could achieve legal recognition there, where imperial laws were not valid. On the other hand, the end of the defensive period of the Catholic Church and the beginning of its own reform provided Ferdinand with the prospect of leading Czech Catholicism out of its protracted crisis. In 1566 the Jesuits were invited to Prague, where they were to educate a new clergy dedicated to the reform programme, the basis of which had been laid at the third session of the Council of Trent (1562–3). Only there, after a delay of almost half a century, were the doctrinal grounds of Catholicism as confronted with Protestantism, defined and the principles of reform of the Church outlined. Ferdinand I did not succeed at the Council with a Catholic reform programme of his own, nor was he successful with his proposal of a joint Catholic–Utraquist archbishopric. Certainly, this was conceded in 1562, but only as an exclusively Catholic institution. The king's request for approval of the lay chalice was denied by the Council. Approval of this concession was given only in 1564 by Pius IV, when the importance of the concession had already been proved illusory. Ferdinand's plan to bring the Utraquists back into the fold of the Church broke down because of the unrelenting attitudes of Catholics already preparing an assault on heterodoxy.[28]

The old Utraquists supported by the king controlled the consistory, while neo-Utraquism was losing legal ground and found itself in a situation similar to that of the Lutherans or the Unity. The demand for a new legal basis presupposed the abrogation of the Compactata, which were a hindrance to further progress. A new religious law was to grant protection to all adherents of the Reformation. The neo-Utraquist Confession of 1562 adhered to the Hussite Confession of 1421, but also classified Lukáš of Prague among the authorities of the Czech Reformation, and it had already ignored the Compactata. The Unity's isolationism was still the main obstacle to unification. In 1560 the Unity established close contacts with Calvin, who was rightly aware of their theological affinities, paving the way for a gradual calvinisation. The Unity's Confession of 1567 (and a Latin version of 1573) represented a mediating attitude towards the most controversial points within contemporary Protestantism. However, it was evident that only the Confession of Augsburg in its melanchthonian interpretation (*invariata*), to which the Utraquists were inclined, would provide a suitable basis for unification. The first success of the as-yet informal non-Catholic front in Bohemia was the abrogation of the Compactata, which took place at the provincial diet of 1567. On the other hand, a neo-Utraquist attempt to have the Confession of Augsburg recognised for Bohemia by pleading that it had been authorised for Austria and by arguing on the grounds of the similarity between the Confession and the Utraquist creed, was rejected by Maximilian II (1564–76). That this occurred without opposition shows that religious freedom was not the foremost of the demands of the non-Catholic nobility. Progress was made when the Unity's nobles overcame the resistance of its clergy and began negotiations with Utraquist representatives about a common Confession to which the Lutherans could adhere, and within which the Unity could preserve its theological and organisational distinctness.

This gave rise in 1575 to the Czech Confession and to an accompanying Ecclesiastical Ordinance as a basis for the legalisation of non-Catholic creeds in Bohemia (in Moravia the local Estates determined their own means of resolving the religious issue). A commission of the Estates, consisting of six members each from the lords, knights and burghers, was entrusted with the drafting. The commission also invited the assistance of some theologians, namely certain professors from the University of Prague. The Unity's representative was to ensure that his Church's Confession was taken into account. It was thanks to him that individual articles did not include a condemnation of other doctrines, which thus precluded any explicit dissociation from Calvinism. The Czech Confession is more or less identical with the Confession of Augsburg of 1530, in its *invariata* version, and incorporates 56 per cent of its text, sometimes sticking to a literal version of the articles, but in an order better suited to the Unity's Confession. A third of the text of the latter was taken over, including the concept of Christian life and order as signs of the true church in which recourse to the secular power was rejected. A smaller section (11 per cent), although remarkable for its contents, was dedicated to the fundamental sources of the Czech Reformation. These were the Four Prague Articles of 1419, synodal resolutions from the period of incipient revolution in 1421, articles of 1524 responding to Lutheran stimuli, quotations from the writings of Hus, and theological views contained in old Czech hymns. The Czech Confession was conceived in such a way as to prove that 'the Confession of Augsburg merely brought to completion the struggle of the Czech Reformation since the time of Hus (Molnár). It is difficult to say whether there were tactical reasons for this, either to prevent resistance expected at the diet from the old Utraquists and from Catholics to 'innovations', or out of real conviction in the continuity of the Czech Reformation and its living tradition. Apparently both reasons played a part. According to the Ecclesiastical Ordinance there were to be fifteen Defenders, five from each Estate, at the head of the new ecclesiastical organisation. However, among the Defenders there were no members of the Unity, which was left with its own organisation, while the Lutherans in Bohemia were also supposed to have their own. The Ordinance was therefore valid only for the neo-Utraquists, whose clergy were placed under the control of regional superintendents. These were to convene every six months at Tábor to deal with the ongoing agenda of the Consistory, and there was to be an annual meeting of the Defenders to resolve major issues.[29]

The non-Catholic Estates did not achieve a complete victory on this occasion either. Maximilian II, on behalf of himself and his successor Rudolf II, authorised the Czech Confession and Ordinance only orally and as valid only for the aristocracy. The nobility did not protest in any way about the exclusion of the royal towns in which the king was overlord. This was a consequence of the principle *cuius regio, eius religio* gaining ground in Bohemia, a principle actually recognised by the provincial diet of 1585. Even so, with this regulation of ecclesiastical affairs the Czech Kingdom ranked among those countries with the most extensive religious freedom.

The Czech Confession provided a successful basis for overcoming antagonisms provoked by both the domestic situation and by the development of religious affairs more widely in Europe. The government tried in vain to exploit differences between the Unity and the Evangelicals, as the neo-Utraquists were increasingly called, and to breach their alliance. Until the end of the sixteenth century the Habsburg policy of recatholicisation had been hindered by the weakness of Czech Catholicism. Despite loud and militant propaganda fed by the papal nuncios and the Spanish envoys at the

Prague court of Rudolf II, the Roman Church held barely one-seventh of Bohemian parishes. Politically more important was a growing number of Catholics among the aristocracy (about a quarter in the early seventeenth century), who sought in conversion better prospects for a career at court. However, the greatest danger for the non-Catholic majority grew out of the increasingly irreconcilable conflicts within European Protestantism itself. The Utraquists increasingly sought Lutheran-style ordination at German universities, which by then mirrored the fragmentation of Lutheranism into several rival tendencies. The differences showed in Bohemia more in a variety of liturgies than in theology, which often led to conflicts. Within the framework of neo-Utraquism, a mediating position was favoured (although less so by theologians), which corresponded to the melanchthonian tendency in German Lutheranism and which was tolerant of the Unity. A smaller but more militant wing inclined to a rigid Lutheranism (Gnesio-Lutheranism in German terms) and interpreted the Czech Confession in the sense of the Formula of Concord. They found a response among the German population of Bohemia, as well as among the Czech aristocracy and clergy who had studied at Wittenberg or Leipzig. This tendency was prejudiced against the Unity, and because of the Unity's positive attitude towards Calvinism, denied it the right to profess the Czech Confession.

Closest to the Unity stood a tendency influenced by melanchthonian Calvinism (the Philippists), which had been rapidly disseminated in both Bohemia and Moravia. This variety of neo-Utraquism (the old Utraquist was heading for extinction) even influenced the development of the Unity. Its seniors tried to maintain close relations with the neo-Utraquist mediating tendency which was favourably inclined to the Unity and to remain independent of the main German currents, the Calvinists and the rigid Lutherans. After the defeat of the Philippists in Saxony, the Unity became more oriented towards west German and Swiss universities, which further reinforced the influence on it of Calvinism, especially among the younger generation, at the expense of the Unity's original doctrine. This shift was also reflected in the epochal new Czech translation of the Bible, based not on the Vulgate but on the original Hebrew and Greek, completed in 1593 and known as the Kralice Bible. It was also later reflected in a new edition of the Unity's Confession which appeared in Czech in 1607 and 1608, and in Latin in 1609 and 1612. Even then, however, the Unity did not fully yield to Calvinism, nor did it accept Calvin's doctrine of predestination.[30]

The reversal of power relationships in Bohemia in the early seventeenth century caused the non-Catholics to cling together again. A group of Catholic nobles educated by the Prague Jesuits took over, with the assistance of the papal nuncios, the most important administrative offices, especially the chancellery, and launched a sharp attack on adherents of the

Unity. The spectre of the Massacre of St Bartholomew not only frightened the aristocratic members, but also stirred up the entire Estates opposition. The dynastic conflict between Emperor Rudolf II and his brother Matthias in 1608–9 seemed to suit this cause most conveniently. The Moravian Estates supported Matthias and secured his approval of an article on religious freedom to be included in a declaration of the provincial diet. The Czech Estates, joined by the Silesian Estates, remained loyal to Rudolf and as recompense demanded that he give written recognition to the Czech Confession on 9 July 1609. Unlike 1575, religious freedom was also to apply to the towns and servile persons, while the enforcement of any other creed was prohibited. Further details were to be set out in an appended *Comparatio*. This law allowing religious freedom, which recognised the equality of the Catholic minority and the non-Catholic majority (at that time nine-tenths of the population) was almost unparalleled in contemporary Europe. On 20 August 1609, freedom for the Confession of Augsburg was also granted in Silesia. After Rudolf's abdication, his successor Matthias (1611–19) confirmed these documents in 1611.

The Czech Church of the Evangelicals and Brethren, entrusted to the protection of non-Catholic Defenders drawn from all three Estates (and who were even in control of the University of Prague), quickly spread to Moravia. The easing of external pressure contributed to greater internal differentiation, especially to the strengthening of the extreme wings, both the rigid Lutherans and the Calvinists. Nonetheless, the Czech Confession did not lose its unifying force. Remarkably, a yearning for a direct union of the Evangelicals and the Unity arose among the younger generation, especially in Moravia, but the Church was not to enjoy any further development under the Czech Confession.

Some vague points in interpretation of the charter of religious freedom were seized upon by the Habsburg government as an excuse for its violation, especially in 1617 by the militant Archduke Ferdinand of Styria, who succeeded Matthias in 1619 as Ferdinand II (1619–37). The reaction was an explosion of anti-Habsburg feeling and the rebellion of 1618–20, which formed the prologue to the Thirty Years' War. The deposition of the Habsburgs and the election as Czech king of Frederick of the Palatinate, son-in-law of James I of England and leader of the German Calvinists, temporarily boosted the adherents of this creed. There was a widespread introduction of a more simplified form of worship, but an independent Reformed Church never emerged in the Czech lands. The one constitution adopted in 1619 aimed to strengthen religious toleration further in the light of past political experience. The Jesuits were expelled from the country, and Catholics who refused to comply with the new constitution were disbarred from public office. But before this constitution could be implemented the rebellion was crushed in 1620 by the Battle of the White Mountain, and the reign of the Habsburg reinstated in the Czech Kingdom until 1918.[31]

Thereafter nothing stood in the way of consistent recatholicisation. Only Silesia was permitted the freedom of the Confession of Augsburg, out of gratitude to Lutheran Saxony, which as a Habsburg ally had contributed to the defeat of the rebellion. As a reward Saxony was also allowed to annex Upper and Lower Lusatia. In Bohemia in 1627 and in Moravia in 1628 the Estates were ordered either to convert to Catholicism or to leave the country. Hundreds of aristocrats and several thousand burgher families emigrated, and despite a prohibition numerous other subjects also joined the exodus. The remaining population were subjected to forcible recatholicisation. Only a small number persisted in adhering to the Reformation on peril of death. Once abroad, the Czech Evangelicals merged with the followers of the Confession of Augsburg. The Unity preserved an independent religious existence until 1656 in Lešno in Poland, where even its last senior, Jan Amos Komenský (Comenius, d. 1670) was forced to take refuge. After Lešno was burned down, the members of the Unity dispersed, especially to Hungary, where they merged with the Reformed Church.[32] In Comenius, who eventually moved on to Amsterdam, the development of the Unity came to an end. In a number of his writings from the last years of his life there can be found a critical account of the development of the Czech and European Reformations. In the Unity he saw an indirect successor to a Waldensian Reformation and a direct one to Hus's Reformation. It went beyond them, however, in that its religious life was realised without the protection of the secular power. The Brethren's ecclesiastical order was therefore considered by Comenius to be exemplary. He greatly revered Lukáš of Prague, whose distinction between things 'substantial' and 'instrumental' he followed. Comenius was critical of the European Reformation. Within the eschatological context of his own thought, he considered its effects to be only relative. He appreciated Luther's impulse to reforming activity as another stage of recognition of the divine will, but held that Luther's followers did not advance the work any further and that it remained incomplete because of their mutual intolerance. He saw a message from his own church for future generations in warning against theological speculation, against emptying the Gospel by even the most expressive slogans such as *sola fide* or *sola gratia*, and in an appeal to acknowledge Christ's rights as King.[33]

Comenius's reflections during the last years of his life pose a question about the place of the Czech Reformation in the cycle of European Reformations. The opinion of an older generation of historians, still held here and there by some theologians, that it was only a 'forerunner' of the Reformation of the sixteenth century, or slightly better, a 'proto-Reformation', cannot hold water today. In its religious content, its ecclesiastical organisation and its far-reaching social consequences, it fulfilled the same tasks as the sixteenth century Reformation, albeit for a hundred years only within national boundaries. More recent Czech research such as that by Molnár or Macek holds that the Czech Reformation can be understood as the first Reformation and that of the sixteenth century as the second. The Czech Reformation was not, of course, the only representative of the first Reformation, but thanks to the Hussite revolution it acquired within its own framework a more persistent and clear-cut representation in comparison with Waldensians, Wyclifism and Lollardy. The relationship between the two Reformations was neither chronological nor evolutionary in the sense that the second was of a higher type that transcended the first. An opinion that seems closer to the nub of the problem holds that each Reformation was different, that they differ fundamentally in their typology, so that it seems more relevant to speak of a twofold Reformation.

The cornerstone of the first Reformation was the authoritative *lex Christi* as a binding norm for the church and all believers, including secular lords. It was mainly derived from a new interpretation of the Sermon on the Mount (Matthew 5–7) and from the eschatological prospect of the coming of Christ's Kingdom. Calvinism was anticipated here in a number of points. The solemnity and the anxious awe of the divine law aimed at a transformation of faith into morality and of Christ into an unrelenting judge. The expectation of the 'end of time', with its leaning towards a prophetic vision and the conviction of the continuing revelation of the Holy Spirit weakened the rightful obligation of the Gospel. The second Reformation, inspired above all by a revealing interpretation of the Pauline Epistles, appreciated more the liberating message of the Gospel that provided new guarantes of individual salvation. On grounds different from those of the first Reformation, it rejected the claims of the institutional church to be the sole instrument of salvation. The two Reformations also differed in their social backgrounds and responses: whereas the first Reformation was more popular, non-conformist and, in its Czech form, revolutionary, the second led to an entirely conservative attitude.

In the sixteenth century both Reformations were confronted one with another, with mixed results. Whereas Waldensianism was integrated into the various currents of the so-called radical Reformation (Anabaptism and similar forms) and dissociated itself from the German and Swiss Reformations, the Czech Reformation in both its varieties – Utraquism and the Unity of the Brethren – was capable of contributing to the second Reformation and of developing alongside it. However, it is not possible to overlook the strong political motives that played their part here. If Utraquism gradually accepted Lutheranism, retaining only the consciousness of its own

historical roots, the Unity of the Brethren, even though it also acknowledged the general points of departure of the second Reformation as the
culmination of its own independent development (Lukáš of Prague), established a basis for dialogue even with Reformed Protestantism, founded on
old Taborite–Waldensianism principles. Moreover, it was capable of preserving that part of its inheritance which, according to Comenius's prophetic words, could hopefully make its contribution where the second
Reformation had left the work unfinished.[34]

There was one further possibility of taking up the fractured religious
tradition of the Reformation, but on the completely different religious basis
of the Enlightenment, thanks to the Patent of Toleration issued by Joseph
II in 1781. It did not renew the church of the Czech Confession, but
recognised only the creeds of the Confession of Augsburg and of the
Helvetic Confession or Reformed faith, not the Unity of the Brethren. It
was not until ordinances of 1848 and 1861 that full freedom and self-govern-
ment was allowed to both these churches, so that they could profess the
legacy of the Unity of the Brethren and republish its Confession. The Czech
Confession was revived only in the free Czechoslovak Republic in 1918,
when the sometime church of the Confession of Augsburg and the
Reformed Church merged and the Evangelical Church of the Czech Brethren came into being.[35]

## NOTES

1 A basic bibliography can be found in J. K. Zeman, *The Hussite Movement and the Reformation in Bohemia, Moravia and Slovakia (1350–1650)* (Ann Arbor, Mich., 1977), A. Molnár, 'Böhmische Reformation', in *Tschechischer Ökumenismus. Historische Entwicklung* (Prague, 1977), pp. 81–144 and more comprehensively in R. Říčan, *Das Reich Gottes in den böhmischen Ländern. Geschichte des tschechischen Protestantismus* (Stuttgart, 1957).

2 Discussed more recently in F. Šmahel, 'Krise und Revolution. Die Socialfrage im vorhussitischen Böhmen', in *Europe 1400. Die Krise des Spätmittelalters*, ed., F. Seibt and W. Eberhard (Stuttgart, 1984), pp. 65–81, *La révolution hussite, una anomalie historique?* (Paris, 1985) and *Husitská revoluce*, vol. I, *Kořeny českéreformace* (Prague, 1990).

3 The problem of the relationship between crisis and revolution, and the character of the Hussite revolution (an 'early bourgeois' revolution, a 'revolution of the Estates', a 'revolution before the revolutions') is discussed in E. Werner, 'Die hussitische Revolution. Revolutionsbegriff und Revolutionsergebnis im Spiegel marxistischer, insonderheit tschechoslovakischer Forschungen', *Sitzungsberichte des Sächsischen Akademie der Wissenschaft zu Leipzig*, Phil.-Hist.Klasse, vol. 129/1 (Berlin, 1989). See also R. R. Betts, 'The Place of the Czech Reformation in the History of Europe', *Slavonic and East Europe Review*, 25 (1947), pp. 373–90, F. Seibt, *Hussitica. Zur Struktur einer Revolution* (Cologne-Graza,

1965) and *Revolution in Europa. Ursprung und Wege innerer Gewalt* (Munich, 1984), H. Kaminsky, *A History of the Hussite Revolution* (Berkeley, 1967), R. Kalivoda, *Revolution und Ideologie. Der Hussitismus* (Cologne-Vienna, 1976) and J. Macek, *Jean Hus et les traditiones hussites* (Paris, 1973) – the relationship of Reformation and revolution discussed in the last item on pp. 204–8.

4 On Hus's predecessors, Říčan, *Das Reich Gottes*, pp. 21–86; their eschatology in more detail in A. Molnár, 'Die eschatologische Hoffnung der böhmischen Reformation', in *Von Reformation zum Morgen* (Leipzig, 1959), pp. 59–187 and 'L'évolution de la théologie hussite', *Revue d'histoire et de la philosophie religieuse* (1963), pp. 133–71.

5 On the interrelations of the works of Wyclif and Hus, see particularly Kaminsky, *The Hussite Revolution* and Kalivoda, *Revolution und Ideologie*.

6 On Hus, see the works mentioned in notes 2–3, basic information only in Říčan, *Das Reich Gottes*, pp. 27–35. The most detailed biography is P. Vooght, *L'héresie de Jean Hus*, 2nd edn, 2 vols. (Louvain, 1975), an attempt to prove Hus's catholicity; a Protestant interpretation in M. Spinka, *John Hus. A Biography* (Princeton, 1968), and A. Molnár, *Jean Hus témoin de la verité* (Paris, 1978).

7 The most detailed discussion so far in P. Vooght, *Jacobelle de Stříbo (1429), premier théologian du hussitisme* (Louvain, 1972).

8 The Hussite doctrine of the chalice in A. Molnár, 'Aspects de la continuité de pensée dans la Réforme tchèque', *Communio viatorum*, 15 (1972), pp. 111–24.

9 For Waldensianism, A. Molnár 'Les Vaudois et la Réforme tchèqué, *Bolletino della Società di Studi Valdesi*, 103 (1958), pp. 37–51 and *Les Vaudois au Moyen Age* (Turin, 1974).

10 The origins of Tábor and the period of chiliasm comprehensively discussed in Kaminsky, *The Hussite Revolution* and Kalidova, *Revolution und Ideologie*; the most recent survey in Macek, *Jean Hus*, pp. 117–58; on the theology, Molnár, 'La théologie hussite' and *I Taboriti. Avanguardia della rivoluzione hussita (sec. XV.). Gli scritti essenziali* (Turin, 1986).

11 Mikuláš Biskupec in A. Molnár, 'Réformation et Révolution. Le cas du sénior taborite Nicolas Biskupec de Pelhřimov', *Communio viatorum*, 13 (1970), pp. 137–53; a critical edition of the 'Confessio Taboritarum', in A. Molnár and R. Cegna, *Confessio Taboritarum*, Fonti della Storia d'Italia, Nr 105 (Rome, 1983).

12 These were: (1) the free unhindered preaching of the Gospel to everyone everywhere; (2) communion under both kinds for all Christians; (3) priests and monks to be divested of property and worldly rule; (4) public punishment of mortal sins, without respect to class or status. Interpretations of the articles in the works mentioned in notes 2–3.

13 The Basel negotiations in E. F. Jacob, 'The Bohemians at the Council of Basel 1433', in *Prague Essays*, ed. R. W. Setton-Watson (Oxford, 1949), pp. 81–123 and P. Vooght, 'La confontation des thèses hussites et romaines au concile de bâle', *Recherches de théologie ancienne et médievale*, 37 (1970), pp. 100–20, the outcome in O. Odložilík, *The Hussite King, Bohemia in European Affairs 1440–1471* (New Brunswick, N.J., 1965), pp. 4–18 and Macek, *Jean Hus*, pp. 178–91.

14 The capitulation of Tábor and the abolition of the Compactata discussed in Odložilík, *The Hussite King*, pp. 64ff. and 132ff., the political conditions of 'double creed' in A. Skýbová, 'Politische Aspekte der Existenz zweier Konfess-

ionen im Königreich Böhmen bis zum Anfang des 17. Jahrhunderts', in *Martin Luther. Leben – Werk – Wirkung* (Berlin, 1983), pp. 463–80.

15 For the religious peace of 1485, see note Odložilík, *The Hussite King*, pp. 64ff. and 132ff.

16 The character of the Utraquist Church discussed in F. G. Heymann, 'The Hussite Utraquist Church in the Fifteenth Century', *Archiv für Reformations geschichte*, 52 (1961) pp. 1–16.

17 The election of John Rokycana in Odložilík, *The Hussite King*, pp. 11ff., his personality in F. G. Heymann, 'John Rokycana. Church Reformer between Hus and Luther', *Church History*, 28 (1959) pp. 240–80.

18 See A. Salač, 'Constantinople et Prague en 1452 (Pourparlers en vue d'une Union des Eglises)', *Rozpravy ČSAV*, 68 (serie spol. ved. fasc.11, Prague, 1958) and Odložilík, *The Hussite King*, pp. 61–5.

19 The origins of the Unity of the Czech Brethren discussed briefly in Říčan, *Das Reich Gottes*, pp.a 68–86, in more detail in J. Th. Müller, *Geschichte der böhmischen Brüder*, 3 vols. (Herrnhut, 1922–31) and most recently in R. Říčan, *Die böhmischen Brüder, ihr Ursprung und ihre Geschichte* (Berlin, 1961) – the concluding chapter on the theology, pp. 283–321, written by Molnár. A brief account of Peter of Chelčice in Molnár, 'La théologie hussite', pp. 159–71, and a translation of selected sections of his works in E. Peschke, *Die Theologie der böhmischen Brüder in der Frühzeit*, 2 vols. (Stuttgart, 1935–40) and R. Kalivoda and A. Kolesnyk, *Das hussitische Denken im Lichte seiner Quellen* (Berlin, 1969); see also H. Kaminsky, 'Petr Chelčický's Place in the Hussite Left', in *Studies in Medieval and Renaissance History*, vol. I, ed. W. Bronsky (Lincoln, Nebr., 1964), pp. 107–36.

20 Unlike earlier historiography, which held the view that Utraquism regenerated into neo-Utraquism under Luther's influence, W. Eberhard, *Konfessionbildung und Stände im Böhmen 1478–1530* (Munich/Vienna, 1981) proved that the reversal had already been striven for earlier by those he called 'left Utraquists', whose origins he described in detail.

21 For the further developments of the Unity, besides the works mentioned in note 19, see on Lukáš of Prague, A. Molnár, 'Esquisse de la théologie de Comenius', *Revue d'histoire et de la philosophie religieuse* (1949), pp. 107–31, 'Luc de Prague édifiant la communauté, 1498–1502', *Communio viatorum*, 5 (1962), pp. 189–200, 'La théologie hussite'; a fundamental work is A. Molnár, *Bratr Lukáš, bohoslovec Jednoty* (Prague, 1948).

22 From a number of works on Luther's links with the Czech Reformation, see S. H. Thompson, 'Luther and Bohemia', *Archiv für Reformationsgeschichte*, 44 (1953), pp. 160–81, Říčan, *Das Reich Gottes*, pp. 87–106; with the Unity of Brethren, F. M. Bartoš, 'Das Auftreten Luthers und die Unität der Böhmischen Bruder', *Archiv für Reformations geschichte*, 31 (1934) pp. 103–20 and 'L'Unité des Frères et le Réformateurs', *Communio viatorum*, 21 (1978), pp. 29–48, and A. Molnár, 'Luther und die Böhmischen Bruder', *Communio viatorum*, 24 (1981), pp. 47–67. Through the Unity of Brethren Luther became acquainted with evidence that St Peter had never been in Rome, see A. J. Lamping, *Ulricus Velenus (Oldřich Velenský) and His Treatise against the Papacy* (Leiden, 1976), supplemented by A. Molnár in *Zeitschrift für Kirchengeschichte*, 89 (1978), pp. 209–14.

23 A detailed account of the early reception of Lutheranism can be found in

Eberhard, *Konfessionbildung und Stände im Böhmen*; on the Unity of the Brethren at this time, Říčan, *Die böhmischen Brüder*, pp. 94–100, its doctrines also in P. Brock, *The Political and Social Doctrines of the Unity of Czech Brethren in the Fifteenth and Early Sixteenth Centuries* (South Gravenhage, 1957), supplemented with revisions by A. Molnár in *Revue d'histoire et de philosophie religieuse* (1959), pp. 375–84.

24 The nature of the Habsburg reign discussed in Fr. Kavka, 'Die Habsburger und der böhmische Staat bis zur Mitte des 18. Jahrhunderts', *Historica* (Prague, 1964), vol. VIII, pp. 35–64, the recatholicisation scheme in Fr. Kavka and A. Skýbová, *Husitský epilog na koncilu tridentském a původní koncepce habsburské rekatolizace Čech* (Prague, 1969).

25 See F. Hrubý, *Die Wiedertäufer in Mähren* (Leipzig, 1935).

26 The Lutherian orientation of the Unity discussed in Říčan, *Die böhmischen Brüder*; links with the Swiss Reformation in A. Molnár, 'La correspondence entre les Frères Tchèques et Bucer', *Revue d'histoire et de la philosophie religieuse* (1951), pp. 102–56.

27 A new view of the anti-Habsburg rising of 1547 and his attitude to the German Reformation is found in W. Eberhard, *Monarchie und Widerstand* (Munich/ Vienna, 1985); the consequences for the Unity in Říčan, *Die böhmischen Brüder*, pp. 127–46. For the Reformation as a political ideology of the Estates opposition, K. J. Dillon, *King and Estates in the Bohemian Lands 1526–1564* (Brussels, 1976) and J. Pánek, 'Das Ständewesen und die Gesellschaft in den böhmischen Ländern (1526–1620)', *Historica*, vol. XXV (Prague, 1985).

28 See note 24.

29 Developments leading to the Czech Confession discussed comprehensively in Říčan, *Die böhmischen Brüder*, pp. 170–7; its significance in A. Molnár, 'The Czech Confession of 1575, *Communio viatorum*, 16 (1973), pp. 241–7. A fundamental work is F. Hrejsa, *Česká konfese* (Prague, 1912).

30 Discussed comprehensively in Říčan, *Die böhmischen Brüder*, pp. 178–89; and in F. Hrubý, *Etudiants tchèques aux écoles protestantes de l'Europe occidentale à fin du 16ᵉ – et la début de 17ᵉ siècle* (Brno, 1970).

31 See Říčan, *Das Reich Gottes*, pp. 127–34, Kavka, 'Die Habsburger und der böhmische Staat', Skýbová, 'Politische Aspekte' and Pánek, 'Das Ständewesen und die Gesellschaft'.

32 See Říčan, *Das Reich Gottes*, pp. 125–48. In the years 1722–77, on the estates of Count Zinzendorf in Herrnhut in Saxony, emigrants from northern Moravia renewed the Unity of the Brethren, which combined certain traditions of the old Unity (but not including the Confession) with pietism. A great missionary activity ensued, and under the name of the Moravian Brethren they crossed the Atlantic to the United States, where they are still active.

33 On Comenius's theology, see Molnár, 'La théologie de Comenius' and 'La théologie hussite'.

34 On the question of the 'first' and 'second' Reformations, see Molnár, 'La théologie hussite', pp. 170ff. and Macek, *Jean Hus*, pp. 306–8.

35 For the fate of the Reformation after 1781, see Říčan, *Das Reich Gottes*, pp. 149–206.

# 9 Hungary

*Katalin Peter*

The Reformation reached Hungary at a time of fairly general interest in the affairs of the Church, whether religious or temporal. The many beautiful tryptych altarpieces dating from the first two decades of the sixteenth century are the most conspicuous reminders of this interest. Nowadays they are cherished treasures preserved in museums, but they were originally shrines of religious worship erected in church buildings all over the country. Commissioned by lay patrons or by guilds, their great number and rich adornment attests the generosity of secular social strata towards the Church. At the same time, by depicting sacred subjects in everyday surroundings, these altarpieces indicate the laity's desire to see themselves as participants in the mystery experienced when attending religious worship. Although the *devotio moderna* did not establish any communities in Hungary, the demand for a more personalised religious experience was apparent. Whole families took lay orders with the aim of sharing in 'the abundance of consolation and attaining the rewards of eternal life more comfortably and more fortunately', as one prior put it in 1521.

The all-embracing interest in personal religiosity is also witnessed by women's lively concern with it. Magnates' wives founded cloisters or donated chasubles, while well-educated nuns such as Lea Ráskai in the 1510s and 1520s composed lives of the saints and copied them into codices for use in nunneries. The cult of the three suffering mothers (the blessed Virgin, St Anne and St Elizabeth), which developed around the turn of the century is as characteristic in this regard as is the fact that the first translation of the Bible to go through the press, the Epistles of St Paul in Hungarian, translated by the eminent humanist scholar Benedek Komjáti in 1533, was made for Countess Katalin Frangepán.

As to the lower strata of society, a peasant revolt in 1514 provides the most striking proof of their deep religious sentiment. The rising actually began in response to the crusade proclaimed by Pope Leo X with a plenary remission of all sins and reconciliation with the Most High. Acting on the pope's words, large crowds gathered for the crusade. When ordered to return home by their frightened lords, they turned against the higher authorities, although the religious spirit of the movement was undiminished. The enemy was now the 'infidel' nobility, and their leader, Geörgy Dózsa, threatened those indifferent to the war with 'the punishment of excommunication and eternal damnation'. By holding out the prospect of influencing a person's fate in the afterlife, the rising made clear how remote the concerns and values of the laity were from those of the ecclesiastical authorities. The latter identified with the secular lords, and the leaders of the suppressed revolt were done to death in body and soul. Their human husk was tortured beyond endurance and their eternal soul was denied the consolation of the Last Sacrament. With this latter gesture, the rebels were officially robbed of their Christianity. However, many contemporaries, whether they had taken part in the rising or not, revered them as martyrs of the church.

The divergence of values was the most deep-rooted problem in the relationship between the official Roman Church and its adherents on the eve of the Reformation. The religion represented by the Church was divorced from the religiosity as lived by the people. Consequently, the Reformation was more a matter of rejection of Roman Catholicism than a struggle against it, and this influenced the decisive role Protestantism played in shaping national culture and vernacular culture.

The dissemination of evangelical teaching began outside the Church, although some of its representatives were willing to meet the laity's demands for more personalised religious experience. Through sermons directed to the intellectual levels of the common people, through voicing their social grievances, and through other means, many parish priests and members of the regular clergy endeavoured to bridge the gulf between the Church and the laity. However, none of these churchmen roughly up to the 1530s took the decisive step of breaking openly with official doctrine. The first preachers of Christian freedom in Hungary were lay people, both men and women. At the very beginning, the new ideas were discussed informally, in places where people were accustomed to meet socially. In many inns 'those who could do so read Lutheran writings' while others listened, as some documents describe the situation. Readers and listeners must have grasped something of this: for example, in a wine cellar there was talk of whether a God who had no hands and feet of his own could have eyes and ears. Probably those engaged in this conversation were musing on Luther's *Sermon on Good Works* which they had either read or heard expounded by someone else. But evangelically minded congregations were also established in the early 1520s. They were congregations in the sense used in Scripture, 'where two or three are gathered together in my name', for these gatherings were not held in church buildings; they worshipped outside, 'under the tree', somewhere 'before the town gates', or in the house of some family. As to the form taken by such gatherings, there is as yet no clear evidence, except that the preachers were 'lay people of both sexes'.

That ordinary men and women should adopt the role of true preachers of the Word was obviously an expression of belief in the priesthood of all believers. Whether this meant a conscious acceptance of Luther's doctrine or was a matter of sheer instinct akin to that of the medieval movements of heresy is a problem for further research. Nevertheless, it shows the great attraction of the Reformation for the common people: evangelical teaching liberated the laity from the burden of approaching the Almighty through intermediaries. Even adherence to that fundamental tenet of the Reformation, 'the just shall live by faith', was in Hungary, unlike in most other places abroad, more a consequence of belief in equality before God than a result of anxiety about the imminence of death. Fear of the Last Judgment was not a feeling one could say was very widespread in Hungary at the turn of the century. The appeal of pilgrimages was modest and saints' relics were not the object of obsessive collecting. But with lay preaching of the Word there followed a break not only with the official form of worship, but also with the entire way of life sanctioned by the Church. 'They scorn ecclesiastical and secular laws equally', commented a high ecclesiastical figure in northern Hungary in 1524. He regarded the 'followers of evangelical doctrine' without hatred, but was deeply concerned for the Roman Church and predicted social unrest and discontent as a result of Lutheran teaching.

Marked symptoms of social unrest, with a peasant rising only recently suppressed and a superficial peace enforced between landowners and tenants, were certainly evident at the time the Reformation reached Hungary. However, the diffusion of Lutheranism did not lead to social disturbance. There was no form of peasant war or rebellion of any kind associated with it. This lack of predicted consequences is striking in comparison with the experience of other lands and was due to three sets of circumstances: the Ottoman conquests in the region; the impact in Hungary of economic conjuncture in the West; and the attitudes of secular authorities towards the Reformation.

The Ottoman incursions eased social tensions in as far as they impinged on all social strata, even the dominant. The Ottomans had taken Belgrade in 1520, the most important border fortress of the country, and in 1526 at the Battle of Mohács, Sultan Suleiman the Magnificent gained a decisive victory over the Hungarian army. Fifteen years later he took Buda and divided the country into three parts. In the face of such events, many penalties imposed on the lower social strata after the Dózsa rising had to be revoked, since their military support was essential. The constant warfare caused a heavy shortage of manpower, so that many 'liberties', that is exemptions from the burdens imposed on their dependents, were granted by many lords to attract people to their estates. Thus, those who survived the incessant warfare experienced an easing of their social burdens and even lived to see economic affluence. Western demands for agricultural produce reached Hungary at the same time as the Ottoman incursions. Throughout the entire sixteenth century, it was possible to export as many cattle and as much wine or grain as could be raised or produced in protected areas and could be spared from the wars, perhaps in the intervals between bouts of armed conflict. Even the poorest parish was extremely rich by later standards. Gáspár Károlyi, the eminent Calvinist churchman, reprimanded the 'princes' in 1592, saying that they acquired gold and silver, houses and plough-land by 'opening their gorges [to eat up] the poor man', implying that there was considerable wealth to be appropriated. There were not many times in Hungarian history when the possession of wealth of this kind was one of the characteristics of 'the poor'.

It seems odd to say so, but from one point of view the most difficult moments at this time were actually experienced by the supreme temporal authority. The kings had struggled since the 1490s without any real royal prestige. The last king for centuries to rule over an undivided country, Louis II Jagellon (1508–26), was a sympathiser of religious reform; nevertheless, when the magnates sought a scapegoat for the abysmal neglect of military preparedness and found one in the 'foreign Lutheran rot', he had to comply. Three laws were passed against Lutheranism in 1523 and 1525, with the grave consequences that many books and persons were burnt at the stake. However, history put an abrupt end to that trend: Louis fell in battle at Mohács in 1526, and two rival kings were elected that same year to succeed him, neither of whom could afford to alienate prospective supporters on religious grounds. The rivals were János Zapolyai, a second-generation magnate, and the Habsburg archduke Ferdinand, both of whom commenced their reigns simultaneously in 1526. Equally simultaneous were their wars against each other, although Ottoman assaults from time to time brought variation to this monotony. Although both kings remained faithful to the Roman Church, they took care not to offend their evangelically minded subjects.

Religious heterodoxy appeared more urgently on the agenda only in the 1530s, as many lay patrons of church benefices began to adopt evangelical convictions and allowed congregations under lay preachers to occupy church buildings. Some of these lay patrons were the same lords who not so very long ago had voted or lobbied for laws against the Lutherans. The sincerity of their change of opinion cannot, however, be challenged without closer examination. Many magnates were sincerely concerned about how to live a religious life. For example, in 1535 Ferenc Révay, a magnate holding high office, turned to Luther himself to resolve his doubts about the

Communion. Some lords corresponded with Melanchthon on matters of conscience, while Countess Orsolya Kanizsai used phrases from Calvin in letters to her husband, so that she must have been well acquainted with that Reformer's works. In any case, it was not by chance that the lower secular authorities began to air their Lutheran convictions exactly in the 1530s. A decisive moment was undoubtedly the presentation of the common Confession of Faith by the Protestant princes in Augsburg in 1530. This event had no direct bearing on Hungary, but by consolidating the status of the Protestant Estates in Germany, it effectively negated the imperial ban on Lutheranism and made membership of this new denomination defensible.

That many had avoided at least open commitment to evangelical doctrines as long as they seemed to stand for heresy was characteristic of relations between the Protestant Estates and the Catholic rulers of Hungary. There were many points of conflict, such as what policies to pursue towards the Ottomans, over the incomes from the mines and on various other subjects, but the enmity was open and the problems were discussed at the Diet. However, the political adversaries only on very rare occasions resorted to religious arguments. The Estates were not faced with a single ruler, although the sultans can be left out of consideration here since the nobility had fled from Ottoman-occupied territory, leaving their tenants to their fate. The Estates thus had to deal only with the rulers of the two unoccupied parts of the country. Once the Estates had lined their pockets from one side, they were able throughout the sixteenth century to turn to the other. Thus, Hungarian Protestantism, which was later to be renowned throughout Europe as the defender of national liberty, did not for the time being get mixed up with politics. The spread of Protestantism had other, social reasons.

When the lower secular authorities began to allow evangelical congregations to take over church buildings for worship in the 1530s, they were prompted by a desire to come to terms with the common people. The congregations moved into the churches, which they then turned into evangelical parishes, mostly under the guidance of lay ministers. As late as 1548, a law was enacted against them and its wording shows clearly that certain authorities accept the lay preachers as official parish priests: 'They do not shrink from executing the office of preachers [assisted by] the obduracy of many lords and nobles'. In other words, the lay patrons had joined their tenants in evangelical worship.

That lay patrons joined evangelical congregations had many consequences, the most obvious of which was that women disappeared from the ranks of the preachers. There is no shred of evidence that women celebrated services inside church buildings, and we know nothing about their further fate. In Hungary a ministry of deaconesses was established relatively late, so that the women preachers of the early Reformation could not even take refuge there. Since the Protestant Churches in Hungary, with the characteristic gesture of the early evangelical movement, also repudiated monasticism, it was in the first instance women of lower social status who were disadvantaged by the development of the Reformation in the 1530s. Female lay patrons of churches remained unaffected by the changes, for if they were heiresses with full legal rights, women had the same standing as their male counterparts.

Another consequence of the intervention of lay patrons in the life of evangelical congregations was to single out and repudiate Anabaptists. These have not been mentioned here earlier because it is far from certain whether their presence in the country was due to the Reformation or to the influence of Hussitism. The only undoubted fact is that lay preachers in the 1520s were able to proclaim the salvation only of the twice-born virtually as freely as any other unordained preachers, but in the 1530s they began to be persecuted by the landowners. At the same time, priests ordained within the Roman Church and disaffected monks began openly to reveal their evangelical convictions. Previously they had been so cautious that even the ecclesiastical authorities could not be sure whether they preached official doctrine or that condemned by the Roman Church. Experts, the best-known of whom was Brother Gergely Szegedi, had travelled from one end of the country to the other to seek them out. After 1530 those clergy who wished to break with the Roman Church, mostly Franciscan mendicants, could now find shelter with Protestant lay patrons, and they became the most fervent propagators of the new faith. Mátyás Dévai Biró and Mihály Sztárai were two of the most famous.

Protestantism was on the verge of forming an organised church by the time the Sultan divided the country into three parts in 1541. The first local synod in which the Protestant clergy on a noble estate signed a Confession of Faith (containing the tenets of the Confession of Augsburg) was convened by a high-born patroness, Anna Báthory, only four years later. Gatherings of a similar kind took place on large estates and among groups of towns, and these synods everywhere became the units of church organisation; the same development occurred in all three parts of the country. The basic similarity in ecclesiastical and cultural processes is obvious, despite the fact that in most other respects the three parts of the country cannot be compared. The Sultan had left the western territories in the hands of King Ferdinand, and here the rule of kings elected from the Habsburg dynasty continued. The eastern part was handed over to the infant son of John I Zapolyai, under the regency of the dowager queen Isabel. From this territory there emerged the principality of Transylvania, a dependency of the Ottomans but under national rulers. Eventually, a third part stretching from north of Buda to the

Adriatic and the lower Danube was gradually incorporated into the Ottoman territories.

None of the rulers did anything to further the cause of Protestantism, nor did they turn against the Roman Church. Nonetheless, by the 1570s it had lost approximately 90 per cent of its adherents. That is, between 80 and 85 per cent of the Christian population were Protestant, with the Greek Orthodox Church and a few Jews accounting for a tiny minority. Thus, Hungary actually became a Protestant country without a nudge from its rulers. There was no royal Act of Supremacy or anything similar proclaiming the Reformation.

Calvinism appeared in all three parts of the country at the same time. Márton Kálmáncsehi Sánta in the 1540s was the first openly Calvinist preacher. He began as a canon in Transylvania, converted there and worked afterwards in the Ottoman territory as well as in the Kingdom. It was the same with the other great Calvinist Reformer, István Szegedi Kis, somewhat later. He also worked in all three parts of the country, but spent most of his working life under the Ottomans. These figures were the founders of Calvinism in Hungary, or rather of the 'Reformed Church' called Calvinist, since its doctrine consisted of a compilation of tenets derived primarily from the works of various Swiss Reformers. It is a telling fact in this regard that the ordinances of the Hungarian Reformed Church were sanctioned, so to speak, by Heinrich Bullinger in 1559. By that time the Calvinists had the same episcopal organisation in all three parts of the country as the Lutherans.

Unitarianism, which was propagated in the 1560s, was the only creed confined to Transylvania. The most important figure shaping antitrinitarian ideas here was Ferenc Dávid. His life was a spiritual odyssey, commencing with Catholicism, going through all the Protestant denominations and ending in Sabbatarianism. For this last belief, Dávid was arrested and died in prison in 1579. His trial represented a rejection of the religious toleration for which Transylvania was famous throughout Europe.

In the persecution of witches, however, there was not the least dissimilarity between the three parts of the country. This peculiar companion of the Reformation had already made an appearance in the 1520s, but it reached its first peak of activity in the middle years of the century. That means that people became increasingly embarrassed by actions which they had earlier regarded as unexceptionable. Later the notion of sorcery was changed, but witches in sixteenth-century Hungary were not usually intimidating. They spoke to the trees or to animals, they gazed into the waters and something happened, more often than not beneficial. The only problem was that there seemed to be no tangible connection between the action and the effect. Instead of consigning such matters to many other inexplicable events, the new rational spirit looked for an explanation. It was found in diabolical inspiration; but it could also be godly: the judges had to decide.

The witches themselves, at least at the beginning, were surprised. They could not understand what was alleged to be wrong with them. Their reactions show that they performed, by the standards of popular belief, quite matter-of-fact operations. The society, or a great part of it, had however lost its belief in mysterious contacts with nature. The most important source on this subject in Hungary, the Debrecen Confession of 1562, drafted by the Calvinist bishop Péter Melius Juhász, indicates that the change in feeling was not prompted by the magistrates. Nonetheless, they utilised it and did not refute unreasonable connections, but rather gave backing to the witchhunt. Even the Ottomans regarded this peculiarly Christian craze with understanding. In return for substantial sums, the inhabitants under their rule instigated as many trials for witchcraft as the citizens in the other parts of the country.

Roman Catholicism, confronted by all the spiritual changes since the turn of the century, withdrew without defending itself. There were only a few attempts made to hinder the dissemination of evangelical ideas, but to no avail. The great mistake was that the measures taken were largely aggressive. Ecclesiastical authorities arrested preachers and the people promptly released them. Miklós Oláh, primate of the Hungarian Catholic Church for fifteen years after 1553, attempted to identify preachers who had not been ordained by Catholic bishops and to prohibit them from exercising their office. By that time, however, they were too numerous and too many of them had been educated at universities abroad. The archbishop's actions earned only widespread hostility for Catholicism.

Catholic authorities did not use persuasion, and did not endeavour to attract people by means of cultural influence. What is much more bewildering is that they lost practically only what they let go: the believers went, but the entire hierarchy of the Roman Church was preserved. By the end of the century, there were only about 300–350 parishes left, but all the prelates kept their dignities. The primate of Hungarian Catholicism was absent for only twenty-four years during the century and bishops were even appointed to those sees which had fallen under Ottoman rule. They resided in Royal Hungary, without ever going near their dioceses. In the Kingdom of Hungary, the ecclesiastical lords did not lose their seats in the Diet, despite near-total Protestant predominance among the secular Estates and the inhabitants of Royal Hungary.

There was no question of Protestantism destroying cultural values in the country, since Catholics were free to hold on to everything. The Ottomans were indifferent towards Christianity, and the rulers of the other two parts of the country, except for a nine-year period in Transylvania, were Catholic throughout the sixteenth century. They would have backed up every cultural effort of the Catholic Church, but there were in fact none at all.

In the first half of the century, three partial translations of the Bible had been published, the last of which, a Hungarian New Testament by János Sylvester, was especially important. But with this endeavour, the work of Catholicism among national culture ceased for a long time. Catholic figures wrote excellent works, for example, on Hungarian history, but they were written in Latin and left unpublished. The first Catholic printing press was only established in 1578. By that time there were seven well-established Protestant presses in action, while the itinerant printers who moved from one customer to another were also Protestant. All this had nothing to do with religious conviction. Catholics were not prohibited by their faith from writing popular verse, but they did not do so throughout the sixteenth century. They did not even continue with the lives of the saints. The most moving works in this genre had been composed in Hungarian at the time the Reformation was reaching the country, but not one was published, let alone put into verse easy to sing or read aloud.

What distinguished Protestants from Catholics was a difference in cultural attitudes, or rather a discrepancy in their values, the same discrepancy that turned people away from the Roman Church. All the social sensitivity and readiness to meet people's demands that had been expressed by many representatives of the Church at the turn of the century had been directed into the Reformation. There remained in the old Church a stiffness, along with an inability to identify with the common people. This led to the absurdity that the efforts of Protestant clergymen in small market towns and villages were far more important in shaping Hungarian culture than those of archbishops who enjoyed royal favour. Later this changed: Protestantism lost much of its cultural flexibility and lack of inhibition, while Catholicism learned to fight for its adherents. For the time being, however, until the first decades of the seventeenth century, the difference in cultural attitudes determined the history of Hungarian culture. Under Protestant dominance, for thirty years after about 1570, a golden age of vernacular culture came into being.

The most characteristic feature of this period was that all people of the country profited from its achievements. In the three decades after 1570 printed books were produced for all the vernacular languages spoken in Hungary. Never before, and not for another hundred years afterwards, had anything like this occurred. There were books to read in Hungarian, German, Rumanian, Slovakian, Slovenian and Croatian. That meant, for example, that the Rumanians of Transylvania received books in their vernacular considerably earlier than their brethren in the Rumanian Vojvodships. On the other hand, the Germans, northern Hungary's Zipsers and

Transylvania's Saxons, took a major role in shaping the spiritual outlook of Hungary. By virtue of the advantage of their language they were surely the first to read pamphlets of the Reformation, and the first modern printing press in Hungary was established in 1529 in the Saxon town of Szeben. Most of the imprints of the sixteenth century in Hungarian were edited by a Saxon Protestant clergyman, Gáspár Heltai (or Caspar Helt in his native tongue), who was at the same time a master of the Hungarian language and the most renowned immortaliser of the glorious Hungarian past. He wrote in Hungarian, of course.

The matter-of-factness with which most intellectuals, regardless of their native tongue, used Hungarian in the sixteenth century at the expense of the scholarly Latin, indicates that the best market for cultural goods at that time was found among the Hungarians. This was due partly to the fact that the Germans, who can be taken as roughly equivalent to the bourgeois layer of society, met their cultural needs from German-speaking territories abroad. The second and perhaps far more important reason was the political and numerical superiority of the Hungarians. Intellectuals born into different ethnic groups usually identified with them up to the eighteenth century. Thus, the study of culture in Hungary in earlier ages is rather like examining a material by taking a sample of it.

The most striking of the cultural goods offered to the Hungarian people by sixteenth century Protestants was that they did not burden believers with theological controversies. The frequent sharp and vehement debates between representatives of different denominations remained locked up in unwieldy Latin tomes, since views on theological doctrines were put into popular editions. Characteristic in this regard are the hymnals, whose religious orientation is usually only identifiable by the person of the editor. The *Songs in Three Orders* of 1582, edited by the Lutheran bishop Péter Bornemisza, is a good example. It contains, besides well-known Catholic psalms, hymns by Calvinist and Unitarian authors but only a few by Lutherans. Among the most frequently sung hymns there were none dealing with the teachings of the different denominations. The editors of the hymnals provided the laity instead with hymns lauding the quietude attained by faith or those desiring the gift of faith. Lamentations on the sufferings inflicted by the Ottomans were sung remarkably seldom in the churches.

The lack of self-pity is a striking and attractive quality in a people living amid unceasing warfare. It is almost unimaginable, but the intellectuals felt quite at ease with their world. They did not complain of the incomprehension of their audience and they worked with amazing speed. The greatest spiritual achievement of the century, the complete edition of the Bible in Hungarian, took only three years. It was a masterly work, directed by

Gáspár Károlyi and printed at Vizsoly in 1590. The Vizsoly Bible had an impact on the Hungarian language and culture unlike any other book written in the vernacular, and was completed in less time than some scholars of the next century were to use in merely discussing problems of phonetics. That the first complete vernacular Bible appeared only at the end of the sixteenth century indicates that the Reformation did not put the Bible directly into the hands of the common people, a fact which has caused some misunderstanding about the cultural impact of the Reformation. Indeed, one eminent Calvinist bishop complained that the Reformation had done little to change the 'total absence of culture' among the lower classes. Similar views have been expressed in connection with the Reformation as experienced in other countries, with many historians pointing to the links between bible-reading and vernacular culture, as Ranke suggested more than a hundred years ago. In Hungary, however, there is no indication that the two factors went together. The people did not really receive the vernacular Bible, but they were nonetheless provided with a rich abundance of reading matter, largely supplied by Protestant authors – even if the culture created by the Reformation in Hungary was a singularly secular one.

The first Hungarian grammar was compiled by the prominent Reformer Mátyás Dévai Biró in 1538, and the first Latin–Hungarian dictionary published in 1590 was the work of Balázs Szikszai Fabricius, a Calvinist teacher at Sarospatak. It was András Farkas, a Lutheran preacher, who in 1538 wrote and published the first history of Hungary written in Hungarian verse, while the Reformer István Benczédi Székely was the first Hungarian to write a world chronicle in his native tongue in 1559. An active Calvinist bishop, Péter Melius Juhász, compiled the first Hungarian herbal in 1572, and two future bishops, the Lutheran Péter Bornemisza and the Unitarian György Enyedi translated classic works of secular literature, respectively Sophocles in 1558 and Boccaccio in 1577.

To return to the golden age, however: its most striking feature was the attention paid to the cultural demands of the people, attested in the immense increase in the amount of popular literature published, an unmistakable trend when one examines contemporary printed material. I call 'popular literature' those imprints published in quarto and no larger in size than twenty-five folios. They were mostly set in large typeface, clearly printed and well composed, with a broad margin. Such popular printed works were eye-catching and obviously designed to attract a less than scholarly public. In other words, they could be called works of popular culture. The change in the proportion of such popular works printed after 1570 is striking. Before that time, a mere 17 per cent of all printed works appeared in such popular editions, but in the three decades after 1570, they accounted for almost half of the output. Hungarian fiction accounted for

8.5 per cent of the works published before 1570, but for 42.3 per cent after that date.

As to the subject matter of such popular literature, it was of a highly variegated character. Stories from the Bible took pride of place, but these were not sanctimonious in tone, and the story of 'Goodwife Judith' was especially popular. It is breath-taking even today to read how Judith stripped before Ahasuerus: will she really go to bed with him? At the end there is the anticlimax, the terrible corpse of the usurper between the bloodsoaked sheets. Such stories represented works of fiction, but there were also travelogues to be found among these popular printed works, telling of faraway countries peopled by exotic inhabitants, as well as popular histories of Hungary and histories of antiquity, or the translated versions of Renaissance novels and of classical literature. Popular pamphlets even reported on contemporary events, such as the execution of Thomas Cranmer at the stake. It is no exaggeration to claim that these popular printed works, 75 per cent of which were published in Hungarian after 1570, mediated culture to all.

The major question, however, is that of their actual readership, a question much discussed in connection with the Reformation pamphlets published in other countries. The latter question is less relevant to the spread of the Reformation in Hungary, because the dissemination of evangelical ideas here occurred mostly by means of oral transmission. Popular pamphlets became linked to Protestantism only when it became a matter of disseminating cultural goods among the people. However, the task of assessing the reception of such printed works is certainly complicated by the tricky problem of literacy. It would be tempting to follow the methods of much research into literacy and to look for direct information on popular literacy, but sources of this kind are extremely rare in sixteenth-century Hungary. In the absence of any firm data on popular reading ability, it would be natural to conclude that these pamphlets did not reach the people because they could not read them.

However, the popular pamphlets do provide some interesting evidence to the contrary, since they reveal some basic facts, the foremost of which is that their authors did not live on university campuses. In any case, the country had no university at that time, and most Protestant intellectuals were usually educated abroad. On returning home, they did not congregate together but lived among the people, serving as teachers and preachers in tiny towns and villages. Thus, they were not ignorant of the lives of their parishioners, whom they often rebuked for negligence and laziness and whom they never idealised. Thus, if the authors of popular pamphlets claimed, either by choosing the medium of popular print for their work, or else by expressly stating in their dedications that the people could read, then we must conclude that the people really could read these works. Nonetheless, this was not reading as we understand it, nor was it even reading as understood by contemporary intellectuals. Yet the contemporary intellectuals had nothing against it. Indeed, from the evidence of popular printed works, they clearly regarded the difference as a mere technicality and met the demands for such popular reading matter with the same sympathy that characterised their attitude towards the religious expectations of the people. If folk needed reading material which could be read aloud easily by some and listened to by others, then they should have it.

The common people responded accordingly Motifs from verses found in popular printed literature became part of Hungarian folklore. King Matthias the Just, who had been the last ruler to keep proper order in the country, Miklós Toldi, the hero victorious over foreign enemies and wild beasts, Szép Ilonka or Beautiful Nelly, who was originally Helen of Troy, all walked out of the verses of such printed literature and straight into the popular imagination. Even 'Blackamoor Country' became a fearful setting for popular tales. This means that people read in the broadest sense of the term: they understood the texts and interpreted them in their own way.

Then sometime after the turn of the seventeenth century, something happened, a symptom of which was a dramatic decline in the number of popular printed works. During the three decades of the golden age, 107 works of Hungarian fiction had been published in popular form, but between 1601 and 1635 only thirty works of Hungarian fiction appeared. It symptomised a corresponding decline in concern for the people's cultural needs. The Reformation lost its impetus, thus opening the way for the Counter-Reformation. It began among lay patrons of the church, who were reconverted first by means of intelligent persuasion and then by politics. Only after this phase, from the 1620s onwards, did the Roman Church turn its attention back to the people. Catholicism worked by means of religious mysticism, while Protestantism defended itself with the intensely subjective religiosity of Puritanism. That, however, was a matter of the 'Second Reformation', which had to face its own problems, very different from those confronted by the first, the original Reformation.

### FURTHER READING

The history of Protestantism in Hungary has received scant attention in English publications. Useful further reading on political aspects can be found throughout the recent volume edited by R. J. W. Evans and T. V. Thomas, *Crown, Church and Estates. Central European Politics in the Sixteenth and Seventeenth Centuries* (London, 1991). A short account that complements that given here is that by David P. Daniel in *The Early Reformation in Europe*, ed. A. Pettegree (Cambridge, 1992), pp. 49–69.

# 10 Poland

*Janusz Tazbir*

The first modern history of the Polish Reformation appeared in English in 1838, but the author of this comprehensive two-volume work was a Polish historian, Walerian Krasinski (1795–1855), who had emigrated to England.[1] In modern accounts of the history of Protestantism, the Reformation in Poland hardly merits more than a few pages.[2] One reason for this neglect is the relatively small numbers of adherents to the Reformation in Poland and in the Grand Duchy of Lithuania, which was united with Poland at that time. It was a 'Reformation episode', as the latest history of the Polish Reformation by Waclaw Urban calls it,[3] rather than a significant epoch in our history.

By contrast with Germany, France or England, where the Reformation movement developed among people speaking the same language, the vast Polish–Lithuanian state, finally united in Lublin in 1569, had a multilingual population. The Poles made up about 40 per cent of the inhabitants, and only some of them were ethnically conscious; their only bond seemed to be a common dynasty. While it was the Reformation that brought about a religious split in most of the Catholic states of Western Europe, in Poland and Lithuania each ethnic group had its own specific creed before the Reformation: the Poles had Catholicism, the Ruthenians (ancestors of today's Ukrainians and Byelorussians) adhered to the Orthodox Church and the Jews to Judaism, while there were also adherents of Islam, the Tartars. The Germans who lived mainly in so-called Royal Prussia were the exception to the rule. The Teutonic Knights lost these territories to Poland after the Treaty of Toruń (1466), and only the Lutheran faith satisfied the German inhabitants' need for the ethnic separateness which was denied them in the common Polish–Lithuanian creed. This was probably one of the reasons for mass defections to the new faith by German burghers from Royal Prussia, Silesia and Greater Poland. Lutheranism began to spread in these areas as early as the 1520s, but in a semi-clandestine manner because of the hostile attitude of the authorities. Certain ecclesiastical circles encouraged Sigismund I the Old, King of Poland and Grand Duke of Lithuania (1506–48), to issue strict edicts against Protestantism. The monarch was wholly convinced of the correctness of these measures: on the one hand, he regarded ecclesiastical institutions as part of his apparatus of power; on the other, he was afraid of the trouble which could be stirred up by Anabaptism. Lutheranism, as a creed advocating obedience to secular authority, was less of a problem in this regard. Anabaptism, which linked religious faith to demands for radical social reform, was mainly adhered to by Germans, and Anabaptist influence was seen to have played a part in revolts by German peasants in Samland in the Duchy of Prussia in 1525, and by plebeians in Gdańsk (Danzig) in 1526. Both revolts had been speedily, ruthlessly and efficiently suppressed.

The last but one of the Jagiellon rulers died in 1548, but the new ruler Sigismund II Augustus (1548–72) at first continued his father's religious policies by issuing severe decrees against the Reformation. However, he soon turned to practical compromise, which can be seen in royal edicts of 1557–8 granting Lutherans the privilege of freedom of worship in Gdańsk (Danzig), Elbląg (Elbing) and Toruń (Thorn). In the following years, this privilege was extended to other towns of Royal Prussia. At the same time Sigismund II Augustus conceded to the gentry the right to abandon Catholicism by a decree of 1555 which suspended the superior power of ecclesiastical over lay courts, and by decrees of 1562–3 which virtually repealed the power of church courts. Thenceforth lay authorities refused to execute verdicts handed down by ecclesiastical courts. This allowed Protestant temples and heretic schools to be established with impunity, and enabled the setting up of printshops on gentry estates. The works of the great reformers, Luther, Melanchthon and Calvin, as well as those of their followers, were printed there. Protestant synods were held on the estates of heretic landowners, thus effectively establishing a Calvinist church organisation in Little Poland as early as 1554, and somewhat later in other regions of the Polish state.[4]

These developments would not have been possible except for the numerous privileges ceded to the gentry at an earlier period. From the late fourteenth century, no member of this class could be punished or his goods confiscated except by due process of law, nor could he be imprisoned prior to being brought to court unless he was caught red-handed (a principle later formulated as *neminem captivabimus nisi iure victum* and equivalent to the English *habeas corpus*). The last of the Jagiellons was too realistic to believe that courts consisting of noblemen would try any of their number for the offence of adhering to the Reformation, since religious fervour was subordinate to a stronger sense of class solidarity, at least during the sixteenth century. Class solidarity was indispensable in the struggle the gentry waged with the magnates, with the episcopate drawn largely from magnate ranks and with the clergy at large. Conflict with the clergy pre-dated the appearance of the Reformation in Poland, and gentry anticlericalism was to survive the defeat of Protestantism until well into the eighteenth century, curiously the epoch of Polish history most famous for attachment to Catholicism and the Catholic Church.

Some scholars have regarded the Reformation as a radical remedy for ills which were either absent in the Polish church or barely existed at all. Thus, it has been said that the Reformation movement was a matter more of reception of foreign ideologies than of protest against the lamentable moral state of the clergy or a reaction to any formalised piety which impeded direct human contact with God. If so, no wonder the movement was not as popular in Poland as it was in Germany, the Netherlands or England. However, there has been little in-depth research on Polish Catholicism of the period immediately preceding the Reformation, so that it is impossible to make categorical statements on this point. Undoubtedly, interest in the Reformation was stimulated by the long struggles over several decades to abolish ecclesiastical jurisdiction over the laity, to achieve a just form of the tithe and to compel the clergy to contribute to defence of the realm. More intriguing is the connection of the Reformation movement with Polish national consciousness, referred to by both sides engaged in confessional polemics.

As early as 1534 the gentry assembled at the Diet of Środa (Greater Poland) demanded that the clergy permit 'publication in Polish of our history, chronicles and laws' and, above all, of a vernacular Bible. It was a matter of great injustice that every nation 'has writings in its own language, while our priests keep us dumb'.[5] The adherents of Rome sought to oppose the Polish Reformation movement as a newfangled idea alien to native traditions of Polish Catholicism deeply embedded in the national past. They alluded especially to the close ties of Lutheranism with German culture, reflected in numerous proverbs such as 'a German is a heretic' or in the identification of Martin Luther's doctrine as the 'German faith', by contrast with that of the 'Ruthenian' (i.e. Orthodox) or Catholic faiths professed by Poles throughout the ages. By the seventeenth century the term 'a Luther' had become a byword for a German and the image of 'Doctor Martin' supplied the collective image for this ethnic group.

German colonisation of Poland since the middle ages had ensured daily contacts between Germans and Poles, in the town-hall, in the street, on the market-place and in the inns. The same cannot be said of the French, so that John Calvin did not become a synonym for members of that nation, although Calvin had numerous followers among the Polish gentry. Moreover, the popularity of Protestantism was qualitative rather than quantitive: barely a fifth of the gentry class adhered to the Reformation, most of them to Calvinism, the strongest of the Reformation creeds. It was this same political and intellectual elite which held sway in the Sejm (Polish Parliament) towards the close of Sigismund I Augustus's reign. On one occasion, at the Sejm of Lublin in 1569, Protestants almost equalled Catholics in the Senate or upper house. There were sixty dissenters, two of whom belonged to the Orthodox Church, while the so-called Papists accounted for seventy seats, fifteen of which included seats officially reserved in the Senate for bishops.

The Bohemian Brethren and the Antitrinitarians, who called themselves Polish Brethren, were even less numerous than Lutherans among the Protestant gentry and magnates. The Bohemian Brethren were exiles from religious persecution in their own land and arrived in the Commonwealth of Gentry in several stages, the first in 1548, and second during the Thirty Years' War. The Antitrinitarians emerged as a separate religious sect following a great schism in the Polish Calvinist Church in 1562–5, when the adherents of Genevan orthodoxy lost a significant part of their intellectual elite to the Arians (so-called after the early medieval heresy). The spiritual leader of the Antitrinitarians, Faustus Socinius, did not become a synonym in the national consciousness for an Italian, but the significant role of the Polish Brethren as a separate church did contribute to the further growth of a pre-existing italophobia. This provided fresh arguments for Catholic propaganda to enrich its theory that the Polish Reformation was an alien growth. The Polish Brethren subsequently gravitated towards the Bohemian Brethren, who doctrinally were a continuation of the moderate wing of Hussitism.

According to the Polish dissenters, it was a Slav spark that laid a fire at a German stake and they saw in Luther a continuation of Hus's doctrine, holding that the truth of the Gospel had first been proclaimed 'in the Slavonic rather than in the German language'. This Bohemian Reformation or 'an improvement of religion corrupted by superstitious papal practices' was then spread not only to noble estates, but even as far as the Cracow Academy, and its influence even reached into the royal court. This light of 'God's Gospel' was rekindled by the outbreak of the German Reformation, as a result of which members of the evangelical church there had been able to follow their Bohemian and Polish forerunners.[6] By calling their Hussite precursors 'evangelicals' the sixteenth-century dissenting polemicists tried to underline a continuity of tradition, a clear progression from Hus and Jerome of Prague, through the Bohemian Brethren to Lutheranism.

Some dissenters then reached back even further into the past, to the tenth century, to plant the traditions of the Polish Reformation even more firmly in native soil. The cult of Polish patron saints provided a point of reference for the discovery of national identity. Protestant polemicists could not, of course, regard the bishops Adalbert (d. 997) and Stanislaus Szczepanowski

(d. 1079) as saints in the same way that Catholics did, but they did attempt to represent both these martyrs as ideological forerunners of the Reformation. In Krzysztof Kraiński's Calvinist *Postylla* (1611) we find the following: 'In short, there was not even one-tenth of the superstitions in St Stanislaus's time as are now found in the Papacy'.[7] It was claimed that in the first ages of Polish Christianity, communion was administered under both kinds, while church services were celebrated not in Latin but in the vernacular. In the heat of their search for the native roots of the Polish Reformation, Protestant scholars even went so far as to deny the existence at the time of St Stanislaus of indulgences, prayers for the dead or the cult of the saints. In the same way, they claimed that there was no belief in transubstantiation, or in the Real Presence of Christ in the Eucharist, so that it was not worshipped nor was it carried in the monstrance during processions. Whether or how far the authors of such views believed them is perhaps unimportant. What is significant for our purposes is that in the polemical struggle for souls, they attempted to identify the essentially native character of the Polish Reformation.

The idea of breaking with Rome and establishing a Polish National Church was in the air for a long time before it was abandoned. Such hopes were fostered by the King himself because of his matrimonial troubles with two successive Habsburg princesses whom he wished to divorce and, as was expected, to follow the lead of Henry VIII. In 1556 Sigismund II Augustus, complying with demands from the gentry sympathetic to the Reformation, sent Stanislaus Myszkowski as his envoy to the Pope to propose convening a National Synod in Poland. Its purpose was to introduce communion under both kinds, to sanction church services in the vernacular and to abolish the celibacy of the clergy. Pope Paul IV rejected the proposal, which would hardly have come as a surprise to the King.

Sigismund II Augustus's attitude towards the Reformation remains a matter of ongoing debate among historians. Some consider him to have been a covert adherent of Protestantism, a fact he wished to keep secret for political reasons. Others see in him an eager Catholic, who wanted to ride out the storm of the Reformation. Both viewpoints concur in their assessment of the ruler's political realism, for he treated matters of religion largely from the standpoint of dynastic interest and reason of state. Sigismund II Augustus was reluctant to change his faith, since he would have gained little thereby, since he already appointed bishops and assigned benefices himself. Nor was he tempted by the English example to secularise ecclesiastical estates and redistribute them among the magnates and gentry. Certainly, he had no wish to use violence in matters of faith, and tried to be 'King of all Poles', continuing the policy of the Jagiellons who sought at any price to avoid disturbance or civil war. A civil war originating in religious division could cause the secession of the Grand Duchy of Lithuania, where the magnates were of great importance. We can mention only the Radziwiłłs, who played the leading role in the Council of the Grand Duchy and who were also the protectors of the Reformation there.

It is difficult to agree with the view that the Reformation would have been a success in Poland if only Jan Łaski (1499–1560), the sole Polish theologian of any renown in Europe, had not died prematurely. As John a Lasco, he became a well-known figure in the history of the Polish and English Reformations. In 1550–3 he was a superintendent alongside others of foreign congregations in London which were structurally and doctrinally independent of the Church of England.[8] He returned to Poland in 1556, four years before his death, and embarked on active measures to unite all the factions of Polish Protestantism. Łaski considered unity as necessary to resist Catholicism successfully, and the ecumenical aims he pursued so tirelessly were continued after his death. But they were only partially successful in uniting the Lutherans, the Calvinists and the Bohemian Brethren in the Union of Sandomierz of 1570 in a common struggle against the growing power of the Counter-Reformation. However, this won growing support from the gentry, and the Confederation of Warsaw of January 1573 enacted 'the greater charter of Polish tolerance' by guaranteeing to the gentry full freedom to practise any religion.

This edict, issued during the Interregnum following the death of King Sigismund II Augustus, gave the dissenting gentry equal access to all posts, offices and profits except for church benefices; however, one should not forget that Catholicism remained the official religion. The edict was confirmed, although not without some objections, by Henry of Valois, who reigned very briefly in Poland in 1574 as an elective monarch – the same Henry of Valois who was an accessory to the Massacre of St Bartholomew. He was followed as king by Stephen Bathory (1576–86), and then by three successive kings from the Vasa dynasty who ruled the Commonwealth of Nobles from 1587 to 1668.

Unlike the Union of Sandomierz, which excluded the Polish Brethren, the Confederation of Warsaw accepted virtually all fractions of Christianity, even including adherents of the Orthodox Church. As a movement for the renewal and revival of Catholicism, the Reformation was not at first very interested in the Orthodox Church, which in its turn did not regard the Reformation, with its close connections to Latin culture, as at all dangerous. It has been said that long before Luther appeared 'half of the population of the Polish Commonwealth adhered to a religion which allowed married priests and communion in both kinds'.[9] If we add to this wholly correct statement of Wacław Sobieski the fact that the Orthodox Church used the vernacular in its church services, it is clear why its believers would not be overly attracted by the main demands of the Reformation, since they had already been achieved.

The situation changed radically, however, in the last quarter of the sixteenth century. First, Reformation propaganda disseminated above all by the Antitrinitarians began to penetrate the eastern territories of the Grand Duchy of Lithuania and to alarm the Orthodox clergy. Second, the proposed union of the Orthodox Church with the Catholics, discussed at the Orthodox Synod of Brest-Litovsk in 1596, became a sore point because the greater part of the faithful opposed its provisions. The question of the separate identity of the Orthodox Church was called into question by this union, and turned Orthodox brotherhoods, printing houses and schools into bastions of 'the true faith'. All these institutions served both religious purposes and to foster Ruthenian culture, which was seen to be menaced by Polish and Latin influences. Every act which attempted to implement progressively the provision of the union was treated as a threat to the national identity of those who confessed the faith of the Orthodox Church.

Those who created the Confederation of Warsaw would not have been aware of all these impending consequences. This edict was intended to protect a state deprived of its monarch against potential political and social conflicts, not least those which might arise from differences of religious faith. Although this edict was issued only for an interregnum, it remained in force, at least formally, until the very end of the Commonwealth in 1795. However the adherents of the waning Reformation soon became aware that the main danger facing them was not the authority of the state but religious tumult in the towns. The Confederation of Warsaw did not propose any sanctions against those who destroyed Protestant churches, attacked Protestant shops and homes, dishonored Protestant funerals or despoiled their cemeteries. Urban authorities dominated by Catholics punished individual perpetrators of such incidents, but they seemed unable (or unwilling) to take any preventative measures. As a result, Protestant churches were finally closed down in Cracow in 1591, in Poznań in 1611 and in Lublin in 1627. In towns under the rule of dissenting magnates they remained untouched: for example, Leszno in Greater Poland, the main centre of the Bohemian Brethren; Raków, the capital of the Polish Arians; and Kiejdany in Lithuania, which was owned by the Calvinist Radziwiłłs. If anyone was persecuted in these places, it was the Catholics, who were forbidden to build churches or chapels. The same is true of the towns in Royal Prussia, where Protestants forbade 'the Papists' to hold public processions or funerals, and denied Catholics the protection of urban statutes or admission to craft guilds. Moreover, monasteries were attacked, especially those belonging to the universally detested Jesuits.

In Royal Prussia the Reformation seemed to function to preserve German culture, and there was a specific form of 'feedback' between ethnic and religious affiliation. The Germans living in Gdańsk or Toruń supported Lutheranism, which was religiously and culturally close to their interests and which in turn strengthened their feelings of national separateness. In the seventeenth-century Commonwealth of the Gentry, the Polish element in Protestant churches decreased significantly. This was due to a new influx of religious immigrants, mostly Lutherans and Bohemian Brethren. They contributed to the development of the towns of Great Poland, and new centres also emerged, such as Rawicz (1658), Szlichtyngowa (1644), Kargowa or Bojanowo. The foundation charters guaranteed the dissenters full freedom of worship for any religion of their own choice, and permitted them to build schools and temples, to settle parishes and to choose their own clergy. The privileges conferred on Jutrosin (1638) and Kamionna (1642) even laid down fines for those who disturbed Protestants in the exercise of their religion. The owners of these centres were for the most part Catholic magnates and gentry, who were only too well aware of the economic benefits that accrued from such foundations.

At the same time, when Polish dissenters were being expelled from many towns such as Lublin, Cracow, or Poznań, their German or Czech co-religionists were accorded full religious freedom. The reason for this divergence in policy is clear: native 'heretics' were treated quite differently from foreign ones. Such differentiations were applied to the Protestants living on private estates and in royal towns such as Lublin, Cracow, or Poznań. Moreover, the commercial and craft centres operated by foreigners, isolated by their language from the rest of the population, were quite different from those centres which represented a danger to the Counter-Reformation because of their active and attractive religious propaganda. Raków was one such; the Socinian temple, Academy and printing office there were closed in 1638, on the basis of a decree of the Sejm which took as its pretext the desecration of a wayside cross by pupils of the local school.

The attractiveness of Polish culture did however contribute to the polonisation of some families belonging to the Lutheran and Socinian churches ('Socinian' was another name used for the Polish Brethren in the seventeenth century). They became very attached to their new homeland, proud of its successes and deeply wounded by its failures. Good evidence for this is found in the ardent 'Prayer on Behalf of the Polish Kingdom', beautifully written in the Polish language around 1632 by Margaret Ruar, the daughter of an assimilated German, Martin Ruar, philosopher and Socinian agitator. But the surest way to become Polish was through ennoblement, the pinnacle of achievement dreamed of by every ambitious newcomer. First, a coat of arms was acquired, followed by a change of name: thus, Statorius became Stoiński, Schoman Ciachowski, Ronemberg Naborowski, and so on. The

Ruthenian gentry living in Volhynia at the beginning of the sixteenth century first left the Orthodox Church for Socinianism and finally adopted Catholicism. This went along with a polonisation that gradually permeated the entire noble class of the Commonwealth, regardless of descent or origin. We can conclude that social status played the vital role here, and different denominations could not hold back the trend of assimilation to the gentry. On the other hand, those classes deprived of privileges were not susceptible to the influences of Polish culture. Here we have mainly in mind the Mennonites from the Netherlands, who settled near Gdańsk and remained faithful not only to their creed but also to their native tongue.

Among those who remained wholly indifferent to the Polish Reformation were adherents to Judaism and Islam. Only a few followers of the radical stream of the Reformation harboured utopian dreams of a unification of the three main religions, Christianity, Judaism and Islam. More down-to-earth thinkers viewed this prospect as unrealistic. The Arian Marcin Czechowic wrote that it was more difficult to convert a Jew than to unaccustom 'a wolf from the habit of killing sheep or a cat from catching mice'.[10] Although Protestant printing houses published books in all languages of almost all the ethnic groups living in the Commonwealth of the gentry, no thought was even given to editions in Hebrew. The only person to attempt to propagate the Reformation among the Jews was Paweł Helicz, who published a translation of the New Testament by Martin Luther in Cracow in 1541. The German text was transcribed by a printer into Hebrew letters, but unfortunately this edition was not read in the Hebrew community. In direct contact Judaism appeared to be stronger than Protestantism: in the second half of the sixteenth century there spread among adherents of the radical Reformation a so-called 'Judaising' tendency, in which the Old Testament was considered the main basis of faith.

The Reformation did not manage to win over adherents of Islam settled in the Grand Duchy of Lithuania. The Armenians living in the south of the Commonwealth and confessing Monophysitism (belief in the exclusively divine nature of Christ), were not attracted either. This group consisted mainly of merchants engaged in trade with the East, whence the Armenians had come to Poland. The Catholic Church did have a certain success here, however, for in 1634 the Armenian Monophysitists agreed to religious union with Rome. Leaving skilful propaganda aside, the ennoblement of many Armenians seems to have been the main factor contributing to their polonisation. Sometimes assimilation was followed by change of religious denomination, but this was not always the case, and it is sometimes difficult to determine what was cause and effect.

The Reformation movement also lost the battle to win over the Polish peasantry. Except for the Oświęcim and Zator Duchy and certain regions in the submontane district of Pogórzew situated in the south of the country, the number of peasant adherents to Protestantism could be counted on one's fingers. Some landlords tried to implement the principle of *cuius regio, eius religio* on their estates, insisting that their peasants adopt the religion of their landlord. It has never been satisfactorily explained whether this principle was intended to be applied to subject peasantry in the edict of the Confederation of Warsaw. Its ambiguous formulations cannot supply any definitive answer as to whether landlords were in 1573 granted the right to impose their own faith upon their serfs.

In any case, whenever propagated by means of a voluntary appeal, Protestantism achieved rather poor results among the peasantry. Some historians ascribe this to the low level of cultural development among the peasantry, arguing that the Reformation would encounter a poor response from the illiterate, the more so since it was spread by German preachers and by printed material in German. Other scholars emphasise the role of the rich ritual life which made Catholicism so attractive; instead of processions and the cult of miraculous images and relics, the Protestants could only offer bare church walls. However, these arguments are unconvincing when one considers that Reformation ideas also reached Poland in native form, since there were publications printed in Polish in Königsberg, the capital of the Duchy of Prussia. Moreover, from the outset the Lutherans in particular and the Bohemian Brethren made great concessions on certain forms of ritual and liturgy. Many Catholic customs were retained for a long time, even in Calvinist churches, in order not to discourage new converts by demanding too sudden a change. Polish peasants did not always appreciate the scope of the radical religious revolution, and even Catholic subjects brought their children to be baptised by Lutheran pastors, who complied with such requests with the approval of their synods.

The reasons cited above for the indifference of the Polish peasantry to the Reformation do not seem to be the most relevant. It should be remembered that in every country, villagers were not those most ready to attach themselves to the new creed. There had to be some stimulus or compulsion from above, that is, from the king of magnates, from towns or landlords. In every state where the Reformation gained the firm support of the ruling classes, it became the dominant religion, whether as Lutheranism, Anglicanism or Calvinism. The peasantry gave allegiance to the movement rather later, regardless of earlier resistance. If the nobility of Poland had been won as adherents of Wittenberg, Geneva or of a National Church, Catholicism would have been negligible among the peasantry: willing or not, they would have followed their masters.

The indifference of common people towards the ideas of a new faith which offered no hope for improvement of their living standards seems to be one of the main reasons for the failure of the Polish Reformation. Among other reasons we can also mention the fidelity of the Polish monarchs to Catholicism and the Catholic Church, divisions among the Protestant dissenters, and last but not least, a genuine lack of interest in the religious ideas of the Reformation. In Poland, the Reformation appeared as a form of ideological fancy dress used in the struggle for noble privilege and as a means of exerting pressure on the Catholic clergy, rather than as a movement of radical reform of the church. It was, then, more a great intellectual adventure than a pursuit of eternal truth about God and the after-life. The strength of the Reformation was clearly weakened when, on the one hand, the gentry realised its objectives in the Sejm and became the real co-rulers of the Polish state, and on the other, the intellectuals began to abandon Protestantism, disillusioned by the intolerance of its leaders, its confessional fragmentation and its increasingly arid intellectual debates reminiscent of the controversies of Scholasticism. In practice Protestantism was left only with an appeal to the national pride and ambitions of the Polish gentry not to let 'Italian prelates' determine their faith. Here Catholic propaganda managed very skilfully to take the wind out of their opponents' sails, since they identified the further development of native Polish culture with an even wider dissemination of Catholicism. Thus, in the century following the acceptance of the decrees of the Council of Trent in Poland (1577), Catholicism became even more widespread than it had been for several centuries previously.

The polonisation of Catholicism did not, however, predetermine Catholic victory, because the major failure of the Reformation had taken place earlier. But an accelerated process of polonisation did bring the Catholic faction final victory and strengthened its impact upon the next few generations. A similar role was played by the geopolitical situation of the Commonwealth of the Gentry. Poland's enemies during the age of the Reformation were almost exclusively non-Catholic countries: the Muslim Ottoman state and a strongly protestantised Transylvania in the south; Orthodox Russia from the east and Lutheran Sweden from the north. In the seventeenth century, the Poles never crossed swords with the followers of Rome. In these circumstances, there grew up the view that Poland played a pre-eminent role as the rampart of Christianity.[11] Let us set aside the problem of how far the gentry itself believed this theory and to what extent it became a legitimating ideology for the status quo; the necessity of repelling the adherents of Islam and the incursions of the Tartars and Turks was undeniable, and was greatly appreciated in the West.

Playing the role of 'defender of the faith' for the outside world could not be reconciled in the long run with continuation of the sixteenth-century

Polish tradition of toleration. As a result, the Arians were expelled, and the Socinians had to seek shelter in neighbouring Transylvania, Prussia, Brandenburg and finally in the Netherlands. Some of them remained in hiding in Poland, but no-one was sentenced to death despite a law which provided for this penalty. Those who were captured were simply sent into exile, while delayed conversions were met with approval and the hesitant were given only token fines. But the expulsion of the Socinians reflects significant changes among the gentry, who began to give greater priority to religious belief over class solidarity. The remaining Protestants quickly followed the Arians; in 1668 the Polish Sejm prohibited repudiation of the Catholic faith. Five years later, it decreed that ennoblement and acknowledgment of foreign ennoblement would be granted only to Catholics. Numerous restrictions were now imposed on freedom of worship of the Calvinist and Lutheran gentry, exempting only those in Royal Prussia. The dissenting gentry gradually became second-class citizens and the following century even saw a temporary loss of their political rights. These were substantially restored in the age of the Enlightenment (1768 and 1773). By contrast, legal restrictions on Catholics were retained in England until 1829 and in Sweden until 1849.

NOTES

1 W. Krasiński, *Historical Sketch of the Rise, Progress and Decline of the Reformation in Poland* (London, 1838–40; reprint, New York, 1974).

2 For example, E. G. Léonard, *Histoire générale du protestantisme*, 3 vols. (Paris, 1961–64), English translation as *A History of Protestantism*, ed. H. H. Rowley and trans. J. H. M. Reid and R. M. Bethell, 2 vols (London, 1965–67).

3 Wacław Urban, *Epizod refoprmacyjny* (Cracow, 1988).

4 S. Kieniewicz, ed., *History of Poland* (Warsaw, 1979), pp. 158ff.

5 *Kultura staropolska* [Ancient Polish culture], ed. Polish Academy of Sciences (Cracow, 1932), p. 414.

6 J. Tazbir, *Szlachta i teologowie. Studia z dziejów polskiej kontrreformacji* [Gentry and Theologians. Studies on the Polish Counter-Reformation] (Warsaw, 1987), pp. 6–7.

7 K. Kraiński, *Postylla* (Laszczow, 1611), fol. 634.

8 See O. Bartel, *Jan Łaski. Leben und Werk des polnischen Reformators* (Berlin, 1981), pp. 100ff.

9 *Pamiętnik zjazdu history czno-literackiego im. Mikołaja Reja* ['Memorials of the Mikolaj Rej Historical-literary Congress'], ed. W. Czermak (Cracow, 1910), p. 86.

10 J. Tazbir, 'Die Reformation in Polen und das Judentum' in *Deutsche – Polen – Juden. Ihre Beziehungen von den Anfägen bis ins 20. Jahrhundert*, ed. S. Jersch-Wenzel (Berlin, 1987), p. 133.

11 See J. Tazbir, *Poland as the Rampart of Christian Europe. Myths and Historical Reality* (Warsaw, 1989).

## FURTHER READING

N. Davies, *God's Playground. A History of Poland*, vol. 1 (Oxford, 1981).

J. K. Fedorowicz, M. Bogucka, H. Samsonowicz, eds., *A Republic of Nobles. Studies in Polish History to 1864* (Cambridge, 1982).

A. Jobert, *De Luther à Mohila. La Pologne dans la crise de la Chrétienté 1517–1648* (Paris, 1974).

S. Kieniewicz, ed., *History of Poland* (Warsaw, 1979).

A. Mączak, H. Samsonowicz, P. Burke, eds., *East Central Europe in Transition* (Cambridge, 1985).

*Nation. Church. Culture. Essays on Polish History*, ed., Catholic University of Lublin (Lublin, 1990), University Handbook Series.

J. Tazbir, *La République nobiliare et le monde. Etudes sur l'histoire de la culture polonaise a lá époe du baroque* (Wrocław, 1986), Polish Historical Library.

J. Tazbir, *A State without Stakes. Polish Religious Toleration in the Sixteenth and Seventeenth Centuries* (New York and Warsaw, 1973).

W. Weintraub, 'Tolerance and Intolerance in Old Poland', *Canadian Slavonic Papers* 13 (1971), no. 1.

G. H. Williams, ed., *The Polish Brethren. Documentation of the History and Thought of Unitarianism in the Polish–Lithuanian Commonwealth and in the Diaspora, 1601–1685* (Harvard, 1980), Harvard Theological Studies, 30.

A. Zamoyski, *The Polish Way. A Thousand-year History of the Poles and their Culture* (London, 1987).

# 11    Italy

*Silvana Seidel Menchi*

## Preliminary considerations

Measured against the Reformation in Central and Northern Europe, the Reformation Italian-style falls short on all counts.

(1) The plan for a Reformation in Italy, designed by a tiny minority, never got off the drawing board. (Only the Waldensian communities, whose origin and development form part of the history of medieval heresies and therefore constitute a separate chapter in the history of the Reformation, managed to achieve a durable confessional organisation.)[1]

(2) This failure was not a defeat bringing to an end the drama of an open struggle.[2]

(3) Italian Protestantism, which took over not a single city or state, never entered the chronicle of European events, except for a few short-term sensations, such as the defection of a few prominent 'heretics' (Bernardino Ochino, General of the Capuchins, who fled in 1542, and Pier Paolo Vergerio, Bishop of Capodistria, who departed in 1549, for example) and the execution of some others who lacked the good sense to get out in time (such as Pietro Carnesecchi, put to death in 1567, and Aonio Paleario, burned in 1570).

(4) The most famous of the 'Italian Reformers', Juan de Valdés, was a Spaniard, whose concept of reform was so subtle that it failed to have institutional consequences and therefore did not make a clear impression, either on most of his contemporaries or on historians of the present day, who continue to have difficulty interpreting it.[3]

Hence this non-event, the Italian Reformation, is difficult to connect to that event of epochal significance, the 'real' Reformation. A marginal phenomenon, which rapidly disappeared from the collective memory of the Italians, Protestantism south of the Alps has little in common with Central European Protestantism, which was and remains fully aware of its *Weltwirkung* and its impact on the periodisation of world history. Such a difference in proportions and effects is reflected in historical writing. Interpretive paradigms worked out by historians of the Central European

Reformation have proven difficult to apply to that microhistory of defeat, the Italian Reformation. A valiant attempt at historiographical linkage was made by Delio Cantimori, who in his fundamental work *Eretici italiani del Cinquecento* contrasted the *epochale Bedeutung* of the Central European Reformation with the *epochale Bedeutung* of the rationalist Italian Reformation, precursor of the Enlightenment, brought about by radical religious emigrants (Camillo Renato, Celio Secondo Curione, Lelio and Fausto Sozzini, Giorgio Biandrata and others) *outside of Italy*. Shifting the terms of the discussion from church history to cultural history enabled Cantimori to evade the problem of the institutional failure of the Reformation in Italy and to argue that the work of the Italian reformers was just as important as that of their northern counterparts.[4] Fifty years after the publication of his book, Cantimori's thesis, which made its way into general historiographical discourse, continues to inform one of the most vital currents of research on 'philosophical religion'.[5]

Nonetheless, it must be recognised that the leading edge of international historiography has completely abandoned the terrain of cultural history, of 'philosophical religion', in which Cantimori's approach was rooted. As opposed to the traditional approaches of church history and history of dogma, which concentrate on the theological and religious aspects of the Reformation, the reigning paradigm in the field is now social history, which considers the Reformation in its relationship to social structures. The focus has shifted from great men to social organisation; intellectual or spiritual biographies of the Reformers have been displaced by analyses of groups and classes. Only in Italy do interpretive schemes shaped by the Cantimorian cultural history approach still predominate. As a consequence of the divergence in historiographical language between scholars who study the Reformation in Central Europe and those who focus on the Italian Reformation dialogue between the two groups has become difficult, even though it has not broken down entirely.

In this essay I have two objectives. First, I shall consider to what extent the concepts most frequently employed by the avant-garde in research on the Central European Reformation can be applied to the Italian Reformation. Then, in the light of this assessment, I shall make a provisional attempt to redraw the map of the Italian Reformation.

## Can there be a social history of the Italian Reformation?

In the last thirty years the methods of social history have dominated the historiography of the Reformation. From Bernd Moeller (*Reichstadt und Reformation*, 1962) to Peter Blickle (*Gemeindereformation*, 1987 and 1990), the interpretation of the Reformation as 'social event' has proven to be the most productive and stimulating methodological approach in this field of study. In fact, treating the Reformation as 'social event' amounts to redefining the historiographical objective: the subject of explanation is no longer the Reformation, but rather the reception of the Reformation. Social historians assume that the explanation of the Reformation's striking success in Central Europe is to be sought in social structures, in the dynamics of social groups struggling to assert themselves. In concrete terms, the two most relevant proposals have identified the locus of this struggle in the imperial city (Moeller) and in the *Gemeinde* or commune (Blickle).[6]

From the perspective of Italian historical writing, it is striking that all these interpretive schemes evade the *coeur religieux* of the problem. In their most explicit assertions, social historians of the Reformation dismiss *homo religiosus* as a fiction. They deliberately turn their attention from *Frömmigkeitsformen und Religionspraktiken* to what they insist are the sole constituent of genuine historical explanation: 'the peasants' and townspeople's actual conditions of life', as Blickle puts it. For these historians, theology and ethics are meaningless unless placed in a dialectical, mutually conditioning relationship with social structures.[7]

To put the matter in what may be slightly oversimplified terms, one can say that during the last thirty years a secularised historiography, addressed to an audience of agnostics, has tended to shelve the theological–religious interpretation of the Reformation. For these historians, religion supplies the ideology for social forces mature enough to come into their own. Most explicitly in the work of Peter Blickle, the 'irrational' of religion is converted into the 'rational' of sociopolitical relationships. Why, Blickle asks, did some cantons and cities embrace the Reformation while others did not? In his view, 'individuals' religious motives' do not represent a satisfactory response to this question. The historian's objective is to discover, beneath the veil of religious enthusiasm in the crucial period 1520–5, the collective reason of a program involving communalisation of religious and political life which is religious precisely because it is political.

That this approach is impracticable for the study of Italy does not require a lengthy demonstration. Here the subject of explanation is not the success but the failure of the Reformation. Philo-Protestants in two Italian cities have been counted. In Venice, John Martin has identified 774 during the period 1547 to 1583, and in Lucca, Simonetta Adorni-Braccesi has found 400 during the period 1530 to 1600:[8] at most, 0.5 per cent of the population. Even if one posits a multiplier of three in order to account for sympathisers who never came to the attention of the authorities, the Reformation movement in two of its most notable Italian strongholds probably never reached, and certainly did not surpass, more than 2 per cent of their population. There could hardly be a more graphic demonstration, which in itself constitutes an explanation, of the failure of the Italian Reformation. What needs to be explained is the solid figure of 0.5 per cent in favour of the Reformation.

Attempts to perform a social analysis of the Italian minorities that proved receptive to the appeal of the Reformation have not yielded much fruit. Of the 400 Protestants identified in Lucca between 1530 and 1600, the largest contingent, 131 to be precise, comprised patricians belonging to the most influential families. Of the 774 'heretics' counted in Venice, the relative majority, 189, were artisans specialising in the production of luxury goods – the aristocracy among craftsmen – all of them literate. But in both cases the philo-Protestant presence was so slight in comparison to the total population that it seems risky to draw a conclusion different from the traditional one: since merchant patricians and the elite among the artisans were the most dynamic, culturally receptive citizens, as well as those most likely to reside for long periods outside Italy, they were consequently the people most susceptible to religious innovation.

If the social analysis of tiny minorities proves inconclusive, then the search for a collective reason behind the episodes of Italian religious dissent is obviously unpromising. Those prestigious merchants, wealthy textile merchants, skilled artisans, and schoolmasters who were the protagonists of the Italian Reformation do not lend themselves to the logic of cost-benefit analysis or to treatment in terms of the conquest of social space. In most cases, their spiritual adventures resulted in social ostracism, economic degradation, significant financial losses, exile, banishment, imprisonment. Rather than the articulation of a collective reason, the outcome of the Reformation in Italy appears as the expression of an individual irrationality. In other words, the Italian evidence vividly highlights that 'irrationality' of individual religious choice, that intuitive and compelling perception of the sacred, which the leading German historians insist is beyond our ken.[9]

The fourteen Italian archives of the Inquisition known to exist (others are continually coming to light) contain several thousand trials for so-called 'Lutheran' heresy. Between 1530 and 1580, the adherents of the Reformation comprised the great majority (around 70 per cent) of those denounced to and tried in these ecclesiastical tribunals.[10] This documentation is quantitatively significant, although – since the trials have not yet been counted – not exactly quantifiable. Its strong point, however, is its quality: Carlo Ginzburg has recently compared inquisitorial documents to anthropologists' field notes.[11] The simile of the anthropologist is apt, at least in the cases of *sponte comparentes* ('heretics' who came voluntarily before the Inquisition without having been denounced or summoned), for inquisitorial procedure allowed *comparentes* to take the initiative in crafting their own 'confessions.' But even in other types of cases the dialogue between the judge and the accused provided the latter ample room for presenting themselves as they wished to be seen. For a variety of motives – at one end of the spectrum, the desire to demonstrate repentance through a detailed confession; at the other, the impulse to answer the call to martyrdom and at the same time propagandise for their cause – persons accused took advantage of this opportunity. Thus Inquisition trial records are rich sources of individual and social information. Complex spiritual itineraries and circumstantial accounts of 'heretics' principled deviations from the prevailing orthodoxy, as well as their attitudes and others' reactions to them expressed in familial and professional settings, emerge from these colloquies, which were seldom conducted in a rigorously programmed, formalistic way.

That is not all. Carlo Ginzburg's studies of popular culture demonstrate that inquisitorial documents lend themselves very well to the anthropological approach to the history of the Reformation, pursued so successfully by English historians.[12] In dialogues between inquisitors and persons accused of heresy, the immediacy of the spoken word is more important than cultural experience mediated through reading and writing, and personal options prevail over doctrine. The absence in Italy of insistence on a single, precise theological stance, furthermore, highlights the spontaneity and immediacy of individual choice. These documents fully meet the requirements of an approach to religion 'from the bottom up': the trial records reflect the course of that Reformation autonomously developed by artisans and merchants, notaries and priests, shoemakers and shopkeepers, who were motivated more by their own needs, emotions, and passions than by what Blickle calls 'the theories of the theological pioneers'.

Nevertheless, as promising as the application of these approaches to the Italian Reformation may appear, the main mode of interpreting inquisitorial documents remains the religious one, which has by no means reached the point of diminishing returns. Religious choice is a primary element that cannot be reduced to something else. The supposition that religious formulations encoded a message of social transformation is difficult, if not impossible, to translate into a new overarching concept analogous to *Reichstadt* or *Gemeindereformation*. Opportunities for an anthropological reading, though numerous, are inconsistent and scattered. That scholars of the Italian Reformation persist in working within the paradigm of religious history is thus dictated, at least in part, by the nature of their sources.

Still, greater attention to the social dimension of the history of the Reformation represents an obligatory response to developments in European historiography. Attention paid by younger scholars to the social contexts shows that a transformation of the field is under way. The work these scholars have done and are doing on the local level (Simonetta Adorni-Braccesi in Lucca, John Martin in Venice) remains to be accomplished on the national level. The job will not be easy, given the fragmentary and discontinuous character of the socio-political situation in Italy and the lack of coordination in the exploration of inquisitorial archives.

What follows is a provisional, investigative attempt to respond to the challenge by reconceptualising the Reformation in Italy in four phases: first, the theological call to arms (the era of the preachers, 1518–42); second, spontaneous diffusion (the era of the artisans, 1542–55); third, repression (the era of the conventicles, 1555–71); and fourth, extinction (1571–88). Each of these can be fitted into an interpretive category developed by the social historians: ways and means of communication (relevant to the first phase), 'the people's Reformation' (applicable to the second phase), discipline (pertinent to the third phase), and the dissolution of the social network (corresponding to the fourth phase).[13]

### The theological call to arms (the era of the preachers, 1518–1542)

The first phase of the Italian Reformation runs from 1518 (the first Italian edition of a work by Luther) to 1542 (the first notorious departures of eminent philo-Protestants). It is characterised by two parallel, related tendencies: a violent, public anti-Lutheran polemic corresponds to the slow, clandestine growth of a philo-Protestant network. In this period we find the largest number of printed Italian works by Luther (just one example: the *Kurze Form der zehn Gebote*, a primitive version of the *Small Catechism*, was published in seven editions); other devotional texts of an evangelical nature, like the *Sommario della Santa Scrittura*, had considerable success in print in the 1540s.[14]

The main means by which the Protestant message was disseminated, however, was not the press but the pulpit. Protagonists of the Italian Reformation in this era were above all friars well trained in theology who earned a reputation as excellent preachers. The thirty-five philo-Protestant preachers whose names emerge from a survey of specialised studies – fifteen Augustinian Hermits, ten Franciscans (most of them Observant), three Augustinian Canons, three Dominicans, two Capuchins, a Carmelite and a Benedictine – are merely indicative of a much broader phenomenon, one which was to have important consequences far beyond this first phase and would become dominant especially in the Augustinian and Benedictine orders.[15]

To a certain extent, the Italian philo-Protestant preaching effort was coordinated, for by the end of the 1530s Italians sympathetic to the Reformation had formed a rudimentary clandestine organisation. They communicated among themselves in a sort of coded language, worked in concert, and managed the appearances of 'evangelical' preachers to advance the common cause. Key links in this organisation were certain prestigious patricians (the anonymous Venetian nobleman who financed the Italian translation of Luther's *An den christlichen Adel deutscher Nation*, for instance) and some prelates, whose strategy appears to have been to conquer the Catholic Church from within (the philo-Protestant bishop of Trieste Pietro Bonomo, the patriarch of Aquileia Giovanni Grimani, the bishop of Bergamo Vittore Soranzo, and others).[16]

For about twenty years, from 1530 to 1550, the corps of dynamic philo-Protestant preachers made the key words 'grace', 'God's mercy', 'the enslaved will', and 'predestination' resound in the churches of such major Italian cities as Milan, Venice, Padua, Vicenza, Treviso, Modena, Ferrara, Genoa, Mantua, Bologna, Florence, Lucca, Siena, Naples, Palermo and even Rome. Smaller towns as well formed part of the evangelical network. In the 1540s evangelical preaching reached its apex: 'everyone in those days was preaching ... evil doctrine', the survivors later testified. This impressive diffusion resulted from the merging, or at least the convergence, of the philo-Protestant movement and the activities of the 'spirituali.' The term 'spirituali' denotes a moderate reforming movement within the Catholic Church, which in the late 1530s and early 1540s coalesced first around Cardinal Contarini and then around Cardinals Pole and Morone. In its most vital form, the programme of the 'spirituali' combined Juan de Valdés's soteriology with Reginald Pole's ecclesiology. Although the reform programme of the 'spirituali' was gradualist and flexible, the line of demarcation between their position and that of the more intransigent partisans of 'new things' was fuzzy, perhaps in many instances imperceptible. In their effort to achieve the broadest possible consensus on irenical positions conducive to compromise, the 'spirituali,' whether or not they planned to do so, assumed leadership of the Italian philo-Protestant movement in all its ramifications, radical and antitrinitarian included. Consequently, at least until 1542 and in some cases thereafter, 'Lutheran' preachers encountered tolerance and protection not only in the Italian episcopate but even in the College of Cardinals.[17]

The various currents of renewal were drawn together by the doctrine of justification by faith alone, which they all endorsed. Cohesion around this platform overcame differences in confessional orientation (Lutheran, Zwinglian, Bucerian, Anabaptist) that had proliferated from the 1530s on. But in 1547 this fundamental plank collapsed: the approval of the Tridentine decree on justification forced those who had not already begun to reconsider their position to make a choice from which there was no turning back.

What influenced the theological choices of the 'Lutheran' preachers? The clues that can be gathered suggest that their choices were more intellectual than religious. Reform-minded theology, which had embraced the main themes of Erasmian biblical humanism, presented itself as modern, philologically sound, dynamic: it was the great intellectual contribution of the period. In particular, the 'paradox' of justification by faith alone presented theological professionals with prospects of dizzying conceptual boldness. It is significant that expressions of an aesthetic character recur frequently in the lexicon of philo-Protestant preachers and their listeners: the works and doctrines of the heretics struck them as 'beautiful' or 'eloquent' even before they endorsed them as 'true'. The beauty of Reformation theology consisted above all in the boldness of its dialectic. Grace/merit, flesh/spirit, spirit/letter, Gospel/human traditions, justice/mercy: these are the great themes of systematic theology which underlay Italian philo-Protestant preaching during these two decades.[18]

It was many years before these preachers were unmasked and denounced. The cautious, convoluted style of preaching which they had adopted represents a fascinating, unexplored problem in techniques of communication. I shall cite a few of its most evident characteristics. First, the preachers avoided direct attacks on the ecclesiastical hierarchy. Anticlerical thunder and lightning – denunciations of immorality, avarice and simony in the time-honoured tradition of Catholic homiletics – are entirely absent. Second, the negative critique of Reformation dogmatics was hidden between the lines of the discourse, which required the employment of ingenious rhetorical techniques: hints dropped but not followed up, reticence, innuendo, partial concealment of crucial phrases by lapsing from Italian into Latin. Third, the positive contribution of Reformation theology was couched in formulas which recur in the sermons with the consistency of hammer blows without being fully explicated: 'Only Christ's passion saves us'; 'He who exalts the merits of Christ is a real Christian'; 'Trust not in your own works, for you will be saved only by the merits of Christ', and so forth.[19]

This was preaching for initiates. Certain astute sympathisers, intent on catching key words, were able to decode the message immediately and draw strength and comfort from it. Catholic theologians, too, though slowly and painfully, learned at last how to interpret this type of discourse. (Of the twenty-four witnesses who gave depositions against Giulio da Milano at the beginning of his trial in 1541, eighteen were churchmen.) But how much did the simple layfolk understand? The documents which might enable us to respond precisely to this question – the summaries of philo-Protestant teaching contained in citizens' chronicles and reports on preaching inserted in trial records, for example[20] – have not yet been analysed. My impression is that most members of the audience had no idea how potentially subversive this kind of preaching was. Unless they had been warned, humble listeners received these 'heresies' as edifying discourses which affected them profoundly by appealing to their emotions. Sermons by so-called 'Lutherans' usually drew crowds so large that the churches could not hold them. Yet members of the audience did not rise up against the ecclesiastical establishment. Products of the philo-Protestant press evoked a similarly 'soft,' passive reaction: the 'ingenuous' reader of the *Sommario della Santa Scrittura* or the *Beneficio di Cristo* did not realize that the type of spirituality promulgated in these books implied the overturning of institutions. As I see it, beyond the narrow circles of initiates, efforts to disseminate the Reformation by preaching bore little fruit. To my knowledge, no philo-Protestant sermon led to action, manifestations of anticlericalism or iconoclasm, as so often happened in Central Europe. The preaching of 'Christ masked' (Bernardino Ochino) quenched some prelates' thirst for reform, and it created 'confusion and scandal' among priests with a scholastic orientation, but it could not move the mass of the faithful to action. Ambiguity was both the strength and the weakness of philo-Protestant preaching in Italy.

### Spontaneous diffusion (the era of the artisans, 1542–1555)

In the early 1540s the philo-Protestant movement broke out of these closed circles into the shops, streets, and squares. The Church's response to this eruption was the reorganisation of the Inquisition (1542). Rather than precipitating the decline of the movement, as historians of the previous generation believed, it ushered in the most vibrant phase of the Italian Reformation.[21]

Closely linked to the change in the early 1540s and fundamental to it was a shift in public opinion. While in the 1520s and 1530s people had reacted aggressively against occasional naive attempts by itinerant artisans from Germany, Croatia, or even the Veneto to make Protestant propaganda,[22] from 1543 on, the sources reveal more ambivalent reactions on the part of common folk: some opposition, to be sure, but also curiosity, anticipation, and even agreement. Inquisitors, too, displayed a certain ambivalence. Fra Marino da Venezia, who passed the death sentence on the Anabaptist Benedetto dal Borgo, was open to dialogue and compromise with other defendants.[23] When Paul IV Carafa ascended the papal throne in 1555, he put an end to such inconsistent behaviour on the part of ecclesiastical judges, as well as closing the spaces in which popular dissent could be manifested.

Documentation from Venice, Modena, Imola, Bologna, Genoa and Siena reveals the existence during the period 1542–55 of some forty dynamic and flexible groups working in the open to spread the Protestant message. They operated almost exclusively in the cities of northern and central Italy.[24] The countryside was barely touched. A few isolated instances of propaganda campaigns among the peasants have come down to us (e.g., Pietro Vagnola in the Polesine, 1547), but are yet to be analysed in their social context.[25]

Artisans predominated in these urban philo-Protestant groups. In second place numerically were professionals and merchants. Taking as a sample a group active in Udine in 1543, we encounter the following social profile: among the twenty-seven members clearly identifiable as philo-Protestants, there were eleven artisans (mostly master craftsmen), two schoolmasters, four clerics (three friars and a priest), a flute-player, a peddler who also pulled teeth, a noble, and six people for whom no occupation is given. The one female in the group, mother of the priest and one of the friars, typifies women's involvement in the movement, which was almost always through kinship ties.[26] Analysis of a group active in Vicenza in 1547 yields practically identical results.[27] The high proportion of artisans in these two groups is paralleled in the quantitative analysis undertaken by John Martin on the whole of the Venetian documentation. That some of the public were curious about and even receptive to such ideas and activities is shown by the allegation, no doubt exaggerated, that the philo-Protestant nucleus in Udine had attracted 400 sympathisers; in Vicenza, 600 sympathisers are mentioned.

The dynamics of communication within and between such groups and with outsiders are abundantly documented, but here again, thorough analyses remain to be made. Forms of communication most frequently mentioned include common participation in religious services and discussion of sermons (both in the groups and with the preachers), discussions in shops and public spaces, propaganda in confraternities. Most important was common reading and diffusion of heretical books: in this period, the book outstripped the sermon as a vehicle of communication. What was new, however, was not books in themselves but the dialectic between the written and the spoken word, that is, common reading and discussion of books. Since trial records usually contain lists of books, it is possible to make a wide-ranging quantitative study of the reform-oriented literature that circulated in these groups. Among members of the Udine group I am using as a sample, thirteen books were passed around, among them an Italian translation of Luther's *An den christlichen Adel deutscher Nation* and the sermons of Savonarola.

References to the use of iconographic material (prints, paintings) are relatively rare. More frequent, and also more interesting, are polemical allusions to traditional Catholic iconography – especially, but not exclusively, depictions of the saints.[28]

This second phase of the Italian Reformation was marked also by the putting of religious convictions into action. In 1544, a public abjuration in the cathedral of Pordenone was transformed by a heretic who was not at all penitent into an opportunity to make Protestant propaganda. A year later, on a fast day in Brescia, a public banquet in honour of a bishop featured meat on the menu. On Palm Sunday in 1546, a group of armed gentlemen stationed themselves in the church square of an agricultural centre to dissuade the peasants from going to confession, telling them that confession was unnecessary. In 1547, a shoemaker in Asolo urged those gathered in church not to have masses for the dead said and contradicted the priest, challenging him to a public debate about purgatory; those present placed wagers on the outcome of the debate. At the end of the decade in Cremona and Gardone, small protestant conventicles supported ministers, established a common chest and attempted to introduce changes in the Catholic liturgy.[29] Open manifestations of dissent can be found on higher levels as well. The French princess Renée, Duchess of Ferrara, financed the philo-Protestant movement and protected religious refugees. In the Venetian Republic, some nobles (not Venetians) plotted a pro-Protestant insurrection.[30]

In this phase, too, the most radical wing of the Reformation movement grew and consolidated to the point of daring in 1550 to convene an Anabaptist summit meeting in Venice. The gap between the radical groups and those oriented toward the 'Magisterial' Reformation was not wide, as is shown by the fact that the clandestine Anabaptist network included a certain number of 'Lutherans'. In 1551 revelations made by one of the heads of the Venetian Anabaptist movement, Pietro Manelfi from the Marche, derailed and dispersed this wing of the Reformation but did not destroy it: as late as the 1570s, Venetian and Friulan Anabaptists continued to swell the ranks of emigres heading for Moravia.[31]

This phase of the Italian Reformation, I think, merits the appellation 'people's Reformation.' Cautious use of this term strikes me as appropriate because not only did the people conduct the movement; they tailored its theological message to fit their own circumstances. If systematic theology had dominated in the previous period, the era of the preachers, what came to the fore now were the practical corollaries, the concrete, everyday aspects of the Reformation message. Inquisitorial sources permit us to measure the appeal of individual doctrinal points by counting the ideas most often put forward in discussions and most frequently utilised in propaganda. A quantitative investigation based on the Udine sample yields the following results. The doctrine most widely diffused, which penetrated most deeply and persisted longest in people's memories, was opposition to veneration of the saints (36 mentions). In descending order come opposition to dietary restrictions (20 mentions), denial of the real presence in the Eucharist and resistance to such cultic manifestations thereof as adoration of the Host (16 mentions) and dismissal of the doctrine of purgatory (13 mentions). The fundamental doctrines, the keystones of systematic theology, which had inspired philo-Protestant preaching in the first phase are virtually absent from my sample. In this dossier justification by faith alone is referred to only once, in a rather unspecific way, and there are two even vaguer allusions to the bondage of the will. Similar results are obtained from analyses I have made of depositions by Istrian and Modenese philo-Protestants, most of them *sponte comparentes*.[32] In Italy, too, then, the people selected from the Protestant message the elements they considered most relevant to their lives and reshaped the Reformation according to their own needs.

The focal point around which the various aspects of this 'people's reformation' were organised was the Gospel – not just the expression, but the book itself. We find it everywhere. It is chained to the work bench in artisans' shops, and passers-by are called in to see the words of St Paul with their own eyes. In private homes it is sometimes present in both Italian and Latin versions. Modest artisans spend their free time comparing one version to the other, that is, conducting Biblical exegesis, in churches, under the galleries in the piazza, and in other traditional gathering places. People use the Gospel to legitimate their dissent, even sometimes when on trial before the Inquisition.[33]

Appropriation of the Gospel by sixteenth-century Italians was an enterprise marked on occasion by flights of fancy. A Roman trial presents us with philo-Protestant Venetian jewellers who invented an evangelical 'jeweller's parable'. Trials from Udine and Istria permit us to identify inclinations to manipulate and rewrite the Bible.[34] The expressions 'evangelical doctrine', 'evangelical way', and 'evangelical preacher', the frequent recurrence of which in the trial records attests to these groups' self-awareness, make clear that 'Italian Evangelism' is to be found here, among the people – not on some vague, equivocal 'middle road' hypothesised by earlier historians.[35]

## Repression (the era of the conventicles, 1555–1571)

What German historians call the process of *Disziplinierung* reached a climax between the pontificates of Paul IV (1555–9) and Pius V (1565–71). From 1559 on, owning, holding, or hiding 'heretical' books was defined as a crime.[36] Around 1560, spies of the Inquisition began to infiltrate philo-Protestant groups.[37] In heresy trials, the employment of torture on reticent defendants became common, especially for the purposes of obtaining the names of accomplices.[38] A fundamental, very delicate, and still unsettled issue is the relationship between the Inquisition and the sacrament of confession. In theory, even the Holy Office should have respected the secret of the confessional. In fact, however, as Adriano Prosperi has shown, confession, too, became a tool for the discovery and repression of heresy.[39]

This situation contributed to the sectarianisation of the movement. Caught in the jaws of repression, philo-Protestants closed ranks and arrayed themselves along confessional lines. Because the circulation of books had become slow and risky, Italian dissidents became increasingly dependent for indoctrination on emissaries from the reformed churches of the North, who visited them periodically. It was above all the church of Geneva which maintained contact with Italian Protestant groups, in part because of personal ties and in part for reasons of doctrinal affinity.[40] Ever since the 1540s, the Italian philo-Protestants had tended to conceive the eucharist as a 'sign', a 'symbol', a 'commemoration' – that is, to deny the real presence. In Italian circles this doctrine was so common that in 1547 the vicar of the bishop of Padua considered it the essence of Protestant theology: the 'Lutheran opinion' *par excellence*, according to the vicar, was the denial that Christ was present in the consecrated host.[41]

Thus a movement that in the 1540s had been spontaneous, polyphonic, and doctrinally flexible was transformed by about 1560 into a network of conventicles oriented for the most part toward Geneva. Here and there we can find traces of a clandestine organisation: messages in code, passwords, ways and means of staying under cover. The best disguise was maintaining the appearance of being an orthodox Catholic. Nicodemite behaviour became most common precisely in the years when Calvin's anti-Nicodemite treatises were spread throughout Italy.[42] 'Heresy' withdrew into private spaces. Every so often it broke out into public in acts of iconoclasm and assaults on a Catholic preacher, but these were actions prepared in secret and carried out by people who concealed their identity.[43]

The social physiognomy of the movement had changed as well. When some of the prosperous pharmacists and skilled artisans tried in the 1540s reappeared before the Inquisition in the 1560s, they were déclassés, indigents who had to rely on charity from their coreligionists.[44] Even the emissaries from Geneva who smuggled in Calvinist books dressed as beggars.[45] Nobles, lawyers, physicians and rich merchants were still to be found in the clandestine network, but they kept to themselves rather than mixing with their social inferiors. The higher a philo-Protestant's social rank, the more cautious his dissent, for a heresy conviction usually meant confiscation of property.

Topics of reading and conversation were different, too. Comments on political events displaced doctrinal disputes. The development of the political-military situation in France was followed with passionate interest; every Huguenot success raised hopes for Protestantism in Italy. Within groups, discussion revolved around the great dilemma – stay or emigrate?[46]

Interrogations under torture reveal a particularly dramatic aspect of this phase: the expectation of a sign. Ever since the 1540s, the movement had been sustained by faith that God would not abandon his own. As the years passed, this faith had been transformed into the expectation that God would reveal himself in history. Now this hope was expressed in the form of prayers and pleas, faithfully recorded by Inquisition notaries. Defendants being tortured cried 'God, perform a miracle!'[47]

## Extinction (1571–1588)

From 1570 on, the statistical profile of Inquisition caseloads reveals a decline in trials for heresy and a corresponding rise in cases of magic and witchcraft, which came to predominate by 1580 (later, toward the end of the century, in border regions).[48] This change in the documentary picture is one of the few trends that emerge clearly from the last phase of my investigation, which is yet to be completed. The following observations should therefore be taken as hypotheses that remain to be verified.

Recruitment of new sympathisers having virtually ceased, the Venetian, Lombard, and Modenese philo-Protestants who came before the tribunals of the Inquisition in the 1570s and early 1580s were survivors from previous phases. They expressed their dissent in a society that by now had been won over to post-Tridentine ideals and values. In Lucca, new associations devoted to unmasking heretics were formed spontaneously; in Faenza, hostility toward 'Lutherans' contributed to the development of new forms of worship.[49]

What little religious dissent remained was an individual phenomenon. With the exception of a few dissident groups in border regions such as Friuli and Istria,[50] very few Protestant conventicles survived. Waldensian communities in Calabria had been ruthlessly wiped out, those in Piedmont hemmed in. Thus the dynamic activities of groups gave way to the monologues of isolated individuals.

But even in these unfavourable conditions, the urge to communicate could not be completely repressed. In the workplace or in the family, the heretic still sought or cultivated an interlocutor. Did dissent find its last refuge between the four walls of the home? That is what recent research suggests. Ties of affection, concern for reputation, and desire to preserve patrimony combined to foster within the family a commitment to confidentiality that outside the home had been eroded by the widespread practice of denunciation. In addition to some cases of domestic cults with Protestant tendencies, the sources reveal heretical 'complicity' between father and son and between brothers.[51] It may well be that in the privacy of some homes, dissent survived beyond my cut-off date of 1588 (the last death sentence against a heretic pronounced in Venice[52]) and continued to produce feeble offshoots until the end of the century.

In the conditions of fragmentation and isolation that characterise this phase, individual dissent sometimes assumed forms so eccentric that including them in the category 'Protestant' becomes problematic. If the term can be used at all, it is in many instances a Protestantism tinged with Anabaptism, and in a few cases combined with millenarian expectation and astrological beliefs.[53]

A notable characteristic of trials for heresy in these years is the tendency for dissent to focus on a material object: one or more printed books, a work in manuscript, a poem learned in childhood. Thirty or forty years earlier, such texts would have been considered more or less innocuous, but now they posed a risk, especially if their possessors had previously been tried for heresy.[54] Such attachment to dangerous material objects seems self-destructive, almost irrational. It can be understood only in the context of dissent that sometimes took the form of quiet madness.

A different, complementary phenomenon identifiable in the last two phases of the movement can be termed 'religious chameleonism.' A group of Sienese trials brought to light by Valerio Marchetti featured highly skilled artisans – engravers, furriers, sculptors – who moved around Europe in search of work and made appropriate religious accommodations wherever they found it: they attended sermons in Protestant territories and comported themselves as Catholics in Catholic lands. In their hearts, however, even these pragmatic, religiously flexible artisans reserved the right to assess the various forms of worship and doctrines they encountered and selectively to combine elements from divergent confessions. The result was theological syncretism, in which the Catholic doctrine of the eucharist might be combined with Calvinist ecclesiology and rejection of the cult of the saints.[55] Thus, even in the harvest season of triumphant confessionalism, dissenting Italy remained a fertile terrain for the cultivation of individual religious hybrids.

*English translation by Anne Jacobson Shutte*

NOTES

1 From the point of view of historical vitality and continuity, the Waldensians occupy a key position within the 'Reformation in Italy', such that the expression 'Italian Protestantism' is practically synonymous with the Waldensian Church. The Waldensians, however, joined the Reformation *en bloc*, as a movement with centuries-old traditions and a pre-established profile: see Giorgio Turn, *Geschichte der Waldenser-Kirche* (Erlangen, 1980). Thus the history of the Waldensian Church has a chronology and shape different from and independent of the history of Reformation ideas in Italy, the theme of this essay.

2 Here again, an exception must be made for the Waldensian communities. On the

annihilation of those in Calabria and on the armed resistance of those in Piedmont, see Turn, *Waldenser-Kirche*, pp. 93–118.

3 After decades of debate, a persuasive interpretation of Valdés's message and its efficacy has been proposed recently by Massimo Firpo, *Tra alumbrados e 'spirituali'. Studi su Juan de Valdés e il Valdesianesimo nella crisi religiosa del '500 italiano* (Florence, 1990).

4 Adriano Prosperi and Maurizio Ghelardi are preparing a critical edition, to be published by Einaudi, of Delio Cantimori's *Eretici italiani del Cinquecento* (Florence, 1939).

5 See Camillo Renato, *Opere*, ed. Antonio Rotondò, Corpus Reformatorum Italicorum (Florence and Chicago, 1968); Carlo Ginzburg, *Il nicodemismo. Simulazione e dissimulazione religiosa nell'Europa dell '500* (Turin, 1969); Lelio Sozzini, *Opere*, ed. Antonio Rotondò, Studi e Testi per la Storia Religiosa del Cinquecento, I (Florence, 1986); Adriano Prosperi, 'Ricerche sul Siculo e i suoi seguaci' in *Studi in onore di Armando Saitta*, ed. Regina Pozzi and Adriano Prosperi (Pisa, 1989), pp. 35–71. A complete list will soon be available in the bibliography compiled by John Tedeschi (see the Further Reading section).

6 Tom Scott, 'The Common People and the German Reformation', *Historical Journal* 34 (1991), pp. 183–92; Tom Scott, 'The Communal Reformation between Town and Country', forthcoming in the proceedings of the conference 'The Reformation in Germany and Europe: Interpretations and Issues' (Washington, 25–30 September 1990). I thank Professor Scott for his kind cooperation in the preparation of my essay.

7 Peter Blickle, 'Die soziale Dialektik der reformatorischen Bewegung' in Peter Blickle, Andreas Lindt, and Alfred Schindler, eds., *Zwingli und Europa* (Zürich, 1987), pp. 71–83; Blickle, *Gemeindereformation*, Studienausgabe (Munich, 1987), pp. 13–21.

8 John Martin, 'Alcuni aspetti di analisi quantitativa dell'Inquisizione veneziana. Primi risultati e metodi' (Martin's total includes 41 Anabaptists and 20 millenarians) and Simonetta Adorni-Braccesi, 'La Repubblica di Lucca e l'"aborrita" Inquisizione. Instituzioni e società', in Andrea Del Col and Giovanna Paolin, eds., *L'Inquisizione romana in Italia nell'età moderna. Archivi, problemi di metodo e nuove ricerche*, Saggi del Ministero per i beni culturali e ambientali (Rome, 1991), pp. 143–57, 233–62. These two articles anticipate forthcoming books, Martin's on the Reformation in Venice and Adorni-Braccesi's on the Reformation in Lucca.

9 I refer to a key passage from the paper given by Peter Blickle at the Washington conference (September 1990): 'I do not know what motives drove people from the Roman Church and to the reformers, nor does anyone else know it. Why did people around 1515 want to see the Body of Christ in the Eucharist, but around 1525 demand to hear the Word of God? No one has produced a plausible answer to this question, much less an adequate one. On this point I admit to being as ignorant as everyone else.'

10 John Tedeschi, *The Prosecution of Heresy. Collected Studies on the Inquisition in Early Modern Italy* (Binghamton, N.Y., 1991), pp. 89–126.

11 Carlo Ginzburg, 'The Inquisitor as Anthropologist', in Ginzburg, *Clues, Myths, and the Historical Method*, trans. John and Anne C. Tedeschi (Baltimore and London, 1989), pp. 156–64.

12 Carlo Ginzburg, *The Cheese and the Worms. The Cosmos of a Sixteenth-Century Miller*, trans. John and Anne C. Tedeschi (Baltimore and London, 1980).

13 The chronology I am proposing here does not work for Piedmont, controlled for all practical purposes until 1559 by the French, where the presence of Huguenot political authorities favoured the diffusion of Reformation ideas and the consolidation of the Waldensian church (see note 1), or for Sicily and Sardinia, governed directly by Spain and subject to the Spanish Inquisition. For Sicily, see Salvatore Caponetto, *Studi sulla Riforma in Italia* (Florence, Dipartimento di Storia dell-'Università di Firenze, 1987), pp. 15–96. It should also be noted that the philo-Protestant movement lasted longer in the Republic of Lucca than elsewhere.

14 Ugo Rozzo and Silvana Seidel Menchi, 'Livre et Réforme en Italie,' in Jean-François Gilmont, ed., *La Réforme et le livre. L'Europe de l'imprimé* (Paris, 1990), pp. 327–74.

15 Here is a list of these preachers. Augustinian Hermits: Giulio della Rovere, Agostino Mainardi, Ambrogio Cavalli, Andrea Ghetti da Volterra, Agostino Museo da Treviso, Nicolò da Verona, Angelo da Crema, Tommaso da Carpenedolo, Paolo da Sant'Angelo, Agostino da Fivizzano, Agostino Fogliata da Cremona, Clemente da Ognio, Ambrogio Quistelli, Aurelio da Scio, Ambrogio Bolognesi; Franciscans: Girolamo Ferrari detto il Galateo, Bartolomeo Fonzio, Alessandro Pagliarino da Piove di Sacco, Benedetto da Locarno, Giovanni Buzio da Montalcino, Antonio della Castellina, Francesco da Cocconato, Barolomeo Golfi dalla Pergola, Francesco Visdomini da Ferrara, Baldo Lupetino; Augustinian Canons: Pietro Martire Vermigli, Costantino da Carrara, Ippolito Chizzola; Dominicans: Bartolomeo Maturo priore, Angelo da Messina (Ludovico Manna), Girolamo da Lodi: Capuchins: Bernardino Ochino, general of the order, and Girolamo da Bologna; Carmelite: Giovan Battista Pallavicini; Benedictine: Marco da Cremona. Information about most of these preachers comes from the following works: Hubert Jedin, *Girolamo Seripando*, 2 vols (Würzburg, 1937); Federico Chabod, *Per la storia religiosa dello Stato di Milano durante il dominio di Carlo V*, 2nd edn. (Rome, 1962); Ugo Rozzo, 'Incontri di Giulio da Milano. Ortensio Lando', *Bollettino della Società di studi valdesi*, 140 (1976), pp. 77–108; Massimo Firpo, ed., *Il processo inquisitoriale del cardinale Giovanni Morone*, I, *Il Compendium* (Rome, 1981); Sergio Pagano, ed., *Il processo di Endimio Calandra e l'Inquisizione a Mantova*, Studi e Testi, 239 (Vatican City, 1991). On the Benedictines in this period, see Barry Collett, *Italian Benedictine Scholars and the Reformation* (Oxford, 1985); I am dubious about Collett's assertion that the concepts of grace and divine mercy diffused throughout the Benedictine Order had their origins within it.

16 A test case of philo-Protestant preaching is Giulio da Milano, whose activities are abundantly documented in the record of his trial (Archivio di Stato di Venezia, Santo Ufficio (abbreviated hereafter as ASV), b. 1).

17 See Firpo, *Tra alumbrados e 'spirituali'*; Gigliola Fragnito, *Gasparo Contarini. Un magistrato veneziano al servizio della cristianità*, Biblioteca della Rivista di storia e letteratura religiosa, 9 (Florence, 1988). The quoted phrase about 'evil doctrine' may be found in Pagano, *Il processo di Endimio Calandro*, p. 251.

18 My main sources for these observations are the published sermons of Giulio da Milano and Bernardino Ochino.

19 This analysis is based on the sample case of Giulio da Milano; see note 16.

20  Among the citizen chronicles, full of judgments about the preaching of philo-Protestants of the evangelical type, is the diary of Tommasino dei Bianchi de Lancellotti of Modena, on which see Albano Biondi, 'Tommasino Lancellotti, la città e la Chiesa a Modena (1537–1554)', *Contributi* 2 (1978), pp. 45–61.

21  Anne Jacobson Schutte, 'Periodization of Sixteenth-Century Italian Religious History. The Post-Cantimori Paradigm Shift', *Journal of Modern History* 61 (1989), pp. 269–84.

22  Archivio Patriarcale di Venezia, Processi criminali, b. 1, pp. 304–5 (1525); Archivio di Stato di Modena, Inquisizione, b. 2, *Contra Henricum Teutonicum* (1530); Franco Gaeta 'Documenti da codici vaticani per la storia della Riforma in Venezia', *Annuario dell' Istituto storico italiano per l'età moderna e contemporanea* 7 (1965), p. 30 (1533).

23  Anne Jacobson Schutte, 'Un inquisitore al lavoro. Fra Marino da Venezia e l'Inquisizione veneziana', in *I Francescani in Europa tra Riforma e Controriforma*, Assisi, Università degli Studi di Perugia, Centro di Studi francescani (Naples, 1987), pp. 166–96.

24  In addition to the works on Venice, Lucca, and Lombardy cited above (notes 8, 15), see Valerio Marchetti, *Gruppi ereticali senesi nel Cinquecento* (Florence, 1975); Susanna Peyronel Rambaldi, *Speranze e crisi nel Cinquecento modenese. Tensioni religiosa e vita cittadina ai tempi di Giovanni Morone* (Milan, 1979).

25  ASV, b. 6, *Contra Petrum Vagnolam senensem*.

26  ASV, b. 1, fasc. Girolamo Venier, Alvise Cavallo and others.

27  ASV, b. 7, *Contra Ricardo pittor et Nicolò dalle Monache*.

28  The trial involving the painter Ricardo, cited in the previous note, is particularly rich in references to iconographic material; see also ASV, b. 7, *Contra Ioannem Donatum della Columbina* (1547).

29  Andrea Del Col, 'L'abiura trasformata in propaganda ereticale nel duomo di Udine (1544)', *Metodi e ricerche* 2, no. 2 (1981), pp. 57–73; Silvana Seidel Menchi, 'Protestantesimo a Venezia', in *La Chiesa di Venezia tra Riforma protestante e riforma cattolica*, ed. Giuseppe Gullino (Venice, 1991), pp. 144–5; ASV, b. 6, *Extractum processus contra hereticos de Asylo* (1547); b. 8, fasc. 29, trial of Girolamo Allegretti (1550).

30  Bartolommeo Fontana, *Renata di Francia duchessa di Ferrara*, 3 vols (Rome, 1888–99); Aldo Stella, 'Utopie e velleità insurrezionali dei filoprotestanti italiani, 1545–1547', *Bibliothèque d'humanisme et renaissance* 27 (1965), pp. 133–82.

31  Carlo Ginzburg, ed., *I costituti di don Pietro Manelfi*, Biblioteca del Corpus Reformatorum Italicorum (Florence and Chicago, 1970); Aldo Stella, *Dall'anabattismo al socinianesimo nel Cinquecento veneto* (Padua, 1967); Aldo Stella, *Anabattismo e antitrinitarismo in Italia nel sedicesimo secolo* (Padua, 1969).

32  Silvana Seidel Menchi, *Erasmo in Italia, 1520–1580* (Turin, 1987), pp. 50 f.

33  These behaviour patterns are documented in the trial records cited in notes 27, 28 and 29. For an appeal to the authority of the Gospel during a heresy trial, see ASV, b. 6, *Contra Ioannem Donatum della Columbina* (1547).

34  ASV, b. 32, *Contra Theophilum Panarelli*, costituto of 23 November 1571 (the jeweller's parable); Archivio della Curia Arcivescovile di Udine, b. 1, fasc. 21, *Contra fratrem Vincentium de Utino* (1560), f. 1r; ASV, b. 40, fasc. Nicolò Guidozzo (1575), f. 19. Both fra Vincenzo da Udine and Nicolò Guidozzo cite a pseudo-Biblical verse ('Quotiescumque ingemuerit peccator, omnium iniquita-

tum eius non ricordabor amplius' [Whenever the sinner groans, I shall cease to remember all his sins]) which I believe to be the product of textual manipulation that can be traced to Pier Paolo Vergerio.

35 The debate about 'Italian Evangelism' is summarised by Schutte, 'Periodization'. It is well to remember that in sixteenth-century sources, Italian as well as transalpine, the term 'evangelical' is regularly employed to refer to the Reformation movement. Here are a few examples: 'evangelical preachers' (as opposed to 'ecclesiastical preachers', i.e., Catholics); 'this preacher is a real evangelist' who follows the 'evangelical way', referring to a preacher with a Protestant orientation (Emilio Comba, 'Giulio da Milano', *Rivista cristiana* 15 (1887), p. 311, p. 315, p. 317); 'evangelical minister', meaning Protestant pastor (ASV, b. 8, fasc. 29, Girolamo Allegretti, letter from the church of Cremona to Allegretti); 'evangelical truth', meaning Protestant doctrine (ASV, b. 14, *Contra presbiterum Faustinum Diaconum* (1559)); 'I know no evangelical preachers except Buzzero,' i.e. Bucer (ASV, b. 4, *Contra presbiterum Nicolaum Rossignolum* (1550)); 'your people, whom you falsely call evangelicals' (ASV, b. 4, letter from Girolamo Muzio to Pier Paolo Vergerio (1548); see also Anne Jacobson Schutte, *Pier Paolo Vergerio. The Making of an Italian Reformer* (Geneva, 1977), p. 231; 'the Huguenots are evangelicals of the Christian truth', 'the evangelical truth [is] persecuted', 'I knew well that you were not a good evangelical' (Archivio di Stato di Modena, Inquisizione, b. 3, *Contra Ioannem Rangonum* (1563)). Catholic controversialists as well used the term 'evangelical' or 'evangelist' for Italian followers of the Reformation. Alvise Lippomano, *Confirmatione et stabilimento di tutti i dogmi cattolici* (Venice, 1553), p. 22v: 'these, our new evangelists'.

36 Paul Grendler, *The Roman Inquisition and the Venetian Press, 1540–1605* (Princeton, 1977).

37 ASV, b. 19, fasc. Pellizzari (1563).

38 ASV, b. 22, *Contra Odoricum Grisonum et complices Anabaptistas et Iacobum callegarium, Baptista tintorem et Valerium tintorem* (1567); b. 24, *Contra Franciscum, Joseph Cinganum, Gabrielem de Stringariis, Aloysium de Coltis* (1568).

39 Adriano Prosperi, 'L'Inquisizione in Italia', in *Clero e società nell' Italia moderna*, ed. Mario Rosa, forthcoming.

40 Edouard Pommier, 'La société vénitienne et la Réforme protestante au XVIᵉ siècle', *Bollettino dell'Istituto di storia della società e dello stato veneziano* 1 (1959), pp. 3–26; Silvana Seidel Menchi, 'Protestantesimo', and in the same volume, Federica Ambrosini, 'Tendenze filoprotestanti nel patriziato veneziano', pp. 155–81.

41 ASV, b. 6, *Exemplum processus contra hereticos de Asyllo* (1547).

42 Carlo Ginzburg, *Il nicodemismo*; Perez Zagorin, *Ways of Lying. Dissimulation, Persecution, and Conformity in Early Modern Europe* (Cambridge, Mass., 1990).

43 For example, ASV, b. 22, fasc. *Contra Vincentium Negronem medicum* (1567); b. 37, *Contra Hieronimo Parto* (1572).

44 One example: the apothecary Zuan Donato della Colombina, who in 1547 had a prosperous pharmacy in Vicenza (ASV, b. 6), reappears in Venetian inquisitorial documents in 1564 as Zuan Donà de paternostri, 'a poor man who makes rosary beads from agate', whom more prosperous coreligionists sometimes invited to dinner (ASV, b. 11, fasc. *Processus contra Andream de Ugonibus Venetiis formatus*, costituto of 22 February 1565). For the identification of the man, see ASV, b. 21,

*Contra Maximum de Maximis*, costituto of 7 September 1566: 'Zuan Donà della Columbina ... now works rosary beads'.

45  See Pommier, 'La société vénitienne'.

46  Seidel Menchi, 'Protestantesimo'.

47  ASV, b. 8, fasc. 29, Girolamo Allegretti (1550); b. 19, fasc. Andrea e Marco Zaccaria (1563); b. 19, fasc. 23, *Contra Sylvestrum, Angelam, Stephanum ... Contra p. Fidelem Vigo marchianum*, costituto Fedele Vigo *in loco torturae* (1568).

48  See Andrea Del Col, 'Shifting Attitudes in the Social Environment toward Heretics. The Inquisition in Friuli in the Sixteenth Century', in *Ketzerverfolgung im XVI. und im frühen XVII. Jahrhundert. Akten des Wolfenbütteler Kolloquiums 1.5. Oktober 1989*, forthcoming. The data furnished by Del Col for the tribunal of Udine are symptomatic of a trend that can be found in all the Italian tribunals, though in most other regions the shift away from heresy toward magic and witchcraft occurred earlier and in a more pronounced fashion.

49  Adorni-Braccesi, 'La Repubblica di Lucca', p. 259; Francesco Lanzoni, *La Controriforma nella città e diocesi di Faenza* (Faenza, 1925), pp. 180–99.

50  Fulvio Tomizza, *Quando Dio uscì di chiesa. Vita e fede in un borgo istriano del Cinquecento* (Milan, 1987).

51  ASV, b. 37, *Contra Hieronimo Parto nodaro* (1572) *et Ioannem Baptistam Michael fratrem eius uterinum* (1573); Archivio di Stato di Modena, Inquisizione, b. 6, *Contra Guidum Rangonum* (1575); Archivio Vescovile di Belluno, Diocesi, Atti vescovili e curiali, b. 11, trial of Agostino Vanzo da Vicenza (1579–80); Trinity College, Dublin ms. 1225, sentence against Giulio Vanzo da Schio (1581). For a family cult with Protestant tendencies, see Archivio Arcivescovile di Udine, Santo Ufficio, b. 5, fasc. 87, *Processo contro Simon Sacardo della villa de Piano* (1580).

52  See the forthcoming study by John Martin listed in the Further Reading section.

53  Archivio Patriarcale di Venezia, Criminalia Sanctae Inquisitionis, b. 2, pp. 183–95 (1573); ASV, b. 50, Achille Rubini da Vicenza (1587); Archivio di Stato di Modena, b. 6, *Contra Guidum Rangonum* (1575).

54  See the documents cited in note 51.

55  Valerio Marchetti, 'Una prova di ricerca. Sulla genealogia della coscienza operaria', *Aut Aut*, fasc. 167–68 (settembre-dicembre 1978), pp. 129–52.

## FURTHER READING

John Tedeschi, in collaboration with James Lattis, is completing work on an exhaustive bibliography, *The Italian Reformation of the Sixteenth Century. A Bibliography of the Secondary Literature* (Binghamton, N.Y., and Ferrara, forthcoming). In this bibliography the Italian Reformation in exile (that is, the Reformation in International Context) is accorded the attention it deserves but could not receive in the present study, devoted to the Reformation in National Context. The critical edition of Delio Cantimori, *Eretici italiani del Cinquecento* (see note 4) will also serve to bring up to date the theme of the Italian Reformation outside Italy. Since these two works will soon be available, the list below includes only the most important works in English on the Reformation in Italy and subjects closely related to it.

Frederic Corss Church, *The Italian Reformers, 1534–1564* (New York, 1932).

Barry Collett, *Italian Benedictine Scholars and the Reformation. The Congregation of Santa Giustina of Padua* (Oxford, 1985).

Paul F. Grendler, *The Roman Inquisition and the Venetian Press, 1540–1605* (Princeton, 1977).

John Martin, *Venice's Hidden Enemies. Italian Heretics in a Renaissance City*, forthcoming.

Philip McNair, *Peter Martyr Vermigli in Italy. An Anatomy of Apostasy* (Oxford, 1972).

Anne Jacobson Schutte, *Pier Paolo Vergerio. The Making of an Italian Reformer* (Geneva, 1977).

In the notes I have cited the most recent Italian studies relevant to my argument. Many of them are evaluated in a bibliographical essay by Anne Jacobson Schutte, 'Periodization of Sixteenth-Century Italian Religious History: The Post-Cantimori Paradigm Shift', *Journal of Modern History* 61 (1989), 269–284.

On the controversial text *Il beneficio di Cristo*, much discussed in recent scholarship, the most important contribution is Carlo Ginzburg and Adriano Prosperi, *Giochi di pazienza: Un seminario sul Beneficio di Cristo* (Turin, 1975).

For a recent assessment of the Italian Reformation as a whole, see Antonio Rotondò, 'Anticristo e Chiesa Romana', in *Forme e destinazione del messaggio religioso. Aspetti della propaganda religiosa nel Cinquecento*, ed. Antonio Rotondò (Florence, 1991), pp. 19–162.

# 12 Spain

*Henry Kamen*

Martin Luther's early career in Germany excited the interest of Spain's intellectual elite. At the Diet of Worms 'everybody, especially the Spaniards, went to see him', confessed one of the Emperor's Spanish entourage, 'but I could never get a step near him'. The same witness testified of the Spaniards that 'at the beginning, when Luther touched only on the need to reform the Church and on the corruption of morals, everybody agreed with him, and even those who now write against him confess in their books that at the beginning they were in favour of him. There was nothing more common then than to hear them saying "Luther is right in what he says"'.[1] There were two areas of common interest: the relevant Spaniards – a select group close to Charles V – were dedicated humanists and adepts of the *philosophia Christi*; they were also, like Luther, sharply critical of the abuses of the papacy. All without exception agreed with the Emperor in rejecting the political implications of Luther's stance, but when they returned with Charles to the peninsula in mid-July 1522 their ideological position was a bit more equivocal.

Spain in 1522 was afroth with ideas. A native tradition of spirituality[2] produced numerous manuals, best represented by the writings of García de Cisneros, reforming abbot of the monastery of Montserrat, and by those of the Franciscan Francisco de Osuna; but there was also an influential current of spiritual writings brought in from Italy (Cardinal Cisneros, the abbot's brother, promoted and translated the works of Savonarola) and from the Netherlands.[3] These trends were further enriched by the first currents of learned humanism from Italy. The visionary nature of much peninsular thought at this period (an aspect closely paralleling the experience of northern Europe) can be seen in the extraordinary role of seers such as the Beata (Holy Woman) of Piedrahita, in the apocalyptic thought both of the Comuneros and of the Germanías of 1520, in the mysticism of religious groups, and above all in the utopian horizons opened up by the discovery of America, which presented the early friars with the millenarian promise of the recreation of a new Christian Church free from the corruptions of the European Church, and the hoped-for establishment of a Fifth Monarchy through the agency of the Emperor Charles.

It was into this rich soil that the thought of Erasmus penetrated and took root with astonishing force. From 1516, when his name was first traced by a Spanish pen, to 1526, when the *Enchiridion* was translated into Spanish and became an immediate best-seller, the advances of Erasmianism were striking. All over Spain, and not just in Castile, Erasmian humanism became the dominant fashion: we can observe its triumphs in the royal court (from which Charles in 1527 wrote to Erasmus assuring him of support), in the highest levels of the Church (both the Archbishop of Toledo and the Inquisitor General were Erasmians), in the small groups of intellectuals in the major cities (Valencia, from which Luis Vives had emigrated long before, was an active centre of humanism), and in the publications of the major presses (that, for example, of Miguel de Eguía at the university of Alcalá, and of the Crombergers in Seville). Ironically, the commitment to Erasmus, at a time when the Reformation was advancing rapidly in central Europe, may well have been one of the major forces that saved Spanish intellectuals from sympathising with Lutheranism.

For there is no doubt that Lutheranism had reached Spain. The flood of Lutheran books into the peninsula (we have no evidence of their nature, nor even any secure evidence that they were in Spanish) forced Cardinal Adrian of Utrecht as early as 1521 to issue the first peninsular ban on possessing or selling Lutheran books 'in Latin or in romance'. By June 1524 it was reported from the court that all the talk was only about Luther.[4] In 1525, faced by indubitable evidence that possibly thousands of books by Luther and his followers had penetrated the country, the Inquisitor General issued a further order for seizure of the forbidden material. All the evidence suggests that these were simple measures of vigilance, and that there was no panic; many loads of books were seized, and others may no doubt have entered the country notwithstanding, but in the absence of any identifiable heretics there was no cause for alarm.

The atmosphere was, however, changing, and the clearest proof was the firm campaign pursued against the illuminists (*alumbrados*), on whom suspicion fell in the prevailing climate, leading to the arrest of some of their leaders in the years 1524–9. It is worth remarking that the illuminists got off lightly, and that none suffered the extreme penalty. But the movement was of fundamental importance, for it opened the eyes of the authorities to possible subversion, and made many deeply suspicious of spiritualising tendencies: in subsequent years other Spaniards, including Ignatius Loyola (in 1527) and Juan de Avila, were to fall victim to suspicions of illuminism, and the problem endured into the seventeenth century. It also deepened doubts about Erasmianism.

Though Erasmianism seemed to be vindicated in a public debate held at Valladolid in 1527, a key event which was in effect a general council of the

Castilian Church, its days were numbered, not because of persecution but primarily because its support derived from the court; and when the court left Spain in 1529 it took with it the major figures associated with European humanism. These were years in which the strong anti-papalism of the humanists came to the fore with Alfonso de Valdés's *Dialogue* on the sack of Rome. Valdés's brother Juan, who was closely influenced by Luther,[5] in 1529 produced his *Doctrina Christiana*, but fled when it seemed the Inquisition might get to him, and settled in the Spanish territory of Naples. In the 1530s a handful of prominent Erasmians began to be arrested. Though none was punished as a heretic, the trend was clear: like illuminism before it, the Erasmian movement carried risky implications.

Erasmus continued to be a lingering but not necessarily a major influence in the development of Spanish thought long after his books were banned in Spain. The search for traces of Erasmus has often become an obsession and has unduly shifted attention from other parallel and native influences affecting Spanish thought at this period.[6] Non-Erasmians were no less capable of appreciating the virtues of reform, peace and tolerance, since all Spaniards were part of a multi-cultural society which many, certainly, were eager to reshape but which some were content to accept. Charles V's Spanish advisers and publicists – many of them non-Erasmians – were in the 1530s and 1540s prominent examples of what may be called the 'alternative tradition', as opposed to the conservative tradition of the Inquisition on one hand and the radical tradition of the Reformation on the other: it was thanks as much to the Spaniards De Soto and Maluenda as to the Erasmians Pflug and Gropper that the Interim of 1548 was issued in Germany.

Throughout the early century, when half of northern Europe had turned to the Reformation and major figures in the public life of Italy and France had done likewise, the peninsula remained immune. In the period up to 1558 there were no more than thirty-nine cases of alleged 'Lutherans' (the authorities used the word to apply to all Protestants) among Spaniards arrested by the Inquisition, and most were merely people who had made careless statements which sounded heretical. Certainly there was little repression in those years, so that the explanation of terror can be rejected at once: when hundreds were perishing at the hands of the Chambre Ardente and the Netherlands Inquisition, and in England the humanist king was executing both papalists and heretics, in Spain it is doubtful if more than one person was executed (in 1530) for identifiable Lutheranism. The Inquisition was not asleep – it rounded up forbidden Bibles, for example – so cannot be accused of negligence. Not until the events of 1558–62 did a real heresy crisis erupt.

The history of the Reformation in Spain is that of the events of 1558–62 and can be soon told. In 1557 a cell of Protestants was uncovered in Seville in the wake of the discovery that they were importing heretical books. The event led to the arrest by the Inquisition in 1558 of the prior and several friars from the monastery of San Isidro, and of a preacher of the cathedral, Charles V's former chaplain Constantino Ponce de la Fuente. In the same year several arrests were made in the Castilian capital, Valladolid; those detained included another former chaplain of the emperor, Dr Agustín Cazalla, as well as the governor of the city of Toro, Carlos de Seso, and some young nobility. The total of accused involved in the two groups was not large, about 120 persons in Seville, about 55 in Valladolid. On the insistence of the emperor, then in retirement at his villa in Yuste in south-west Spain, a harsh policy was put in hand (Philip II was in the Netherlands and was kept informed, but did not make the decisions). *Autos de fe* at Valladolid in May 1559 and at Seville in September began the bloody repression, which continued with a series of further *autos* up to 1562. With these executions, Protestantism in Spain was almost totally extinguished. In subsequent years an occasional self-confessed heretic was found and burnt for 'Lutheranism', but possibly less than a dozen Spaniards suffered for it in the second half of the sixteenth century. Several Protestants fled from the country in mid-century, but their history forms part of the European rather than of the Spanish Reformation.[7]

Were these harsh measures the reason why the Reformation did not happen in Spain? It would be foolish to pretend that they were not of some importance. But two simple considerations must be borne in mind. First, the real issue is not why Protestants were found and repressed in 1558, but why no Protestant movement of any description had taken root in Spain in the forty years since the beginning of the Lutheran Reformation. Second, as events in England, France and the Netherlands had already demonstrated amply, persecution usually served to stimulate rather than to annihilate heresy, and the *autos de fe* cannot by themselves explain the failure in Spain.

Traditionalist Catholic historiography has always maintained that Spain was too firmly Catholic a society ever to be susceptible to heresy. The great scholar Menéndez y Pelayo argued in 1880 that the Castilian mind of that time was incapable of heresy, that Spain preferred a 'noble and saving intolerance', and that 'the language of Castile was not made to utter here-sies'. This view offers a watertight explanation for the failure of the Refor-mation, and is often accepted even by those who do not share the author's ideological premises. In reality, Spanish society was more pluralist than the uncompromising conservatism of Menéndez y Pelayo allowed, and several relevant issues deserve a brief consideration.

Spain was not an illiberal society. Given the rich confusion of thought throughout peninsular history, and the freedom for philosophers like the thirteenth-century Catalan Ramón Llull to draw on all the cultural traditions of the peninsula, especially the Arabic, it is not surprising to find that Spaniards were eager to receive ideas from every quarter. Netherlands spirituality, represented by Herp and Ruysbroek, was particularly influential; but the rapid reception of Italian influence, from the spiritual to the humanistic, was in the end more lasting. The illuminists, for their part, drew on multiple influences, and only the fear of Lutheranism on the part of the Inquisition acted as a check on their activity. It was a feast of ideas: 'we interpreted everything freely', a friar was to comment later, looking back on those days. It is not surprising that one of the most popular spiritual writers of the mid-century, fray Felipe de Meneses, sympathetic to Erasmus and a close friend of Archbishop Carranza, should have warned in his *Light of the Christian soul* (1554) that 'I find more inclination to liberty in Spain than in Germany or any other nation, a desire not to be subjected and to live free ... If the drum of Lutheran liberty were to sound in Spain in this conjuncture, I fear that it would rally more people than it did in Germany'. Even as he was writing, Lutheran ideas had taken root; but despite his fears they did not succeed. Indeed, nowhere in Spain was there any coherent reception of the doctrines of Luther. Though the illuminists were certainly heterodox, they were innocent of Lutheranism and were never castigated as heretics. The 'Protestants' of 1558–9 are more difficult to analyse. Though triumphantly claimed for the Reformation by pro-Protestant scholars and denounced as heretics by Menéndez y Pelayo, only a small core of the accused, particularly those associated with Carlos de Seso, can be accurately identified as 'Protestants', and it is virtually impossible to find any systematic adherence to Lutheranism in their tenets. Nothing in the life or writings of Constantino indicates any heterodox leanings.

Spain had a strong reformist and independent tradition. Spanish clergy had shared in the conciliarist movements of the fifteenth century, but by the early 1500s conciliarism was almost dead, its last gap being the Council of Pisa (1511), when the Castilian cardinal Carvajal pressed the cause of Church reform. Though Spaniards were supporters of papal supremacy, like clergy of other nations they objected to papal manipulation of provision to benefices, papal taxation and papal pretensions to a supreme power that derogated from the powers of bishops (the last of these points was to lead in 1562 to celebrated scenes of disorder in the Council of Trent). In the early century Charles V actively encouraged his publicists to attack the papal position, notably in the writings of his secretary Alfonso de Valdés, whose *Dialogue on the events in Rome* (1527), a brilliant epitome of all the vices of the unreformed Church, argued that the sack of the Eternal City was not the fault of the emperor but a judgment by God. While still in manuscript, the work was rapidly copied, circulated from hand to hand, and delighted educated Spaniards throughout the peninsula. An infuriated Baldassare Castiglione (then in retirement in Spain, writing *The Courtier*) denounced the work to the Inquisition, and warned that it would convert Spain to Lutheranism. A few years later, in 1536, Alfonso Alvarez Guerrero published his *Treatise on the Reformation of the Church*. Guerrero was a jurist who served in Italy and ended his professional career as president of the supreme court in Naples, then retired from that, became a priest and was created bishop of Monopoli by Philip II. His tract, written probably at the behest of Charles V, questions the nature of papal secular authority, insists that in some cases the General Council of the Church is superior to the pope, and asserts unequivocally that the emperor has the right to summon a Council if the pope fails to do so. In two chapters he bluntly condemns the extent to which the greedy see of Rome is bleeding Spain: 'nearly a million in gold leaves the realms of Spain each year for Rome, and it would be an endless task to tell the sorry state of Church affairs, and how everything in Rome is run on the money that comes from Spain'. Another chapter is devoted to 'some unjust things that are done in Rome, whereby religion and the Church are scorned by lay-people, and the universal Church is thoroughly scandalised'.

It cannot be said that Spain did not need a Reformation. The wholly unacceptable argument once put forward by historians, that the reform of religious orders undertaken by Cardinal Cisneros in the 1490s helped to strengthen Spain's defences against the Reformation, ignored the reality that few religious houses were affected, and then only in Castile; that the reforms were hasty and superficial; that no reform was made either of clergy or of episcopate; and that no reform took place in the daily religion of the people. The Spanish clergy by the 1520s were as lax and ignorant as any in Europe, with prelates regularly absent, parish churches neglected, monasteries empty, convents unregulated. Precisely because of this, urgent moves were made by Charles V in 1531 and by Philip II in later years, to bring about a satisfactory reform at all levels, and by mid-century some progress was being made. But these reforms took place largely after the Reformation, and in no way pre-empted the possibility of a revolution in the Spanish Church.

Spain of the early century was not a closed society. For the two decades between the Diet of Worms and the emergency measures of 1558 not a single step was taken to cut Spain off from outside ideas, and even after 1559 the controls were only partially effective. Spaniards were active as traders in the major ports of western Europe, served as soldiers in Italy, the Netherlands and Germany, studied at several foreign universities both within (such as Louvain) and outside of (such as Montpellier) the monarchy. Nor was the peninsula geographically isolated: it was open to access by sea from every quarter, and the land frontier was used incessantly, the western Pyrenees by migrants in search of a living and by pilgrims going to Santiago, the Roussillon border by French settlers and pilgrims to Montserrat. Above all, books of every description came over the frontier with no hindrance at all.

The book trade, a virtually unstudied topic, is one of the biggest problems facing our enquiry, for its existence is incontrovertible proof that the peninsula was not shielded from foreign ideas. There was a continuous entry of Lutheran material into the country, though there is no firm evidence of Luther's works being translated into Spanish until the 1530s, despite various references to such books at a much earlier date. 'From one hour to the next', the Inquisition commented in 1532, 'books keep arriving from Germany'; but it was unable to stop the flow. Legislation on book control was out-of-date (the operative law was one of 1502), there was no guide to what books should be stopped, and there were no officials to deal with the matter. Since Spain, with its limited printing resources, was largely an importer of books (most books on sale in Barcelona, for example, had been published in Venice or in Lyon), the situation was impossible to control. The pious Catholic in Spain was still heavily dependent on foreign presses for essential manuals such as mass-books, breviaries and Bibles: in 1552 in Seville alone the Inquisition seized 450 Bibles printed abroad.

Ideas, then, were not stopped from entering the country, and in addition literary repression was usually ineffective. Though the Inquisition had issued its 1521 decree against Luther's works it was not until 1551, thirty years later, that adequate information on disapproved literature was made available, when the Inquisition issued its first guide (*Index*) to forbidden books, essentially a copy of one issued the previous year in the Netherlands; and even at this late date there was astonishingly no system of censorship in existence. Only with the decree of 7 September 1558, issued in Philip's absence by his sister Juana, was an apparently ferocious range of measures issued, an obvious reaction to the discovery of the Valladolid Protestants. This was accompanied in 1559 by the first of several famous Indexes of prohibited Books issued by the Inquisition.

Inexplicably, historians have assumed that with these measures Spain slipped into the grip of intellectual tyranny. The apparatus had not existed in the preceding half-century yet heresy failed to materialise then; it was surely no more likely to materialise now. The truth is that the censorship apparatus was far less effective than its creators might have wished. In Seville, one of Spain's principal printing centres, the censorship rules functioned more in theory than in practice[8] and had no visible impact in themselves on the fortunes of publishing. In many parts of the country, it took decades to implement the rules. Suspicious book shipments were seized, then not examined for years because the inquisitors did not have the personnel or the linguistic knowledge to read them. Above all, it is important to stress that the 1558 decrees applied only to the crown of Castile and not to the crown of Aragon, where steps to introduce similar laws were not taken till about 1570, so that for the best part of the sixteenth century the Mediterranean realms and the Pyrenean border had no official system of censorship.

Why then was there no Reformation, given these appalling gaps in the curtain? Our inability to understand the phenomenon is paralleled by that of the Castilian inquisitor of Barcelona, who in 1569, after touring the whole of northern Catalonia, concluded of Catalans living there that 'all are very Catholic ... their Christianity is such that it is cause for wonder, to see how they live next to and among heretics, having dealings every day with them', yet none was contaminated. They might, he conceded, be trying to deceive him; but he doubted it. There was no identifiable frontier between Catalan Roussillon and the French province of Languedoc; people came and went freely between the two, and occasionally Catalans out of curiosity slipped into Calvinist meetings. Yet no heresy entered Catalonia.

The fundamental difference between Spain and the rest of western Europe, one that may be vital to any explanation, was that Spain was a multi-cultural society where the coexistence of Muslims and Jews with Christians for several centuries had created a quite different perception of heresy. When religious conflict occurred, it was between communities that were easy to recognise, for each had a legally recognised position. At the same time, elements and concepts of the three faiths penetrated each other, and dissent when it occurred took on the lineaments of the other communities, and could be perceived as cultural rather than ideological, racial rather than theological. Islam was still a legally recognised religion in Spain a decade after the Lutheran Reformation had commenced in Germany, and continued to be practised by up to 5 per cent of Spain's population during the sixteenth century. But it was the Jewish situation that was apparently more conflictive. Forced conversions of Jews in 1391 and after, heightened religious sensibilities and made Spaniards see dissent as coming from mainly one direction: the converted Jews (*conversos*). When Charles V in the 1520s planned to introduce (as he did) an Inquisition into Flanders, his Spanish advisers tried to dissuade him on the grounds that, in the emperor's own words, 'there were no Jews among them'; in 1556 Philip II expressed his own belief that 'all the heresies which have occurred in Germany and France have been sown by descendants of Jews'. It is significant that what the inquisitors, who in theory were looking for Lutheranism, seem to have found most suspicious about the Castilian illuminists of the 1520s were their Jewish antecedents. It may be that this cultural identification of heresy limited its appeal to non-semitic Spaniards and impeded understanding of the Reformation. Some *conversos*, by contrast, gravitated to the Reformation: in 1556 *conversos* in the Netherlands, among them Marco Pérez, were reported by the regent Margaret of Austria to be translating and planning to send into the peninsula '30,000 books by Calvin'.

The cultural difference between northern and southern Europe may therefore be a relevant point. In the north, the parameters of dissent were historically limited to official Christianity and its unofficial deviations ('heresy'). In the south, beyond official Christianity existed the rich horizons of Arabic and Jewish tradition, and throughout the sixteenth and seventeenth centuries in Spain examples could be found of 'renegades' who embraced Islam as the most accessible alternative to official Christianity.[9]

Precisely because religious confrontation in the peninsula was directed against the Muslims and Jews, medieval Christianity in Spain was too busy to produce dissent of its own. Like Menéndez y Pelayo in his massive history of heterodoxy in the peninsula, one has to go back to the sixth century to find a heresy (Arianism).[10] For the next ten centuries there appears to have been nothing, apart from sporadic infiltration across the frontier from movements like the Albigensians. This astonishing freedom from heresy was matched by an absence of repressive institutions. Since 1232 papal commissions to inquisitors had been issued in the crown of Aragon, to combat the Cathars of Languedoc, but their activity was negligible, and by the fifteenth century they were all but defunct. In Castile no such commissions existed, and the first proposal (as late as 1461) to set up a tribunal suggested an 'inquisition into heretics such as they have in France'. In general, then, the peninsula had no memory of heresy. Both in Germany and in England, there were traditions – Hussitism, Wycliffism – to which the reformers could appeal and on which they could build; in Spain there was nothing, apart from *converso* heterodoxy. Was this, perhaps, a major obstacle to the success of the Reformation in the peninsula?

Certainly, when the first cells of Protestants were found in Castile, the alarm aroused reflected the deep shock that after so many centuries, and after forty years of the Reformation, heresy should have been able to penetrate the country. 'Before that time', a Dominican said of the year 1558, 'Spain was wholly untouched by these errors'. 'There was no need at that time to be suspicious of anyone', an abbot observed of the previous decades.[11] Yet this immunity had not come about because of a protective curtain, quite the reverse: only after 1558 did the government attempt to set up a curtain of defence against heresy. Prior to that time, Spaniards at the highest level mixed on good terms with foreign Protestants, representing as these did a heresy that was unknown in the peninsula. At the 1551 session of the Council of Trent Archbishop Guerrero of Granada, head of the Spanish delegation, invited the German Protestant delegates to his residence, and Charles V's ambassador don Francisco de Vargas drank amicably with them in his house.

If we look not at the roots of popular support but at the mechanisms through which the Reformation in northern Europe was institutionalised, they reduce themselves to three: elite support, urban support and state support. None of these three was readily available in Spain. The Renaissance nobility in Castile had a good cultural grounding, based mainly on contacts with Italy, and some families such as the Mendozas[12] made outstanding contributions in all fields. Nobles were open to new ideas, and the vogue for spirituality encouraged the duke of Infantado, in his palace at Guadalajara, and the marquis of Villena, in his residence at Escalona, to patronise the illuminists in the 1520s. Precisely in that decade, the great popularity of Erasmus swept all levels of the educated elite, but faded when the court left with Charles V in 1529. In the provinces Erasmianism was virtually unknown: in Barcelona there was very little trace of it, and the most ardent Erasmian Catalans were those who accompanied the Emperor. But though the Spanish elite travelled widely, and had a respectable contact with humanism, not a single significant member flirted with the Reformation, and only lesser members of the nobility were involved with the Valladolid group of Protestants in 1559.[13]

The possibility of urban support has unfortunately never been explored, since the culture of urban elites in the Renaissance remains unstudied. In any case, the peninsula seems to have lacked the evolved urban structures to be found in northern Italy and central Europe. Without an adequate social or urban soil to receive it, the message of the Reformation, even had it entered, would have found a void in which it could not take root. At state level, to contrast with the Reformation states of England and Scandinavia, it is important to observe that despite ongoing distrust of the papacy the Spanish crown never required political gains, since it possessed almost total control over the Church within Spain and its dominions. The papacy issued to the Spanish crown in July 1508 a bull giving it the Patronato or right over all appointments to the Church in America. Within Spain the king was in 1523 granted by Adrian VI (the former Adrian of Utrecht), in two separate Bulls of May and September, a Patronato of appointment over all the churches of Navarre, Castile and Aragon. Implicit in all these concessions was crown control over much Church revenue, and in addition the crown exercised rigid control over the papal right to publish Bulls in the country, and over the right of appeal by clergy to Rome. The last monarch in Europe to wish to use the Reformation for political advantage was the king of Spain: quite simply, he did not need it.

But did the people not need reform? Spanish popular religion in the early sixteenth century was comparable to that of much of Europe. Nominal adherence to the practice and beliefs of the Church was combined with regular resort to agrarian and community rites that often held greater validity because they arose out of local traditions. Few dogmatic imperatives operated in this environment (the sacraments were seldom used, even marriages did not have to take place in church), and religion remained powerful not for its tenets but because it supplied the only cultural context with which the community could identify itself. The situation seemed ripe for reform, and since the late fifteenth century many bishops had held diocesan synods in which they lamented the poor contact of their people with Christianity. In 1526 in Granada a government committee debated what to do about the prevalence of witchcraft in the countryside of northern Spain; when the Jesuits first began preaching in the peninsula in the 1540s they were reminded that the 'Indies' of Spain required more urgent attention than those of America.

Spanish Catholic reformers were the first in Europe to apply themselves to the problems they identified in their country's religions. This was because from the 1520s two crucial mission fields offered themselves: the first was America, where groups of friars went out armed with the purpose not merely of taking the faith but of reforming the fabric of both Church and society and bringing back the lost innocence of the early Church; the second was Granada and Valencia, where the massive concentration of a Muslim population challenged the complacency of Christian belief. Thus already in the first decade of the Reformation, and a full generation before the Counter Reformation that followed Trent, the clergy were attempting to missionise, an effort they also later extended to their own people. Whether they succeeded in America is still a matter of controversy, but they certainly failed among the Muslims of Spain; and their impact on the nominally Christian population remains to be investigated.

The Inquisition, finally, should not be forgotten. Spain was the only European country to possess a national institution dedicated to the elimination of heresy, and however inefficient it may have been we would be rash to discount it completely as a possible barrier to the entry or spread of dissenting ideas.[14] It would also, of course, be a mistake to exaggerate its role, since the existence of an Inquisition in the Netherlands did not impede the rapid spread of heresy there.

A massive movement for reform was eventually undertaken in the peninsula after the 1560s, in what scholars have identified as a 'Counter-Reformation': there is certainly no reason to consider that Spain was impervious to change. But the hopes of a godly Reformation imported from Germany faded in the

Mediterranean, evidence perhaps of a conscious inability by the south to accept the parameters of cultural dissidence proposed by northern civilisation.[15]

## NOTES

1 Juan de Vergara, cited in Marcel Bataillon, *Erasmo y España* (Mexico, 1966), pp. 110, 454.

2 The most systematic study of spiritual ideas is by Melquiades Andrés, *La Teología Española en el Siglo XVI* (Madrid, 1976).

3 Pierre Groult, *Les Mystiques des Pays-Bas et la Littérature Espagnole du Seizième Siècle* (Louvain, 1927).

4 Augustin Redondo, 'Luther et l'Espagne de 1520 à 1536', *Mélanges de la Casa de Velázquez*, i (1965), p. 133.

5 Carlos Gilly, 'Juan de Valdés. Übersetzer und Bearbeiter von Luthers Schriften in seinem *Diálogo de Doctrina*', *Archiv für Reformationsgeschichte*, 74 (1983).

6 A point made by E. Asensio, 'El erasmismo y las corrientes espirituales afines', *Revista de Filología Española*, XXVI (1952).

7 Ernst Schäfer, *Beiträge zur Geschichte des Spanischen Protestantismus und der Inquisition im sechzehnten Jahrhundert*, 3 vols. (Gütersloh, 1902), gives a profile of the Protestant community.

8 Clive Griffin, *The Crombergers of Seville* (Oxford, 1988), p. 123.

9 B. Bennassar, *Los cristianos de Alá. La fascinante Aventura de los Renegados* (Madrid, 1989).

10 M. Menéndez y Pelayo, *Historia de los Heterodoxos Españoles*, 8 vols. first published 1881 and since available in several editions.

11 J. I. Tellechea, *El arzobispo Carranza y su Tiempo*, 2 vols. (Madrid, 1968), vol. II, pp. 241, 255.

12 Helen Nader, *The Mendoza Family in the Spanish Renaissance* (New Brunswick, 1979).

13 Doña Isabel Briceño, a distinguished Mendoza lady, flirted with the Reformation, but in Italy, where she formed part of the Juan de Valdés circle.

14 J. Contreras, 'The impact of Protestantism in Spain', in S. Haliczer, ed., *Inquisition and Society in Early Modern Europe* (London, 1987), considers that the Inquisition deliberately exaggerated the threat from heresy in order to maintain social control.

15 See F. Braudel, *The Mediterranean and the Mediterranean World in the Age of Philip II*, 2 vols. (London, 1972), vol. II, p. 768.

## FURTHER READING

The following brief list is restricted to items in English and French.

A general survey with some bibliography is given in Henry Kamen, *Inquisition and Society in Spain in the Sixteenth and Seventeenth Centuries* (London and Bloomington, 1985); and the older Henry Charles Lea, *History of the Inquisition of Spain*, 4 vols. (New York, 1906) has a full if outdated presentation. There is a useful bibliography by Gordon Kinder, *Spanish Protestants and Reformers in the Sixteenth*

*Century* (London, 1983). John E. Longhurst devoted several short studies to the subject, principally *Luther and the Spanish Inquisition. The Case of Diego de Uceda 1528-1529* (Albequerque, 1953); 'Luther in Spain 1520-1540', *Proceedings of the American Philosophical Society*, 103 (1959); *Erasmus and the Spanish Inquisition. The Case of Juan de Valdés* (Alberquerque, 1950). The thesis of Juan C. Nieto, *Juan de Valdés (1509?-1541)* (Michigan, 1968) had not found general agreement. There are interesting essays on the spirituality of the alumbrados and the 'Lutherans' by Nieto and by Melquiades Andrés in A. Alcalá, ed., *The Spanish Inquisition and the Inquisitorial Mind* (Boulder, Colorado, 1987), but the best short introduction to the alumbrados and their religious context is by Alastair Hamilton, *Heresy and Mysticism in Sixteenth-Century Spain. The Alumbrados* (Cambridge, 1992). The fundamental and essential survey of the intellectual background is Bataillon, cited in the notes.

Edward Boehmer, *Bibliotheca Wiffeniana. Spanish Reformers of two centuries, from 1520*, 3 vols. (London, 1864-1904) is a basic source. Emigré reformers are discussed in studies such as P. J. Hauben, *Three Spanish Heretics and the Reformation* (New York, 1967), and A. G. Kinder, *Casiodoro de Reina* (London, 1975); the best known of the émigrés has been studied by Roland Bainton, *Hunted Heretic. The Life and Death of Michael Servetus* (Boston, 1953). J. M. de Bujanda has produce a splendid (French-language) edition of the Index of Prohibited Books of 1559, *Index de l'Inquisition espagnole* (Sherbrooke, 1984).

For the general historical context see Henry Kamen, *Spain 1469-1714. A Society of Conflict* (2nd edn, London, 1991) and John Lynch, *Spain 1516-1598. From Nation State to World Empire* (Oxford, 1991). William Christian Jr. in his *Local Religion in Sixteenth-Century Spain* (Princeton, 1981); and his *Apparitions in Late Medieval and Renaissance Spain* (Princeton, 1981) gives excellent insight into unofficial aspects of peninsular religion. For an aspect of the tradition of freedom see Henry Kamen, 'Toleration and dissent in sixteenth-century Spain: the alternative tradition', *Sixteenth-Century Journal*, 18, no.4 (1987).

# 13    A Comparative Overview

*Bob Scribner*


Contributors to this volume were all set an identical task: to reflect on what was distinctive about the Reformation as it appeared in the 'national context' assigned to each author. The essays were intended to be exercises in interpretation, rather than comprehensive surveys of the Reformation in the regions under discussion. No model or paradigm of the Reformation or its development was prescribed, no chronological boundaries were imposed, nor was any approach privileged over another – authors were free to emphasise religious, intellectual, cultural, political or social aspects as they thought fit. The result has been a collection that highlights the complexity and diversity of the Reformation as it spread out from its German origins across most of Europe during the course of the sixteenth and well into the seventeenth century.

There can be no doubt about the strongly 'national' character of the Reformation's appearance in different territories, states or localities. For varied reasons, and as a result of widely differing influences, the Reformation certainly had a distinctive face in Germany and Switzerland, which produced two major variants of religious reform, the Lutheran and the Helvetic. In Scandinavia and in England, it was primarily a matter of royal policy, of top-down state action which virtually ensured a slow mass diffusion. In France, it seemed from the outset doomed to no more than a disruptive minority existence, while in the Low Countries it enjoyed a pyrrhic victory by opening the way to a principle of toleration that undermined its claim to exclusiveness. In Scotland, its rapid success after a hesitant beginning was achieved by political compromises that led to two generations of internal turmoil. In Poland, ethnic diversity played a predominant role, while in Hungary, political divisions determined the possibilities of its organised (or rather disorganised!) development and ultimate fragmentation. Three somewhat unique cases also stand out. In Bohemia we find the strongest claims that the Reformation of the sixteenth century was in reality only a 'second Reformation' in succession to the religious reform attached to the name of John Hus (accepting the terminology would entail a consequent renumbering of that wave of calvinising movements of reform in the 1570s and 1580s that we are just learning to call the 'Second Reformation').[1] In Spain and Italy, despite the existence of religious and ecclesiastical problems no less vulnerable to the impulse of reform, we find Reformations which failed to happen, events which are still far easier to describe than to explain.

Moreover, it is not simply the diversity of local circumstances that constitutes the distinctiveness of each 'national' Reformation. Local and regional varieties of Reformation somehow became linked to questions of group identity, whether national or ethnic. At a national level, the case of Bohemia speaks most eloquently for itself, as does the example of England, described in persuasive detail here and in other publications by Patrick Collinson,[2] while the notion that 'the [Protestant] nation had made a covenant with God' produced a characteristically Scots tradition of radical and revolutionary religion. Sometimes Protestant identity took ethnic-linguistic form, so that German Lutheranism became the creed of the germanophone populations in Prussia, Lithuania, Poland and Hungary, while the Slavic basis of the Hussite Reformation at one stage looked like forming a bridge for the dissemination of evangelical opinions into Poland via the Bohemian Brethren. But whereas in Poland ethnic diversity hindered the reception of Reformation ideas, which were regarded as alien to Polish native traditions, a no less complex linguistic-ethnic mix in the Hungarian Kingdoms (comprising German, Hungarian, Rumanian, Slovakian, Slovenian and Croatian) did not prevent large numbers turning to Protestant belief. Here it was the cultural dominance of Hungarian which mattered, once the means had been found of translating the new religious ideas into a Hungarian context. Finally, ethnic diversity seems to have played its part in preventing the Reformation enjoying more than a fleeting existence in Spain, which Henry Kamen reminds us was a multi-cultural society where Christians, Muslims and Jews had coexisted and interpenetrated for many centuries. Religious energies were channelled into confrontations with Muslims and Jews, so that Spanish identity became defined in opposition to these non-Christian faiths and not in terms of doctrinal disputes internal to Christianity.

Modern historians' perceptions of this striking ethnic and national diversity may derive from the benefit of hindsight, whereas many contemporaries were more conscious of the international and trans-ethnic character of the Reformation impulse. We may adduce a number of reasons for this latter awareness, not least of which was the dominance of a small number of central personalities in the shaping of Reformation thought: Luther, Zwingli, Calvin, Melanchthon and Bullinger make up the remarkably short list of theological eminences who may be said to have been internationally significant. Patrick Collinson's reference to the alleged 'theological mediocrity' of the Reformation in England might with equal justice be applied to the movements elsewhere. There may have been persons of considerable intellectual stature in all the local contexts reviewed in this volume, but they were rarely able to match the intellectual contribution made by these central figures. Even among what we might call the 'famous five',[3] not all were of the same calibre. Luther, Zwingli and Calvin contributed the major Reformation doctrines; Melanchthon gains his place because of his important modifications to Luther's theology, producing internal disputes which were to weaken Lutheranism more than any of the efforts of Luther's Catholic opponents; Bullinger joins the list because of his pivotal role in disseminating Helvic doctrine throughout Europe in ways that made him as influential as Calvin in the shaping of the Reformed tradition. This meant that the problem of spreading the Reformation was essentially one of translating the theology of these few men into different linguistic and cultural contexts. This was, in turn, a problem in the transmission of ideas, involving modes of communication, questions of translation, reception and adaptation to local context, and politically charged matters such as propaganda and opinion formation. Depending on whether we emphasise the points of origin of these ideas or the process of their reception, we could discern a unitary Reformation or one fragmented by the peculiarities of local context.

Before we look more closely at such matters, we should emphasise a further important internationalising element, the mediating role of humanism, which provides one of the most significant connecting threads between the varying national contexts of reform. Humanism tilled the ground in which the seeds of reform were to germinate not only in Germany, but in Switzerland, France, the Low Countries, England, Scotland, Denmark, Hungary and Poland. Even in Spain and Italy, where no Reformation took place, humanism functioned to direct attention to the need for religious reform and to shape its agenda. This is scarcely surprising, given the international character of humanism as an intellectual movement founded on Latin as a language of universal learning. We could even speak of a 'humanist international', a body of like-minded scholars joined in a common campaign to reform European intellectual, cultural and religious life, and increasingly aware of its historic mission as its members attempted to implement humanist ideas within a national context.

Yet humanism experienced the same tensions between universality and localism, indeed even more so once its largely Latin-based programme confronted the problem of vernacular culture. In as far as humanism provided essential intellectual and cultural presuppositions for the evangelical movements everywhere, it also undoubtedly contributed to the schizoid nature of the Reformation as a movement which emphasised the importance of vernacular languages for proper access to religious knowledge, but which also came to promote book-learning in Latin in ways that enshrined the cleavage between 'lay culture' and 'learned culture'. Of course, once we raise the question of humanist Latin, we encounter the dominating figure of Erasmus, who defined and inspired the linguistic programme that was to have such an important impact on the intellectual character of the Reformation as a whole. The prevailing tone of international humanism in mediating ideas of religious reform was undoubtedly Erasmian, although it is worth noting Kamen's judgment that an Erasmian orientation in Spanish humanism may actually have deflected Spanish intellectuals from sympathising with Lutheranism.

The contributions of humanism can be found in several very specific characteristics: its educational emphasis, its programme of literary and textual revival, its penchant for social and political criticism, and its distinctive religious stance, critical of the more emotional and irrational aspects of pre-Reformation religion. Julian Goodare has rightly called attention to the anti-ritual and anti-magical emphases in humanism, which placed at the centre of its programme 'intellectually satisfying religion based on the primary text of Christianity'. The appeal to the Word of God as found in the Bible was an emphasis common to humanism and Reformation alike, especially to those movements of reformation that took place well before the sixteenth century, so persuasively described by Frantisek Kavka. This community of emphasis did not create an automatic affinity of humanist and Reformation ideas, but it certainly helped influence the attitudes of Zwingli and Calvin and made humanists susceptible to Reformation thought.[4] Humanist textile criticism was of vital importance for the development of Reformation theologies, and many of the emphases in Luther, Zwingli, Calvin and others would be unthinkable without its influence. Its educational programme passed easily into the educational heritage of the Reformation tradition, and its social critical cutting edge provided much of the incisiveness of Protestant programmes of social reform. Finally, the preaching revival of the sixteenth century that most effectively transmitted Reformation theologies was begun by Erasmian humanists, and enabled Reformation preachers to make an effortless transition from evangelical preaching in an Erasmian sense to more explicitly Lutheran and later Protestant preaching.

The humanists were also responsible for harnessing the printing press to the cause of religious reform. There has been in Reformation historiography a tendency to link printing and the Reformation too closely and too exclusively, as though humanists had not previously realised the propagandist and educational potential of the printing press, nor put it fully into service in the cause of their own programme. A vigorous printing press may have helped the dissemination of the Reformation in Germany, but was manifestly less influential in France and even less so in Italy, while in some countries (most noticeably Hungary), it is scarcely in evidence at all. The influence of printed religious literature in the vernacular may have been a more significant feature, not least the availability of a vernacular Bible. If England and Germany stand out as regions displaying high degrees of interest in the printed Bible, it was undoubtedly because of their well-established pre-Reformation traditions of a vernacular Bible. The most striking example of all, the Czech lands, possessed a Czech Bible from 1370 and a printed Bible only from 1488, while the normative Czech edition dated from 1506. However, in other parts of Europe printing necessarily took a back seat compared to other means of disseminating ideas – through forms of oral transmission as yet unexplored in Reformation historiography: for example, via the personal networks created by mobile merchants, humanist scholars or itinerant students, through preaching campaigns or through the informal transfer of news and rumour prior to appearing in print. The power of oral dissemination is attested by the reception of evangelical thought in Hungary, as well as by the effectiveness of its propagation in the Gaelic-speaking highlands of Scotland, for which there was virtually no printed matter to transmit the evangelical message, not even a Gaelic Bible.[5] This further complicates the counter-example of Spain, which may have lacked an indigenous printing press but was certainly not isolated from a flow of books or travellers across its borders. Neither printed nor oral transmission was denied to any Spaniard interested in new religious ideas, and if humanists, merchants, pedlars, students, scholars, pilgrims or other travellers served to carry the Reformation virus elsewhere, it was not for want of carriers that it failed to infect the Spanish in the epidemic proportions it achieved in other parts of Europe.

Pondering this problem, Henry Kamen has fixed on the absence from Spain of what he calls the 'mechanisms through which the Reformation was institutionalised': elite support, urban support and state support. The term 'mechanism' may be less than adequate to describe the complex socio-cultural and political context in which each of these three came to influence the reception of Reformation ideas, but all three certainly deserve closer examination. Urban support had undoubtedly received the lion's share of attention in the research of recent years, with studies of the 'urban Reformation' in German begetting imitators in almost all lands touched by reform. Julian Goodare concludes for Scotland that 'popular Protestantism was a largely urban affair, despite its considerable attraction for lairds who shared its values, and the Reformation cemented an urban cultural hegemony'. This drive for urban control is no less remarkable in Switzerland, where the Reformation had very distinctive urban origins, both in the attempts of towns to invade monastic and ecclesiastical privilege and in the established urban control over the rural church. The mere fact that the leading Swiss towns functioned as territorial lords allowed the incipient reform immediately to spill over into the countryside. The Reformation further benefited from the territorial ambitions of urban cantons such as Zurich or Berne, and it was the expansionist policy of the latter that favoured its spread into francophone Switzerland. Thus, the Swiss model of Reformation was one based on urban hegemony, and for this reason it aroused anxiety in southern Germany. 'Turning Swiss' means both urban anti-feudal republicanism and the dangerous propagation of heresy, and the clear appeal of evangelical ideas in the cities of Germany revealed the enormous potential of urban ambitions for disruption of the entrenched aristocratic hierarchical society of the German-speaking Holy Roman Empire.[6]

Switzerland and Scotland both reveal the links between receptivity to evangelical reform and desire for urban political and cultural hegemony. Elsewhere the 'urban moment' was significant in providing a bridgehead for evangelical reform, but was not decisive in determining the outcome of the Reformation. In the Low Countries, that most urbanised of landscapes, the spread of the Reformation was necessarily urban, as it was in Scandinavia for the very opposite reason: political, cultural, economic and ecclesiastical life was concentrated most densely in the few major cities and in market towns. In France, England, Germany, Austria, Bohemia, Hungary and Poland the towns provided a major focus for evangelical activity, and what little potential there was in Italy and Spain was also urban. But in all these places, other contexts were also of signal importance in deciding the fate of the evangelical movements – that of the court, gentry or aristocracy, and above all the ecclesiastical hierarchy and the clergy.

This looks ahead in the next major point of discussion, elite support, but first there is one other issue to mention about the urban context which leads us into this theme. Should we think of urban support for evangelical reform across Europe as a whole in terms of an instinctive urban affinity, as has been suggested in various ways for the German Reformation? Urban communalism, the drive to rationalise religious life to accommodate the demands of the urban economy and life-style, the desire to make better use of scarce resources (implicit in the pre-Reformation 'purchase of paradise'), the desire to laicise the church and place it firmly under secular control (a concomitant of the anticlerical impulse), a reaction of the urban artisan and mercantile classes against a church and religion dominated by the aristocracy and aristocratic privilege: these are all interpretations of the appeal of the Reformation that focus heavily on its urban location and depend on notions of compatibility of mentality or mindset.[7] Some of these affiliations may depend on mere historical coincidences, that religious reform 'took off' first and most easily in towns because, after all, a new movement has to start somewhere and towns were natural concentrations of population, nodes of communication and significant locations for intellectuals and important churchmen.

Yet the important contrast is not between townsfolk and elites – the story of the Reformation's progress in towns is more often than not the story of its acceptance and/or promotion by an elite, as we shall see in a moment – but an implicit contrast between urban culture and rural culture that has surfaced several times in essays in this volume. Mark Greengrass has commented on how the Reformed religion was unsuccessful because of the challenge it presented to the way of life in rural France. Notoriously, French Protestantism made little headway among agrarian producers, and even its spread in the few rural areas where it took root easily depended on reception by rural artisans such as those in the outworking cloth villages of Normandy or the leatherworkers of the Cevannes, the latter a source of amazement even to the ardent Theodore Beze.[8] There is no doubt that the Reformation confronted radically the belief system and cultural presuppositions deeply rooted in the way of life of peasant producers. They experienced a more drastic challenge to their notions of a magico-sacramental universe than the average town dweller, and it is not without significance that the Reformation was to make considerably slower progress in rural areas where it collided with such an entrenched belief system. If its task in the urban cultural context was merely one of seeking 'affinities', in the rural world it would be forced to proceed by a process of 'acculturation', by eroding presuppositions about the nature of the cosmos and its interpenetration with the texture of daily life.[9] The process of desacralising, deritualising and demystifying was one which would have administered a traumatic shock to European rural culture, and which was only possible under a number of limited conditions. The eschatological and chiliastic moment in the Reformation movements was capable of producing the radical change in mentalities entailed, as was the more secular 'utopian moment' experienced during the German Peasants' War. Yet a long-term shift in mental attitudes may have been more elusive, even for the more rigorous type of reform associated with Helvetic Protestantism. Here there were two basic approaches adopted. Lutheranism proceeded with characteristic moderation, stressing the need to allow time for 'those weak in conscience' to experience the effects of the Gospel message and meanwhile permitting 'adiaphora', nonessentials to faith, to continue where they did not seriously mislead the faithful or give cause for scandal. This permissive approach allowed large segments of rural religious culture to survive intact, if not in overt form, at least in mental outlook. The Reformed religion took a more drastic line, not dissimilar to that of the early radical reformers, in demanding a dramatic break with the old mental world, often symbolised by iconoclastic activity. Here reformation meant uprooting, rather than redirection, confrontation rather than gradual accommodation.

For a long time, it seemed as though the latter strategy had been more effective, but radical protestantisation could effect the dramatic change in rural culture that of the folklorist Richard Weiss claimed to have perceived in the Swiss context, producing a Protestant popular rural culture as different from the Catholic version as chalk from cheese.[10] This might seem to document the notion that peasants can be told what to believe, and that deference to authority will in the course of time lead them to accept and internalise what they cannot change. We might see this kind of process as underlying the gradual transformation of England over three generations into a Protestant nation. However, we have not yet begun to probe the 'hidden transcripts' of popular mentalities that made cultural continuity as potent as cultural transformation and inhibited the 'decline of magic'. Evidence is now beginning to surface that reveals that the process may not have been as thorough or complete as was once thought, and that even an outward appearance of thorough protestantisation may have masked deeper and more complex processes of syncretism.[11] In short, Protestantism in all its forms was no more successful in uprooting a magico-religious view of a sacramental universe than pre-Reformation Christianity had been in displacing paganism.[12]

This is a subject for analysis in another context. Its relevance here is to indicate unmistakably that urban culture proved a more fertile ground for the implanting and luxuriant growth of the reformation impulse than its rural counterpart.[13] This in turn illuminates the problem of national context. Undoubtedly, the Reformation made slower headway in those countries where national identity was closely tied to a pervasive rural culture or where there had been, for whatever reasons, no considerable leavening of this identity by urban cultural norms. France, Poland and Spain stand out as three very different examples which bear out the observation. In France, royal charisma and the tradition of sacral kingship, perhaps the most powerful weapon in its monarchs' armoury, presupposed a sacramentalism inherently alien to reformation ideas. In Poland, native traditions stretching back well into the middle ages ultimately had an acculturating effect even on Protestant polemicists who attempted to assimilate national patron saints such as Stanislaus and turned a blind eye to religio-magical traditions in Polish Christianity. And despite an extensive protestantising campaign throughout the latter half of the sixteenth century to provide new religious literature in the vernacular, the net effect was to promote the status of Polish as a literary language, but with little noticeable impact on native popular culture.[14] In Spain, the role of traditional religion in the life of the people had never really been challenged by anti-sacramental heresies and was not to be called into question during the age of the Reformation. Indeed, it was probably only the missioning impulse of the Counter-Reformation that first confronted rural religion with notions of 'superstition', but even then within the framework of a Spanish Catholicism in which royal devotion mirrored a 'local religion' that left little to choose between the 'geographies of grace' of town and country.[15]

On the other hand, Bohemia and Hungary confirm the insight by their orientation in the opposite direction. In Bohemia, a religious heterodoxy became closely associated with national identity, regardless of urban or rural context. In Hungary, according to Katalin Peter, the reformation impulse first prospered because of its ability to address the needs of Hungarian popular culture, its leading advocates of necessity immersed in rural and market town life; it later withered because of growing remoteness from this milieu. We might add here the interesting example of the Habsburg Austrian lands, where the Reformation first found response in an urban setting, even stronger support from the mobility and later among the peasantry, but which was ultimately routed by the ruling dynasty's ability to identify itself with a form of essentially rural sacramental religion.[16] Here we have not raised, of course, the question of how, and by whom, such a thing as 'national identity' is constructed, although we might suspect that even the very notion itself indicates the important role played by elites, a theme to which we should now turn.

The role of elites has been relatively neglected in the history of the Reformation, although it is striking how often its progress in one context or another depended on the support of various kinds of elite groups. In an urban setting, the response of cultural elites such as intellectuals and higher members of the clergy, or of political elites, such as town councillors, city mayors and secretaries was often crucial. Administrative or bureaucratic elites such as princely councillors, judges or district officials provided protection, status and often ecclesiastical patronage that gave a foothold for the new preachers. The adherence of the gentry and the aristocracy was also as important for the penetration of the countryside as dissemination from the towns, even in Germany, where we are accustomed to think of the Reformation as an 'urban event'. This was especially the case where such members of the rural propertied classes appropriated for themselves the principle that subjects should adopt the same religion as their rulers (*cuius regio, eius religio*) and insisted on their tenants or dependents conforming to their own religious choices. Even where that was not the case, the political prestige and control of patronage exercised by the aristocracy, especially over ecclesiastical benefices, made them indispensable for the advance of the Reformation. The case of Hungary illustrates the point admirably, where gentry patronage transformed the prospects of Hungarian Protestantism in the 1530s.

Perhaps the most significant manifestation of elite support in several 'national contexts' was that of the Estates, the politically organised form of the politically privileged classes of any polity. The role played by the Estates in the fate of the Reformation in many German territories has long been a matter of common knowledge, but has somewhat dropped out of view in recent discussion. There was a dual tendency: on the one hand, a prince enthusiastic for reformation was sometimes inhibited by the caution of his Estates, not necessarily because they are unwilling to follow him along a path of protestantisation, but because they may have had reservations about the character of the ensuing reformation, which may have encroached on their privileges or given too much power to the prince. On the one hand, a conservative prince may have been pushed along by the Estates, which were rather more enthusiastic for reform than he. In either case, the Reformation cause and the issue of Estates constitutionalism easily became entangled. This was even more the case outside Germany, most notably in Bohemia and Hungary, where the issue of Estates constitutionalism was somewhat 'hotter' than elsewhere. It certainly played a significant role in Sweden at the end of the sixteenth century, when a revived aristocratic constitutionalism found its arm strengthened by a defence of Sweden's Protestant traditions against the Catholic and counter-reforming Sigismund III.[17]

This calls attention to a final point of comparison, namely, that between the different polities involved in our case studies. It is noticeable that the religious situation was sometimes least complicated in monarchies with relatively strong personal rulers, although this counted both for and against the reformation cause. Once a monarch such as Francis I had set his face against Protestantism in the 1530s, the path of reformation became one tied to the experience of persecution and exile. On the other hand, tough-minded rulers such as Henry VIII or Gustavus Vasa were able to promote reform of the church as an extension of their firm control over their state. However, hereditary monarchies were better placed than elective ones, where the rough and tumble of agreements with the Estates made religious changes imponderable at best. Monarchies with powerful or politically ambitious Estates, such as those in the Habsburg lands of eastern Europe, provided an invaluable foothold to the Reformation once they perceived that their political solidarity was strengthened by a new common religious identity in opposition to the belief of their monarch.

We should also mention several examples of federal states, the most obvious of which are Switzerland and that peculiar phenomenon, the 'Holy Roman Empire of the German Nation'; but we should also not forget that Spain and the Netherlands were in effect federated states. It is interesting to reflect that the Reformation actually made little real headway in capturing, totally and with unqualified success, any of the federated states. Federal states were most likely to experience contrary tensions in which religion easily became embroiled and from which it was best kept distant in the interests of preserving overall unity. In Switzerland, the best example of this principle, further expansion of the Reformation was checked by the Battle of Kappel of 1531, but even beforehand, the thrust towards reformation took different directions according to the influence of Zurich or Berne, while the later emergence of Geneva as a 'third force' in the Helvetic Reformation steered in yet another direction. Religious coexistence between Catholic and Protestant was favoured over any weakening of the Confederation, so that there was probably as little chance of a unified Protestant Switzerland as there was of a wholly Protestant Germany. Thus, if it is generally true that 'the evangelical movement was much more likely to flourish in areas of weak or dispersed political control',[18] it was also exactly such dispersed control that often hampered its complete institutionalisation.

Beyond calling attention to such obvious generalisations, it is difficult to discern any more reliable politico-constitutional pattern. Political forms were an integral part of 'national context' and as such seem to partake of the same diversity and local variation that we have perceived in the ethnic and cultural fields. If it is possible to summarise a movement as internationally and locally complex as the essays here have shown the Reformation to be, we must concede that diversity is a *leitmotif*. National context counted because it was exactly in the realm of local circumstances that the phenomenon of reformation was domesticated, made meaningful for people of different national, cultural or ethnic groups. Thus we might say, to return to an example used in the introduction, if 'the Reformation in England' was to have an enduring existence, it had to become the 'English Reformation', to be assimilated to national context. The dictum holds true if we replace 'English' with any other adjective identifying the national contexts discussed in this volume; and for the same reason we can speak of 'the Reformation in Italy' but scarcely of an 'Italian Reformation'. Such conclusions remind us forcibly that the historian's task should always involve comparison, closely followed by that other imperative of the discipline, cautious qualification.

## NOTES

1 See Heinz Schilling, 'The Second Reformation – Problems and Issues', in *Religion, Political Culture and the Emergence of Early Modern Society* (Leiden, 1992), pp. 247–301. We are also reminded by Ann Hudson, *The Premature Reformation. Wycliffite Texts and Lollard History* (Oxford, 1988) that English Lollardy could also claim a place in this lineage.

2 *The Birthpangs of Protestant England* (New York, 1988); *The Religion of Protestants* (Oxford, 1982).

3 Some might like to include Martin Bucer in the list to round it up to a half-dozen, others might include Carlstadt or Thomas Müntzer as founders of the radical tradition.

4 For an interesting statement and summary of the relationships between humanism and Reformation, see Peter Matheson, 'Humanism and Reform Movements', in *The Impact of Humanism on Western Europe*, ed. Anthony Grafton and Angus Mackay (London, 1990), pp. 23–42. See also Alister McGrath, *The Intellectual Origins of the European Reformation* (Oxford, 1987), pp. 32–68.

5 To Julian Goodare's comments on these points, we must add the illuminating discussion by Jane Dawson, 'Calvinism and the Gaidhealtachd in Scotland', paper delivered at the international conference on 'European Calvinism', Oxford 1–4 September 1993, and forthcoming in the conference proceedings edited by Alistair Duke, Gillian Lewis and Andrew Pettegree.

6 The now classic statement of this view is Thomas A. Brady, *Turning Swiss. Cities and Empire 1450–1550* (Cambridge, 1985).

7 Many have been succinctly and tellingly criticised by Euan Cameron, *The European Reformation* (Oxford, 1991), pp. 293–311, although he does not deal adequately with the explanatory power or problematic aspects of the concepts of 'affinity' (Weber's notion) or 'affiliation' (Cameron's). Nor does he discuss in more than a passing way Peter Blickle's notion of 'communal Reformation', now available in English in *Communal Reformation. The Quest for Salvation in Sixteenth-century Germany* (Atlantic Highlands, N.J., 1992), but his possible critique might be inferred from his comments on the 'Moeller thesis', pp. 303–4.

8 E. Le Roy Ladurie, *The Peasants of Languedoc*, translated by John Day (Urbana, Ill., 1974), p. 165.

9 Although I do not accept the validity of Robert Muchembled's 'acculturation' thesis, set out in his *Popular Culture and Elite Culture in France 1400–1750* (London, 1985) – and even he has now begun to modify some of its force, for example in his *L'invention de l'homme modern* (Paris, 1988), where the term is not mentioned – his point of departure in the cultural clash between urban and rural culture was undoubtedly a useful insight. For a succinct summary of the advantages and disadvantages of the term, with further literature, see Peter Burke, *History and Social Theory* (Cambridge, 1992), pp. 155–7.

10 For the comments by Richard Weiss, alluded to above by Kaspar von Greyerz, see the former's *Volkskunde der Schweiz* (Zurich, 1946), pp. 309–10; the contrasts discussed in more detail in R. W. Scribner, 'The Impact of the Reformation on Daily Life', in *Mensch und Objekt im Mittelalter und in der frühen Neuzeit*, Österreische Akademie der Wissenschaften, Phil.-hist. Klasse, 568 (Vienna, 1990), pp. 315–43, especially pp. 315ff.

11 For these points see Scribner, 'Impact of the Reformation on Daily Life' and 'The Reformation, Magic and the "Disenchantment of the World"', *Journal of Interdisciplinary History* 23 (1993), pp. 475–94. Similar points have been made by Richard Godbeer, *The Devil's Dominion. Magic and Religion in Early New England* (Cambridge, 1992); for 'hidden transcripts', James C. Scott, *Domination and the Arts of Resistance* (Yale, 1990).

12 On the latter point, see Valerie Flint, *The Rise of Magic in Early Medieval Europe* (Oxford, 1991).

13 Notwithstanding the peculiar variation introduced by Peter Blickle into the theme of 'communalism' under the title of 'christianisation', see *Kommunalisierung und Christianisierung. Voraussetzungen und Folgen der Reformation 1400–1600*, ed. P. Blickle and J. Kunisch, *Zeitschrift für historische Forschung*, Beiheft 9 (Berlin, 1989).

14 Besides the comments by Tazbir above, see also Mieczysław Szymczak, 'Protestantism and the Development of the Polish Language', *Polata Knigopisnaja* 16 (August, 1987), pp. 48–55. I am grateful to Steven Rowell for calling my attention to the special issue of this journal devoted to 'Early Protestantism in Eastern Europe'.

15 On Spanish urban 'local religion', and on kingship, W. A. Christian, *Local Religion in Sixteenth-century Spain* (Princeton, 1981), pp. 148–53, 153–58 respectively.

16 For the urban response in Austria, see Corina Marta Herrera, *The Ambiguous Reformation in the Territorial Cities of Upper Austria, 1520–1567* (Ph.D. dissertation, Yale University, 1980); on the reaction of the Austrian Estates up to the 1550s, Winfried Eberhard, 'Bohemia, Moravia and Austria', in *The Early Reformation in Europe*, ed. Andrew Pettegree (Cambridge, 1992), pp. 43–47; see also more generally, Peter F. Barton, *Evangelisch in Österreich* (Vienna, 1987), chapters 2–3. The seventeenth-century policies of recatholicisation through fostering vernacular and popular culture, admittedly building on the forcible expulsion of recalcitrant Protestants, in R. J. W. Evans, *The Making of the Habsburg Monarchy 1550–1700* (Oxford, 1979), pp. 186–91.

17 See Michael Roberts, *The Early Vasas. A History of Sweden 1523–1611* (Cambridge, 1968), pp. 338–48.

18 The perceptive comment by Andrew Pettegree in *The Early Reformation in Europe*, p. 14.

# Index